The Jesus People Movement

The
Jesus People
Movement

A Story of Spiritual Revolution among the Hippies

Richard A. Bustraan

PICKWICK *Publications* · Eugene, Oregon

THE JESUS PEOPLE MOVEMENT
A Story of Spiritual Revolution among the Hippies

Pickwick Publications
An Imprint of Wipf and Stock Publishers
199 W. 8th Ave., Suite 3
Eugene, OR 97401

www.wipfandstock.com

ISBN 13: 978-1-62032-464-6

Cataloguing-in-Publication data:

Bustraan, Richard A.

The Jesus people movement : a story of spiritual revolution among the hippies / Richard A. Bustraan.

xxiv + 238 pp. ; 23 cm. Includes bibliographical references and index.

ISBN 13: 978-1-62032-464-6

1. Jesus People—United States. 2. United States—Church history—20TH century. I. Title.

BV3773 .B87 2014

Manufactured in the U.S.A.

to God my Savior, who alone is wise.
with loving affection to my earthly treasure, my Khasi princess.

Contents

Preface

THIS BOOK IS A revised version of my PhD thesis conducted during the years 2008–2011, in which I examined the Pentecostal and Charismatic nature of the Jesus People Movement (JPM). While I never was part of the JPM, my life was affected by Jesus People (JP) like Keith Green and by the Calvary Chapel Movement. I am a pastor of Calvary Chapel Birmingham in the UK and as such could be considered an insider to some of the beliefs and practices of the JP. Although the JPM was a Pentecostal and Charismatic movement, it has been omitted from the history books of American Pentecostalism. Hence the aim of this book is to describe and locate the JPM in Pentecostal historiography and as such it is not primarily cynical or hostile against the beliefs and practices of the participants. My goal is to be sympathetic to the testimony of the JP, while not becoming a cheerleader for all their claimed experiences.

Following Allan Anderson's Family Resemblance analogy, and applying a multidisciplinary approach, the book demonstrates that the JPM has historical links to Pentecostalism and it also shares a similar sociological and theological focus.[1] In addition to many books and journal articles, I read over 270 newspaper articles, all issues of the *Pentecostal Evangel* (*PE*), *Christianity Today* (*CT*), and *The Christian Century* from 1967 to 1977, and five PhD theses on the JPM. I travelled to California, Georgia, and Florida to visit churches and find resources and also interviewed just over fifty people—twenty through email and thirty-three by phone or in person.

Methodology

Academic research involves more than examining sources and as such it is also necessary to discuss how I handled the above data and to admit some of the complexities and potential pitfalls with my methodology. To begin,

---

1. Anderson, "Varieties," 27.

while I did not approach every source with cynicism, I did recognize that historical sources are often tainted with ulterior motivations. Books and newspaper, magazine, and journal articles can be written as self-promotional materials, as rebuttals, and as legitimization tools for their expected primary audience. Newspapers and magazines are established to promote conservative or liberal ideologies or denominational agendas. The sources' allies and enemies, financial supporters, and denominational affiliates can influence the historical information reported. Claims to have "coined," to be the "first" or "the most significant" can be ways of intentionally ignoring evolutionary, borrowed, and antecedent factors and creating heroes who were free from outside influences—except God of course. And "in-house" literature can be a mixed bag of behind-the-scene details as well as overstatements.

In interviews, I sought an equal proportion of women and men, but was only able to interview eleven women. Ten interviewees were leaders in the JPM and the others were common participants; although several have since taken more prominent leadership roles. Three were from JP musical groups, six now work outside America in a missionary capacity, and four work in leadership positions in missionary organizations. I selected interviewees from different JPM communities including those from the east coast and the west coast of America. They comprised non-Charismatic JP, classical Pentecostal JP, and Charismatic JP. I limited my selection of Calvary Chapel interviewees to five persons, hoping this would avoid skewing my conclusions. I conducted the interviews by asking four open-ended questions, in which I allowed the interviewees the freedom to talk—or write in the case of email—about their experiences without interruption, with the exception of clarifying questions.

The use of interviews as a source is not as cut-and-dried as it may appear on the surface. I had to recognize that interviewees' thoughts are not perfectly logical and are sometimes self-contradictory. Also, motivations may have been at times self-seeking, ex-members may have had an axe to grind, or with the passing of time, the fading memory of events may have affected their present interpretation of the past. In addition, American Pentecostal and Evangelical Christians use value-laden, rhetorical phrases like, "born again," "saved," "baptized in the Holy Spirit," "tongues," and "Satan" that carry much of an assumed and implied understanding. Sharing a somewhat similar belief could be equally as harmful as helpful in understanding these terms, as working with assumed meanings for biblical jargon could have obscured an individual's actual meaning. For this reason, I often probed further in interviews by asking clarifying questions about the meanings of these rhetorical terms. All interviews were not warm and friendly conversations and ranged from those who were amicable and polite, to those who were rather blasé, to a few who were aggressively antagonistic and cynical against the JPM, Evangelicalism, and Pentecostalism. In spite of these inherent weaknesses, my objectives with the interviews were to be able to have an additional tool for triangulation and for gaining a better grasp on the insiders' experiences and interpretations.

Finally, there are pros and cons with using the Internet as a research tool. On a positive note, many JP groups have begun to publish the details of their particular community, and the Internet has increased the accessibility to many films, photos, magazines, and newspapers that would not have been easily available a couple of decades ago. However, the potential for self-propagandistic misinformation on the web is exacerbated by the fact that anyone can publish anything, by the perfunctory nature of information, and by the extremely fast pace at which posted information can be changed or removed altogether. Individuals and religious organizations can make exaggerated claims of numbers of adherents that are difficult to confirm. In the cases where I have relied on the websites of religious organizations for qualitative data, I have tried to be careful to state that this is their claim. Also, due to the anonymous nature of articles posted on Wikipedia and the lack of academic credibility often associated with the site, I have chosen not to use it as a source for information.

Limitations

This book is not an encyclopedic list of all organizations, ministries, and people in the JPM; if indeed such a list were even possible. The limitations of space as well as the focus on Pentecostalism were the primary criteria for deciding who was included and excluded from this account. For example, Evangelical groups that were famously associated with the JPM, but did not participate in the Pentecostalism of the JP, may only receive a minor mention. The church movements, music, and communes are discussed, but are too enormous to receive exhaustive coverage and far more attention is deserved from a book focused on each. Some groups like the Metropolitan Community Church (MCC), The Children of God (COG)— The Family—The Alamo Foundation, Salem Acres, and Jim Jones' People's Temple, were part of the JPM and did participate in its Pentecostalism. But these were regarded by most JP as marginal and as such receive only minor attention. I realize this runs the risk of merely supporting the opinions of the majority JP, but due to the limitations of space, and the emic nature of this book, the mainstream beliefs and practices of the majority of the participants has been pursued.

Definitions

Finally, there are a few important words and phrases that need to be defined. To begin, because the word "revival" carries an inherently positive interpretation, the word "movement," and the phrases "religious movement" or "phenomenon" will be used in its place. Second, the word "Pentecostalism" is a term that refers to the phenomenological and theological, Christian experience of the baptism of the Holy Spirit (BHS) or Spirit empowerment, and the emphasis on the gifts of the Holy Spirit such as tongues, prophecies, words of knowledge, words of wisdom, visions, dreams, signs and wonders, and healing. My use of Pentecostalism is very inclusive of the many variations on this same theme. Further, I use "Pentecostal" or "Pentecostals" to refer to the beliefs and practices of Pentecostalism and also to refer to the people who adhere to these beliefs and practices.

I use the term "charismatic," synonymously with Pentecostal, to refer to those who claim to be gifted with gifts of the Spirit and who practice these gifts. The word "Charismatic" is applied to the movement of Pentecostalism within the mainline or historical churches and "Charismatic(s)" to the individuals who belong to these particular movements. The phrases "classical Pentecostal" and "classical Pentecostalism" refer to the churches, organizations, and individuals that trace their historical roots to the Pentecostal movements of the early part of the twentieth century. The classical Pentecostal churches included in this research are the Assemblies of God (AG), and the International Church of the Foursquare Gospel (ICFG); the Church of God, Cleveland (CG) does receive a minor mention. This was due to the limitation of time and the availability of source information. Generalizations from these two denominations are applied to all classical Pentecostal churches with reservations.

As for the Charismatic Movement (CM), I follow Peter Hocken's definitions that interpret the whole as divisible into two renewal movements: the Charismatic Renewal (CR) that took place in the mainline Protestant Churches, and the Catholic Charismatic Renewal (CCR) that took place in the Catholic Church beginning in 1967.[2] The word "neo-Charismatic" aligns with David Barrett's taxonomy as a descriptive of the Pentecostal movements that occurred outside the historic churches, and outside the classical Pentecostal churches beginning from the 1960s and 1970s.

In addition, this book assumes that Fundamentalism, Evangelicalism, and Pentecostalism are three large umbrella terms that describe distinctly separate movements that overlap at certain historical, sociological, and

---

2. Hocken, "Charismatic Movement," 477–519.

theological junctures. They are not used interchangeably or synonymously, and I intentionally maintain a distinction between the three throughout the book. I draw a strong line of distinction between Fundamentalism and the JPM and will show the reasons for this in chapter 4. I use Evangelical(ism) most often to indicate the communities and people in the JPM that did not participate in Pentecostal(ism) and at times, the terms "Conservative Evangelical" or "non-charismatic Evangelical" are also used to indicate the same. On occasion Evangelicalism is used more inclusively of all Evangelical and Pentecostal groups and individuals and it is hoped that the context for each of these uses is clear. In chapter 5 the word "restoration" is used as a very loose descriptive of the thematic resemblance in the theology and theopraxis of some churches to "restore" the "fivefold" ministry of Apostles, Prophets, Evangelists, Pastors, and Teachers.[3]

Although the phrase "Jesus Movement" was commonly used in the seventies, it has since been adopted by the field of study interested in the social history of early Christianity around and after the time of Jesus (Horsley and Hanson, *Bandits, Prophets, and Messiahs*; Stegemann and Stegemann, *Jesus Movement*). In order to avoid any confusion I have chosen to use the label "Jesus People Movement" instead of "Jesus Movement."

I have spent hours cross-examining sources to seek precision and accuracy in my statements. It is hoped that this research demonstrates enough reflexivity to hold in balance the need to be empathetic to the JP's own narratives while not becoming completely uncritical of the JPM. I also hope that this book is as educational and inspirational for the reader as it has been for me to research and write it.

3. Althouse, *Spirit of the Last Days*, 52.

Acknowledgments

I COUNT IT A privilege to have worked under Allan Anderson's supervision over the four years of my PhD research. Now it is a pleasure to know him as a friend. Mark Cartledge and Andrew Davies also offered timely advice during this same season. James Richardson ever so kindly helped me locate difficult to find articles. Many Jesus People took time from their busy schedules so that I could hear their stories and ask lots of questions. *Challenge Weekly* in New Zealand helped me locate archived articles and gave me the location of a hidden treasure of resources on the Jesus People in New Zealand. The patient and knowledgeable staff at the University of Birmingham libraries, Oxford Bodleian Reading Rooms, Central Library in Birmingham, and the David Allan Hubbard Library greatly facilitated my research efforts. The Flower Pentecostal Heritage Center and the Pathway Press assisted my search of archives in the *Pentecostal Evangel* and the Church of God *Evangel*. My parents' moral support over the last five years of research and writing only comes second to that of my three beautiful children and my lovely wife.

Introduction

What Is the Jesus People Movement?

The Jesus People Movement (JPM) was a religious movement among White American youth in which the participants wed certain values of the 1960s American counterculture, namely hippiedom, together with values of Christianity, namely Pentecostalism. The JPM was not homogenous in nature, it did not have a founder or central character, neither did it emerge from a single location. Instead, it would be more accurately described as a heterogeneous family or collection of smaller movements, polycephalous in leadership, and ploynucleated—birthed from a myriad of multiple geographical locations. It exhibited a broad variance in the particulars of beliefs and practices while being harmonized by a nearly universally shared set of charismatic and hippie characteristics. The movement lasted from 1967 to the end of the 1970s and its aftermath has continued to grow, diversify, and influence American Christianity into the present day. The participants of the JPM were commonly referred to as Jesus People (JP).

Accounts of the Jesus People Movement

During the height of the movement, the years 1970 to 1973, a flurry of newspaper and magazine articles were published that followed the JPM all across America, giving a flavor for how ubiquitous the movement was. Many short books were also published, like Plowman (*Jesus Movement*) and Michelmore, *Back to Jesus* (1973), which highlighted a random selection of individuals and ministries from various states across American. Others were more thematic in their approach, like that of Ward, *The Far-Out Saints of the Jesus Communes* (1972), Ellwood Jr., *One Way* (1973), and Enroth et al., *Story of the Jesus People* (1972), Enroth's probably being the most popular and most cited work to date.

However by 1973, when the movement was in full swing, the publishing of books, newspaper, and magazine articles swiftly ended and the storyline of the JPM fell abruptly silent. Only a very few, extremely brief articles by Enroth, "Where Have All the Jesus People Gone?" (1973), P. King, "What Ever Happened to the Jesus People?" (1974), and Beaty, "Jesus People" (1992), offered anecdotal suggestions to the question of what happened to the Jesus People. Since 1973, the JPM has suffered from having neither academic nor popular storytellers who continued to chronicle and analyze the movement. James Richardson is rather exceptional in that he has followed and assessed certain sociological elements of the JPM on his own and in collaborative works from 1972 to 2005. In 1979 he wrote this observation; one that is still true today. "There has been little attention given to the [Jesus People] movement since the early years of its development, especially in the more scholarly publications . . . Few people realize that the movement is alive and well. Several of its groups have achieved a remarkable degree of strength and stability and must now be considered more or less permanent fixtures on the religious scene in America, and even around the world."[4] Consequently, without storytellers committed to understanding and chronicling its broad narrative, the JPM, which is primarily an account of American Pentecostalism and Evangelicalism, has been omitted from most Pentecostal and Evangelical historiographies.

Since 1973, abridged accounts of the JPM have been written in three basic ways. First, it has been included as an entry in an encyclopedia, as a single chapter in a book, or as part of the discussion in a single chapter. In this case the JPM is positioned alongside other movements and is merely cited as an exemplary illustration of the editor's or author's major theme. Since it is not the author's intention to offer extensive coverage, the broad storyline of the JPM is severely abridged and grossly oversimplified. For example, Allitt, *Religion in America* (2003), incorporates the JP into a chapter entitled "Alternative Religious Worlds: 1967–1982." Tracing several post-World War II trends in American Christianity, he discusses the JPM alongside feminism and Asian spirituality as a phenomenon that thematically resembled New Religions or "cults." Jenkins, *Mystics and Messiahs* (2000) makes a minor mention of the JP as one of the many "cult" groups to rise in the 1960s and 1970s, locating them within a long "cult" trajectory that he believes reaches into America's earliest history. Or again, Balmer (*Mine Eyes*) includes a one-chapter overview on the iconic JP mega-church, Calvary Chapel in Costa Mesa, California. Balmer is not concerned with the entire JPM, so he places Calvary Chapel alongside a sampling of other

---

4. Richardson et al., *Organized*, xvi.

groups in an attempt to frame a portrait of what he believes to be conservative Christianity in America.

Second, the JP story can be found in qualitative, micro-analysis of single JP communities. In this case, the author's eye is focused upon the details of a single JP community and the larger storyline of the JPM becomes the overarching narrative that is often very briefly overviewed in the introductory chapters. As should be expected from qualitative studies, they offer multifaceted, in-depth examinations of the beliefs and practices of one particular JP community. However, by projecting the findings from a single JP community upon the entire JP phenomenon, the broad story of the JPM becomes over homogenized and robbed of its multidimensionality. Perhaps the best example of this is Richardson et al., *Organized Miracles* (1979), a thorough, sociological analysis of one JP communal collective, the Shiloh Youth Revival Centers (pseudonym Christ Communal Organization), from 1968 to 1978. Another example would be Tipton, *Getting Saved* (1982), who examined a small JP community called the Living Word Fellowship and placed it alongside a Zen Buddhist meditation center and a human potential training organization. Tipton argues that people, including JP, join New Religious Movements to make moral sense of their lives. Then there is Warner, *New Wine* (1988), who incorporated the JP into part of his historical assessment of a local church called the Presbyterian Church of Mendocino, California from 1959–1986.

The third way that the JP story has been told is through studies that analyze how the religious phenomenon affected political, religious, or denominational trends in America. More often than not, these studies are more concerned with the broad JP storyline with the intention of establishing connections between the JPM and the institution or trend under consideration. For example, Romanowski, "Rock'n'religion" (1990), explored the rise of the Christian Contemporary Music Industry (CCM) that emerged from Jesus Music, the JP's musical expression. Reid, "Impact of the Jesus Movement" (1991), examined the impact of the JPM on the Southern Baptist Convention (SBC), concluding that the JPM was causal of the largest rise in baptisms in the history of the SBC as well as other qualitative impacts on their seminaries and mission structures. Then there is D. Miller, *Reinventing* (1997), who analyzed three JP church movements—Calvary Chapel, The Association of Vineyard Churches, and Hope Chapel—labeling them as "new paradigm churches." Or again, Shires, *Hippies* (2007), established connections between some JP, Evangelicalism, and the rise of the "Religious Right" in the 1980s.

It is only in recent years, however, that there has been a renewed interest to return to the 1960s and 1970s and investigate the entire JPM phenomenon. Perhaps the most notable is Di Sabatino, *Jesus People Movement* (2004), which catalogued a lengthy list of resources for researchers of the JPM. Since his book is an annotated, bibliographical resource, his analysis is limited to sixteen pages. But the book also includes three helpful articles, and copious annotated comments. More recently Philpott, *Awakenings* (2011), published his own account of the movement and attempted to answer the question of whether or not the JPM was a Fourth Great Awakening. While the book is limited to his own biographical narrative and personal experiences in San Francisco from 1967 to the present, it does offer insight into his travels across the country and his interaction with Protestant and Catholic Church leaders that also participated in the JPM. Kevin Smith (*Origins, Nature, and Significance*) published a revised version of his Doctor of Missiology, a work in dialogue with Max Weber and with Anthony Wallace's Revitalization Theory. Smith makes an important contribution to the story of the JP by analyzing several groups that flourished in Australia. Finally, Larry Eskridge's PhD dissertation, "God's Forever Family" (2005), has been one of the only attempts since the early 1970s to maintain a thorough and focused eye upon the broad storyline within America. Eskridge updates and builds upon the Evangelical players in the JPM and locates it in a trajectory of youth movements in American Christianity.

Revivals and Awakenings: Differing Evangelical and Pentecostal Lenses

The overlap between American Pentecostalism and American Evangelicalism is so great that it is impossible to perfectly untangle the two. Nevertheless, dissimilarities can be observed in the way that their historiographies have been framed and the contrasting religious stories are maintained by the emphasis on different dates of origin, different religious "revivals," and different characters. For example, Evangelical historical accounts rarely include the Azusa Street revival or the names of A. J. Tomlinson, Charles Parham, and William Seymour. Likewise, Pentecostal accounts commence with the latter years of the nineteenth century or early years of the twentieth and omit the people and revivals that Evangelicals consider sacred.

When American Evangelicals examine the JP story, it is located within a longer historical trajectory than Pentecostalism, one that begins with the early days of the nation of American. While revivalism is rhetorically significant to both, American Evangelicals are often preoccupied with answering the question of whether or not the JPM was a third or fourth "Great Awakening." The answers to these questions are based on definitional differences between "revivals" and "awakenings" and establishing comparative similarities to the JPM and these earlier revivals. Evangelicals cherish these relatively short-lived "revivals" and "awakenings" as exemplary, high water marks in American History; times in which they believe the collective soul of the nation is brought back to the God of the Bible and his providential, historical purposes for the United States. This kind of historical presentation can be found in Philpott, *Awakenings* (2011), McLoughlin, *Revivals* (1978), and Lovelace, *Dynamics* (1979); all of which present the JPM as a "fourth Great Awakening."

American Pentecostal and Charismatic historiography is preoccupied with a different set of questions; ones that focus on the narrative of what is believed to be the restoration of the experience of Pentecost as found in Acts 2. It traces the individuals, movements, and denominations that emerged from the revivals of the early twentieth century and that emphasized the experience of the baptism of the Holy Spirit and gifts of the Holy Spirit. The analysis of the JPM in this book does not attempt to answer questions of Evangelical revivalism and awakenings, but is instead concerned with the historical, sociological, and theological connections to American Pentecostalism. This book breaks new ground in the historiography of American Pentecostalism by including, for the first time, the JPM into its twentieth century American story.

Abbreviations

Reference Works and Literature

CNS	*Copley* News Service
CT	*Christianity Today*
DPCM	*The Dictionary of Pentecostal and Charismatic Movements.* Edited by Stanley Burgess et al. Grand Rapids: Regency Reference Library, 1988.
HFP	*Hollywood Free Paper*
JSSR	*Journal for the Scientific Study of Religion*
NIDPC	*The New International Dictionary of Pentecostal and Charismatic Movements.* Edited by Stanley M. Burgess and Eduard M. Van der Maas. Grand Rapids: Zondervan, 2002.
PE	*Pentecostal Evangel*
NYT	*New York Times* News Service
SC	*Social Compass*
TCTS	*The Cross and the Switchblade*
LGPE	*The Late Great Planet Earth*

Names

AG	Assemblies of God in America
BHS	The Baptism of or in or with the Holy Spirit
CCC	Campus Crusade for Christ

CCM	Christian Contemporary Music
CCR	Catholic Charismatic Renewal
CM	Charismatic Movement
CG	Church of God (Cleveland)
COG	The Children of God (The Family)
CR	Charismatic Renewal in Mainline Protestant Churches
CWFL	Christian World Liberation Front
EFC	Eugene Faith Center
FGBMFI	The Full Gospel Business Men's Fellowship International
GO	Gospel Outreach
ICFG	The International Church of the Foursquare Gospel
IPHC	The International Pentecostal Holiness Church
IVCF	InterVarsity Christian Fellowship
JPA	Jesus People Army
JPM	Jesus People Movement
JP	Jesus People
MCC	Metropolitan Community Church
MCM	Maranatha Campus Ministries
NAE	The National Association of Evangelicals
PHCF	Potter's House Christian Fellowship
SM	The Shepherding Movement
TC	Teen Challenge
TCC	Teen Challenge Centers
VoE	The Voice of Elijah

Chapter 1

The 1960s and the Hippies

The 1960s—The Decade of Change

WHEN THE DOME OF Alaskan volcano Novarupta exploded in 1912, it famously became the largest volcanic eruption of the twentieth century. The valley below was transformed by the pyroclastic ash flow and thereafter renamed the Valley of Ten Thousand Smokes. In much the same way, the cultural revolution of the 1960s and 1970s abruptly and violently tore large fissures across the landscape of American society, leaving behind what could be argued as a pre-sixties America and a post-sixties America.[1] For if the period of the sixties and the seventies was the volcanic eruption, then the remainder of the century, the 1980s and 1990s, was the spreading and cooling of the pyroclastic ash flow and a period of resettling and rebuilding around this new feature in the landscape of American society. Metaphors aside, many scholars of American history have noted that the 1960s was the most significant decade of change in the twentieth century. It was during this era that alternative religious, political, and social movements that had been fermenting in the margins of American society moved into the mainstream and battled for legitimacy. By the eighties and nineties they were attaining increasingly acceptable positions as viable competitors for shaping American cultural values. Francis Fitzgerald summarized it in this way, "There were very few periods in American history in which the dominant sector—the white middle class—transformed itself as thoroughly as it did in the sixties and seventies; transformed itself quite deliberately, and from the inside out, changing its customs, its sexual mores, its family arrangements, and its religious patterns."[2]

---

1. The idea of pre-sixties and post-sixties is inclusive of the two decades of the 1960s and the 1970s.

2. Fitzgerald, *Cities on a Hill*, 390.

The following snippet from hippie forefather Allen Ginsberg under-scores how deeply acrimonious the rift was between the marginalized and the mainstream in American society. His tone is unabashedly provocative, enunciated in the taunting, warfare-like language of an intruder who has dared to trespass and lay down the gauntlet for cultural transformation. He wrote, "I am in effect setting up moral codes and standards which include drugs, orgy, music and primitive magic as worship rituals—educational tools which are supposedly contrary to our cultural mores; and I am pro-posing these standards to you respectable ministers, once and for all, that you endorse publically the private desire and knowledge of mankind in America, so to inspire the young."[3] Many churches in the West felt the ef-fects of the 1960s, especially in the erosion of their taken-for-granted place in the public arena and in the unabated attrition of membership. In Hugh McLeod's bold appraisal, the sixties were comparable to a "rupture as pro-found as that brought about by the Reformation."[4] The JPM was birthed in 1967, in the midst of this tempestuous, historical season and was animated in particular by two important twentieth-century movements—American Pentecostalism and the hippies.

That there were antecedent and contextual factors at work within American culture from before the sixties is of little doubt, but divergent opinions exist among scholars over how far back to draw the boundary lines. Those like Robert Ellwood (*Sixties*) draw attention to the more im-mediate influences of the 1950s upon the 1960s, whereas others like Charles Taylor (*Secular Age*) argue for the long range societal changes that date back to the Protestant Reformation. Hugh McLeod (*Religious Crisis*) strikes a balance between the long-term evolutionary influences of the twentieth century and the immediate, revolutionary movements and key people of the 1960s. Agreeing with McLeod, it is necessary to consider the evolution of several trends afoot from the early part of the twentieth century to make more sense of the revolution of the sixties.

Twentieth-Century War and Economics

Twentieth-century America was a nation that had experienced two major world wars that claimed the lives of over half a million US military service-men. World War II seamlessly transitioned into the Cold War era in which the new enemy was communism and especially communist Russia and China. The US government adopted a general strategy called "containment"

3. Ginsberg, *San Francisco Oracle*, quoted in T. Miller, *Hippies*, 1.
4. McLeod, *Religious Crisis of the 1960s*, 1.

that included large financial investments in the Marshall Plan for rebuilding Western Europe, the nuclear arms race, the space race, and the resistance to communism in Southeast Asia that culminated in the Vietnam War. Closer to American shores, the threat of the Cuban Missile Crisis gave further credence to the government's anti-communist rhetoric. Though WWI and WWII had ended, a posture of war was aggressively maintained throughout much of the century.

Twentieth-century America was a nation that experienced extreme economic highs and lows. The post-WWI economic boom of the Roaring Twenties that resulted in America being classed as the world's richest nation, was followed by the 1929 stock market crash and the Great Depression that brought financial deprivation to many. Recovery was slow until America's entry into WWII in 1941, after which time the nation entered a period of unprecedented economic growth that lasted through the end of the century. The generation of children born in this post-WWII economic recovery has been labeled "Baby Boomers," and this was the generation of the hippies and the JP. Growing up in this period of uninterrupted economic growth and prosperity, the Baby Boomer generation stood in stark contrast to the generation of their parents who had come through the deprivation of the Great Depression. Some optimistically envisaged the dawning of a utopian era of "post-scarcity" in which food and basic necessities would become in abundant supply and work would become more balanced with leisure.[5] The result was a new generation of youth with money to spend, new blossoming youth markets in which to spend it, and an increase in youthful leisure time.

Six Marginal Movements of the Twentieth Century

Twentieth-century America was also a nation that experienced a transformation in conventional gender roles and gender identities. The Roaring Twenties initiated trends for women to sport less traditional fashions and short haircuts, to work in jobs outside the home and to enter university. In 1920 Congress had enacted the Nineteenth Amendment giving women the right to vote and run for elected office and during WWII unprecedented numbers of women went to work in factories to manufacture war supplies or to serve in various branches of the military. After the war, many women remained in the labor force and increased the acceptability of women in the workplace, but not without many pejorative stereotypes and inequalities. Beginning in 1966, women's groups like the National Organization for Women were formed to battle for equal status against what they perceived

5. Bookchin, *Post-Scarity.*

to be the oppression of women. The 1972 Equal Rights Amendment and the Supreme Court's 1973 decision in *Roe v. Wade*, which protected a woman's right to have an abortion under the 14th Amendment, seemed at the time to be evidence that the women's liberation movement was gaining ground.

As pointed out by George Chauncey, the 1920s also sowed the seeds of tolerance toward heterosexual and homosexual liberation.[6] Bohemian values that decried segregation, materialism, and strict sexual mores were promoted through jazz music, alternative art forms, the literature of the Lost Generation, plays like *The Drag*, and in locations like Greenwich Village and the Cherry Lane Theatre. What had been originally promoted with the double entendre of song lyrics in jazz music and the tongue-in-cheek of cross-dressing in the 1920s was advocated with greater earnest through the Beat Generation movement in the 1950s and in the sexual revolution of the 1960s and 1970s. The sexual revolution jettisoned conventional American taboos on heterosexual and homosexual relationships in exchange for the ethics of "free love." By the 1970s events like the Gay Pride Day Parades that sprung up from the Stonewall Riots of 1969, "gay" neighborhoods like that of Castro in San Francisco, and movements like Lesbian Gay Bisexual and Transgenderism (LGBT) were growing in influence all across America. The degree to which the sexual revolution had mainstreamed its values by the close of the century is a matter open to interpretation. For example, while it is true that by the early 1970s the field of psychiatry no longer considered homosexuality to be a mental disorder, according to Ilan Meyer discussions on mental health among lesbians and gays is still tainted by the legacy of pre-seventies terms.[7] And while the United States Supreme Court decision in *Lawrence v. Texas* struck down several state sodomy laws and decriminalized same-sex relationships, American laws on same-sex marriage remained unchanged.

Twentieth-century America was also a nation of extremes regarding intoxicating substances. According to David Farber, the Mental Health Act, passed by Congress in 1946, legitimized the mental-health practice and helped to boost the number of practicing psychiatrists from 3000 in 1940 to over 15,000 by 1956.[8] In 1943, Albert Hofmann synthesized a drug called lysergic acid diethylamide, otherwise known as LSD or "acid," which Sandoz Pharmaceuticals, in Basel, Switzerland, manufactured and marketed to the burgeoning field of American psychiatry. By the 1960s the American public had become accustomed to the field of Psychiatry and to the use of drugs as

---

6. Chauncey, "Long-Haired Men," 151–63.

7. Meyer, "Prejudice," 674.

8. Farber, "Intoxicated State," 21.

an acceptable form of Psychotherapy, at times known as psychedelic therapy. According to Farber, the hippies' parents consumed more drugs than
the hippies in the 1960s, with an estimated 123 million patient prescriptions
for tranquilizers and 24 million prescriptions for amphetamines being written in 1965 alone.[9] University campuses also witnessed high rates of LSD
exposure as, according to Imperi et al., 20 percent of students they surveyed
admitted to using hallucinogenic drugs and an additional 25–30 percent
had considered using drugs.[10]

A rather interesting twist in psychedelic therapy developed in 1961,
when a Harvard professor named Timothy Leary, who had been researching
the effects of psilocybin on personality, began to take LSD for personal experimentation. Almost immediately he touted its value for spiritual discovery. To him, LSD was no longer a mere psychotherapeutic aid for treatment;
it became a sacramental practice, an entheogenic tool for transcendence to
higher, spiritual plateaus of consciousness, and the key for searching out the
new frontier of the inner self. With evangelistic fervor he converted many
to LSD's spiritual potential and together with the likes of Allen Ginsberg,
William Burroughs, Aldous Huxley, and Alfred Hubbard, they "utilized the
insights gained from their LSD-enabled neo-childhoods in the service of
erasing adult, middle-class programming."[11] Leary soon became both a national hero and a national villain. Richard Nixon branded him as "the most
dangerous man in America," (MDMA). Leary appreciated the label for its
double entendre, as the acronym "MDMA" is also another name for one of
Leary's favorite drugs—"love drug."[12] He also gained a cult following among
many young people and he coined the phrase that became the central theme
of the Hippie movement: "Turn On, Tune In, Drop Out." It is difficult to
understate how deeply the religious value of LSD colored every fabric of the
Hippie movement and it was the very reason they were called the psychedelic generation. However, the apostles of LSD and hippiedom encountered
a major setback on October 6, 1966, when the US Government declared it
to be illegal to possess, to manufacture, or to sell LSD.

Twentieth-century America was a nation fraught with racial tensions between blacks and whites. The Emancipation Proclamation of 1863
marked the beginning of the end of slavery in America, but civil liberties for
African Americans continued to be denied until the 1950s and 1960s. Early
in the twentieth century the National Association for the Advancement

9. Ibid., 19.

10. Imperi et al., "Use of Hallucinogenic," 1022.

11. Braunstein, "Forever Young," 253.

12. Seesholtz, "Remembering Dr. Timothy Leary," 106.

of Colored People was formed and became a catalyst for challenging the inequalities and segregation during the first half of the century. The admission of African American officers into service during WWI, The Harlem Renaissance, and the fusion of white and black music in the jazz clubs of the twenties were small signs of change. However, even greater momentum for civil change in American culture was gained through the Supreme Court's decision of *Brown v. Board of Education* in 1954, the Montgomery bus boycott of 1955, the Civil Rights Acts of 1957, 1960, and 1964, the Voting Rights Act of 1965, and the famous protest marches of Martin Luther King Jr. The legal battles won in the fifties and sixties became a battle for the hearts and minds of Americans through the seventies, eighties, and nineties. By the end of the century opinions remained divided over defining and assessing the "progress" made in racial equalities, as some saw the LA race riots of 1992 as evidence that little had changed.[13]

Twentieth-century America was a nation whose beliefs became increasingly more pluralistic and more influenced by eastern religions. From the turn of the twentieth century, Zen Buddhist teachers began arriving from Japan to teach at universities and to establish Buddhist centers in various locations across America. The Immigration Act of 1965 increased the quotas for immigrants from Asia and bolstered the numbers of adherents to Asian religions through demographical changes in the population. Also, during the fifties and sixties, three notable Indian teachers immigrated to America: in 1959, Maharishi Mahesh Yogi, the founder of Transcendental Meditation (TM); in 1966, A.C. Bhaktivedanta Swami Prabhupada, the founder of International Society for Krishna Consciousness (ISKCON)—more popularly known as the Hare Krishna movement; and in 1966 Sri Swami Satchidananda, founder of Hatha Yoga (Integral Yoga). The alien nature of these religions did not impede their ability to attract large followings. Their success in America lay in their methodology that promoted a message of self-improvement, with the religious beliefs and practices having been more subtly communicated as a means to the end.

The hippies were introduced to these teachers by the Beat Generation, who themselves explored and celebrated the alluring and exotic nature of these unconventional American religious. Allen Ginsberg, for example, was a disciple of both Swami Satchidananda and Bhaktivedanta Swami, lived in ashrams in India for more than a year, and spent time at the Zen Buddhist, Dai Tokuji Monastery in Japan.[14] Gary Snyder's poems and Jack Kerouac's 1958 novel *Dharma Bums* captured the imagination of many readers and

13. "Black Demographics."
14. "Chicago 7 Trial."

opened them to Zen Buddhism's spirituality. Stephen Warner and Judith Wittner estimated that by the end of the century the number of mosques and Islamic centers in the United States were around 1,000 to 1,200, the number of Buddhist Temples and meditation centers between 1,500 and 2,000, and Hindu temples around 400.[15] This, they claim, was more attributable to the growth of new immigrant communities and than the result of conversions to these new religions.

Twentieth-century America was also a nation that experienced the birth of Pentecostalism and its spread into every sector of its Christianity. Pentecostalism is most often understood to be the teaching about the Baptism of the Holy Spirit (BHS) and the gift of tongues that was probably first introduced by Charles Parham and first experienced by Agnes Ozman in 1901. This teaching and experience was thought to have been popularized through the revival meetings, known as the Azusa Street Revivals, led by William Seymour at Azusa Street in Los Angeles, California, in 1906. More recent Pentecostal and Charismatic scholarship (Dayton, *Theological Roots*), however, has unearthed an array of nineteenth-century, proto-Pentecostal, theological themes found in Wesleyan Holiness, in nineteenth-century healing movements, in Dispensational premillennialism, and in Reformed and Keswick theologies (Menzies, "Reformed Roots"). Connecting the theological themes of Pentecostalism to the nineteenth century has helped to diminish the notion of an ex-nihilo spontaneity of the 1906 Azusa Revivals. In addition, scholars like Grant Wacker ("Golden Oldies"), Joe Creech ("Visions of Glory"), and Allan Anderson (*Spreading Fires*) through his "polynucleated" theory, have challenged the over-centralization of Azusa Street in Pentecostalism's history.

Nevertheless, Azusa Street's role in early American Pentecostalism cannot be understated. The "revivals" occurring in and around 1906 influenced and birthed many denominations that are most often identified as "classical Pentecostal." These would include the Assemblies of God (AG), the Church of God Cleveland Tennessee (CG), The International Pentecostal Holiness Church, the Church of God in Christ, the Church of God of Prophecy, and The International Church of the Foursquare Gospel (ICFG). In addition to these, there also emerged a plethora of independent Pentecostal churches and ministries that focused on healing, evangelism, and spreading the Pentecostal message of the BHS into other Christian denominations. Among them were people like David du Plessis, Glenn Clark of the Camps Farthest Out, Oral Roberts, Demos Shakarian—the founder of the FGBMFI, and David Wilkerson.

---

15. Warner and Wittner, *Gatherings*, 5.

By the late 1940s, due to the success of classical Pentecostals and independent Pentecostal churches and ministries, the experience of BHS began to spread more readily among Protestant denominations in America, and, by 1967, among the Roman Catholics.[16] This phenomenon is commonly referred to as the Charismatic Movement (CM) collectively; the Charismatic Renewal (CR) among the Protestants and the Catholic Charismatic Renewal (CCR) among the Roman Catholics. Pentecostalism's more notable beginnings among American Protestants can be traced to 1946, when a Lutheran minister named Harald Bredesen received the BHS and spread the experience to many others, both inside and outside his denomination. Later, with the help of Jean Stone, he coined the phrase "Charismatic" as a descriptive of the movement. Other names synonymous with the early years of the CR were the Lutheran minister Larry Christenson and Episcopalian ministers Dennis Bennett and Graham Pulkingham.

The CCR began in February 1967 at Duquesne University, where a group of students and professors gathered to discuss and to receive the experience of the BHS that they had read about in David Wilkerson's book *The Cross and the Switchblade* (*TCTS*). The movements of Pentecostalism among the Protestants and Catholics flourished in the sixties and seventies, but not without controversy. Two other strongly influential and controversial, pan-Charismatic movements arose in America during the 1960s and 1970s called the Shepherding Movement (D. Moore, *Shepherding Movement*) and the Word of Faith Movement (Coleman, "Faith Movement"). The JPM began in 1967 and experienced a relationship of mutual interchange with these other movements of American Pentecostalism, both influencing and being influenced by them. By the end of the twentieth-century Pentecostalism had crossed into nearly every arena of American life with such a broad array of hybridizations and overlap that no one person, organization, or church could stand as a representative voice and even the broadest descriptive statements were fraught with limitations.

The Rise of the Hippie Movement

In 1967, Haight-Ashbury, an enclave of San Francisco, was instantaneously raised to national fame by becoming the birthplace of the hippie movement. Beginning in January of that year, local and national media organizations subjected the American public to a daily barrage of images and stories that focused on a rapidly emerging new movement of young people called

16. For Assemblies of God growth from the 1940s to 1970s, see Blumhofer, *Restoring the Faith*, 4, 7, 50, 176; and Poloma, *Assemblies of God at the Crossroads*, 243.

hippies. The hippies sought a different way of life, wore distinctive fashions, conversed with a unique vocabulary, listened to an unfamiliar style of music, and openly flaunted the merits of drugs and sexual freedom. The graphic images embarrassed, enraged, and frightened mainstream Americans, but they also served to inspire and recruit thousands of youth to join in the new movement that would impact American culture for many years to come.

Haight-Ashbury, also known as "the Haight," or "Hashbury," became the staging area for the hippie movement primarily because of its low cost housing and its geographical location. According to Helen Perry, Haight-Ashbury was a neglected district of San Francisco which had suffered steady economic decline since the end of WWII and consequently many of its large Victorian homes had been converted into inexpensive, shared accommodations.[17] In the late 1950s, students from the nearby San Francisco State College discovered that these homes in the Haight offered them both the convenience of a short commute to class and more affordable housing compared to the surrounding districts. For two years previous to 1967, a growing number of Beat influenced, Bohemian young people also began to migrate into the Haight, drawn by the affordable rents and its close proximity to North Beach; the Beat's west coast home. From 1965 to the end of 1966, this eclectic confluence of students, graduates, drop outs, and Beat devotees bourgeoned to approximately 15,000. During these two years they became increasingly self-aware of their underground movement and insiders began to describe themselves with the sobriquets of "freaks" and "hippies."

Many have traced the etymology of the name hippie to a derivative of "hipster" or "hip" a slang used among Beats and others linked with the Greenwich Village jazz scene in New York; a word used to describe someone who is "in the know" or "aware."[18] It caught on as a self-descriptive nickname used by the young Beat aficionados of Haight-Ashbury during the rather short lived, organic period in the movement's history from 1965 to 1966. Outsiders were a little late to discover the term. According to Charles Perry, the earliest known reference in print media of the name hippie was found in *The San Francisco Examiner*, September 6, 1965, and researcher John Howard claimed to have first encountered the hippies in the autumn of 1966.[19]

The original hippie coterie often eulogize about the movement in the Haight-Ashbury between the years 1965–1966 as being the convivial, communal maelstrom of a new phenomenon and the stage upon which any new alternative expression could be freely acted out. To them it was a glorious

17. H. Perry, *Human Be-In*, 17–20.
18. McCleary and Jeffers, *Hippie Dictionary*, 246.
19. C. Perry, *Haight-Ashbury*, 14; and Howard, *Flowering*, 382.

insider's secret. However, it is the hippie movement from 1967 onward that is most stereotypically etched in the perception of the American public. By contrast the hippie movement from 1967 was the one associated with the squalor and desperation caused by thousands of naïve, teen runaways, and the accompanying circus of sociologists, journalists, drug dealers, and commercial marketers. Based on interviews with famous hippies like Bob Seidemann, Pat "Sunshine" Nichols, Carl Gottleibm, Jerry Garcia, and the Diggers, Alice Echols argues that the post-1967 hippie movement was so profoundly distinct that many of these "hippie forefathers" disdain the name hippie and the popular hippie movement.[20] Many of them confessed their loyalty to the Beats and preferred to call themselves freaks or Beats, if anything at all. Although the original hippie dream was altered by its rise to popularity, elements of its formative ethos remained intact throughout the popularized movement.

When listing the people and groups that influenced the hippie movement two cannot go without mentioning: The Beats—Beatniks or Beat Generation—and Ken Kesey and the Merry Pranksters. Historians of the hippie movement write unequivocally of the inspiration the hippies received from three particular Beats; Allen Ginsberg, William Burroughs, and Jack Kerouac. In the 1940s the three men first banded together as poets and a novelist in the jazz clubs of America's famed Bohemian community, Greenwich Village, New York. Thomas Albright claimed they were the "last of the Bohemians," and the "first large-scale, self-conscious and widely publicized group of middle-class dropouts."[21] Jack Kerouac is credited with coining the phrase "Beat Generation," but the man from whom they gained their inspiration was Herbert Huncke—a "short-Shift, hustler, petty thief, con artist, convicted felon, parasitic leech, [and] lifelong junkie."[22] Ginsberg's and Burroughs' poetry was bold and controversial and, according to Theodore Roszak, it paralleled the impulsive and improvisational style of jazz musician Charlie Parker.[23] Their content and tone were an expression and celebration of their own lives: an anti-establishment, sexually liberated, independent life which owed nothing to anyone, cultivated alienation, participated in eastern religions, and used drugs as a tool for spiritual exploration. Their nomadic lifestyle led them to North Beach's cafés and jazz clubs where a west coast community of Beats was established in the 1950s. It was the popularity of Kerouac's book *On The Road* and the controversy surrounding the

---

20. Echols, *Shaky Ground*, 32–33.

21. Albright, "Visuals," 354.

22. L. Lynch, "Originator," 287–89.

23. Roszak, *Making of a Counter Culture*, 127.

infamous 1957 obscenity trials, centered on Ginsberg's poem "HOWL!" and Burroughs' poem "Naked Lunch," that launched the Beats into the public limelight. In its day, "HOWL!" was so significant that Mark Doty calls it "a manifesto of the counterculture."[24] The hippies saw the Beats as something far greater than a mere contrast to the austere and banal way of traditional white America; they offered an invitation to taste and experience an intoxicating, alternative lifestyle.

While the Beats gave ideological and lifestyle inspiration, it was Ken Kesey and the Merry Pranksters that brought the psychedelic experimentation out of the closet and into the public domain of the Haight. From the proceeds of his bestselling book *One Flew Over the Cuckoo's Nest*, Kesey purchased a house in La Honda, California just outside San Francisco.[25] From his house and in other locations around San Francisco, he held what he called "acid tests;" parties that included strange sounds, Day-Glo colors, and the invitation to try LSD. Then in 1964, taking this same idea to the streets of America, Kesey and his friends The Merry Pranksters bought a school bus that they painted in Day-Glo colors and symbolically named "Further." They travelled from California to the World's Fair in New York and along the way stopped at towns across America and invited people to "get on the bus" and try LSD. Consequently, in the counterculture the phrase "get on the bus" became synonymous with those who had decided to join the celebration of LSD. The wild tale is chronicled in Tom Wolfe's *Electric Kool-Acid Test*.

All this served as a precursor to a three-day event, January 21–23, 1966, called the Trips Festival held at the Longshoremen's Hall in San Francisco.[26] A brainchild of Stuart Brand, the Trips Festival was a large scale Merry Pranksters styled acid test that brought together an estimated 6,000 hippies under one roof to "trip" on LSD to a display of lights and music.[27] Kesey and the Merry Pranksters had taken the LSD of Leary and the lifestyle of the Beats, and in place of the Beats' grim pessimism, had injected a powerful dose of celebration and merriment into the newly forming Hippie movement of Haight-Ashbury. At the event, participants were astounded to discover the large numbers of other freaks that had been privately cultivating a similar lifestyle.[28] The Haight-Ashbury's inexpensive, run down halls provided perfect locations for subsequent Trips Festivals to flourish and gave rise to famous

24. Doty, "From the Poem That Changed America," 5.
25. Whelan, "'Further,'" 67, 72.
26. "Trips Festival," 9E.
27. Wolfe, *Electric Kool-Aid Acid Test*, 224.
28. *Trips Festival Movie Introduction.*

venues like the Avalon Ballroom and the Fillmore. The Trips Festivals also made famous the iconic hippie bands like Jerry Garcia's The Grateful Dead, Janis Joplin's Big Brother and the Holding Company, Country Joe and the Fish, Quicksilver Messenger Service, and Jefferson Airplane.

The hippies self-consciousness as an alternative and subversive movement was promoted through all things being dubbed "underground." For example, Owsley Stanley, who supplied large amounts of homemade acid to the Haight-Ashbury, was called the "underground chemist." Allen Cohen's *The San Francisco Oracle*, the newspaper that acted as a networking tool for the freak community, was called the "underground newspaper." And the "acid rock" songs—which were intentionally too lengthy to air on the radio—were called "underground music." In several cities across America, enclaves sprung up of hippie communities connected with the underground, alternative happenings of San Francisco. City authorities, however, kept a close eye on the underground activity and soon after the Trips Festivals police raided Kesey's house in search of drugs.[29] With public pressure mounting lawmakers began to tighten the reins on the free use of LSD and in October 1966, the drug was declared illegal. By outlawing LSD, the central, psychedelic propellant was removed, the hippie experiment was impossible, and their movement declared illegal.

On January 14, 1967, in San Francisco's Golden Gate Park, a free event called the Human Be-In marked a new phase in the movement's history. Billed as the "Gathering of the Tribes" and drawing a crowd of at least 20,000, the Human Be-In was a one-day celebration that brought together what had been brewing in the Haight for the previous two years.[30] The celebration featured music from Santana, The Steve Miller Band, and The Grateful Dead and speeches from Timothy Leary, Richard Alpert, Dick Gregory, Allen Ginsberg, and Jerry Rubin.[31] For insiders, the Human Be-In was a protest against the illegalization of LSD only three months earlier in October 1966. As an amazing testimony to the stealthy influence of the underground newspapers, the Human Be-In was announced in the *San Francisco Oracle* and by word of mouth on the streets of the Haight, but was completely undetected by the mainstream media. The event itself caught most of the nation and the national news media off guard as the hippies seemingly appeared from nowhere. Most importantly, The Human Be-In, marked the beginning of the large-scale migration of American youth who flocked from every corner of the country to see what was happening in San Francisco.

29. "Kesey Klan in South," section II, 11.
30. "American Experience."
31. From the "Human Be-in poster."

As universities and high schools closed for Spring Break, Haight-Ashbury's streets swelled with an ever increasing influx of enthusiastic, curious youth. At first, city officials, fearful of what the city might become by summer, adopted a negative posture threatening those who intended to come to San Francisco. Realizing this had only served to strengthen anti-establishment resolve and attract more youth, the city officials decided instead to leave matters in the hands of the people of San Francisco. Several Haight-Ashbury groups formed the Council for the Summer of Love and decided on a more optimistic and accommodating strategy, even adopting a name, "The Summer of Love."[32] However, as The Summer of Love approached and the crowds continued to grow in Haight-Ashbury, a deep sense of foreboding developed and the *San Francisco Oracle* even wrote articles to discourage young people from pilgrimaging to San Francisco.[33]

The Summer of Love was officially inaugurated on June 16, 1967, with the three day Monterey Pop Music Festival. Often called the precursor to Woodstock, it drew crowds of 30,000 to 60,000 to see the most popular hippie bands of the day. The Beatles timed the release of "Sgt. Pepper's Lonely Heart's Club Band" to coincide with the festival dates as did Scott McKenzie and his version of "San Francisco." The Diggers—a self proclaimed "anarchist, guerrilla street theater" that took their name from the original English Diggers—were on hand offering free food, sponsoring a free shop, and a free health clinic as models of the new utopia. An optimistic euphoria, fuelled by LSD and marijuana, heightened the anticipation among the new arrivals for what the summer would hold. Yet, as the summer progressed and the throngs of young revelers peaked at 100,000, Haight Street, the main artery, resembled little more than a bizarre carnival of free sex, drugs, and colorful fashions. The sites became so strangely alluring that San Francisco tour operators included a "hippie tour" of Haight Street to give curious outsiders a gander.

University students in their droves, with no intention of dropping out, also joined in the Haight party and returned to their studies once the summer was over. "Weekend hippies" came to participate in the activities and then returned to their places of work and study during the week.[34] Most tragically, however, were the large numbers of 13–17 year-old runaways who were ill-prepared for life and found themselves homeless, hungry, sexually abused, and at the mercy of street level drug dealers pushing LSD, speed, cocaine, and heroin.[35] Poor hygiene in communal homes and the sharp rise

32. "American Experience."
33. Ibid.
34. Howard, *Flowering*,
35. Moses, "Runaway Youth Act," 228.

in the number of young hippies contracting sexually transmitted infections produced health care concerns. In response, some doctors gave their time and hippie bands donated money from rock concerts to operate free clinics in San Francisco. One doctor who volunteered time in a free clinic reported that 100 percent of those he had attended to were using drugs, nearly all had upper respiratory infections, and very high percentages had contracted hepatitis and venereal disease.[36] The rising deprivation transformed the Diggers free food utopia into a soup kitchen for homeless and hungry youth.

When the Summer of Love came to a close idealism and beauty had given way to despair and rancid squalor. The Haight resembled a grim ghetto and the hippie dream had turned into a frightful nightmare. This famous, chilling snippet depicts the atmosphere that summer. "Pretty little 16-year-old middle-class chick comes to the Haight to see what it's all about & gets picked up by a 17-year-old street dealer who spends all day shooting her full of speed again & again, then feeds her 3000 mikes [of acid] and raffles off her temporarily unemployed body for the biggest Haight Street gang bang since the night before last."[37] On October 6, 1967, one year after LSD was declared illegal, the Diggers performed a mock funeral as a street drama entitled "Death of the Hippie" that symbolically expressed their disgust with the summer fiasco and the end of the 1965–1966 hippiedom.

In spite of the mayhem at the Summer of Love, hippiedom was instantaneously exported from Haight-Ashbury to the nation's youth and, as early as July 1967, *Time* magazine was claiming that enclaves thrived in every major US city.[38] Over the ensuing years, as it spread it also diversified and fragmented and much of its original ethos and ideology eroded. There are two commonly accepted reasons for this. First, hippiedom was an eclectic and existential phenomenon and as more people "dropped out" and "got on the bus," its ideologies seemed to be in a constant state of flux, shaped by each person's own interpretation of what it meant to be a hippie. Second, the neo-"hip" music, fashion, hair, art, film, and dialect succumbed to commercialization. For example, hippiedom was scripted into "rock opera," theatre productions like *Hair* (1968) and *Jesus Christ Superstar* (1971) and Hollywood films like *Easy Rider* (1969). Television also jumped on the bandwagon and, as Aniko Bodroghkozy points out, attempted to bridge the gap between the establishment and the counterculture with programs like the *Smothers Brothers*, *M*A*S*H**, *The Monkees*, and *The Mod Squad*.[39] Consequently, a majority of the Baby

36. W. Harrison, "Hippies Find Golden," 14.

37. "Uncle Tim'$ Children."

38. "The Hippies," 18.

39. Bodroghkozy, *Groove Tube*, 61–199.

Boomer youth may have embraced little more than a well packaged, hippie brand, a hippie image, and a marketed product.

John Howard describes this category of popularized hippiedom as the "plastic hippie." He wrote, "Plastic hippies are young people who wear the paraphernalia of hippies (baubles, bangles, and beads) as a kind of costume. They have entered into it as a fad, and have only the most superficial under-standing of the ideology the visionaries sought over a two-year period in Haight-Ashbury to implement their view of the good society."[40] The com-mercialization of "plastic" hippiedom helped to solidify the concept of the generation gap and set in place the process by which the synthesis of some hippie values would be more readily assimilated into American mainstream society. Although "plastic," some hippie ethics had been embraced by large percentages of the under thirty population and would be carried with them into the next decade as the generation aged.

The Primary Characteristics of the Hippie Movement

Demographics

Observers unanimously commented that the hippies were mostly white, middle, and upper class youth, ranging in age from 15 to 30. These demo-graphics indicate a generation gap, hence the hippie expression "trust no one over thirty," as well as an ethnic and economic gap. The hippies in many cases were from families that enjoyed the post WWII economic prosperity. White, middle, and upper class youth, aged 15–30 could afford to "drop out," to be nomadic and to experiment with building new, ephemeral, utopian so-cieties. African Americans, on the other hand, were entrenched in the battle for their civil liberties and the newly arriving Asian and Latino immigrants were striving to establish themselves and their communities. The establish-ment that white hippies despised was the same establishment that held the key to prosperity and social justice for Asians, Hispanics, and African Americans. Peter Braunstein and Michael Doyle discuss the tensions that existed between the hippies and other ethnic communities and brand the hippie experiment as "virtual poverty" and "fantasy Ghettos."[41] One black resident of New York's East Village said, "the hippies really bug us, because we know they can come down here and play their games for a while and then escape. And we can't, man."[42] The hippies were not racist, but they were

40. Howard, "Flowering of the Hippie Movement," 43.
41. Braunstein and Doyle, "Historicizing," 12.
42. *Village Voice*, 43.

indifferent to the causes of other racial communities. African Americans, Latinos, and Asians were scattered throughout their ranks, but the hippie movement was predominantly a white American youth movement.

Determining the number of participants is very difficult as most estimates were little more than guesses. For example, Lewis Yablonski's often cited "fulltime participants" of 200,000 and "part time" participants of 200,000, as well as *Time* magazine's estimate at "300,000 total participants" were not based on qualitative statistical analysis.[43] In addition they were written very early in the movement's history. Later numbers like the 500,000 who reportedly attended the Woodstock music festival in 1969 and the rising numbers of youth runaways reported by the FBI that peaked at 204,544 in 1972, should also be considered.[44] The level of participation in the hippie movement, as Howard ("Flowering") points out, further complicates attempts to count hippies.

Spiritual and Alternative Political

Among the various movements of the American counterculture, the New Left and the Hippie movement were perhaps the closest cousins. Both the hippies and the New Left shared a common discontent with the American establishment and both primarily consisted of young, white people. Both were aware of each other and could be found at times at each others "happenings." Yet there was little else they held in common and their feelings toward each other ranged from sympathetic to antagonistic. The New Left was politically motivated and tended to be non-religious, while the hippies held alternative political views and were very religious. New Left groups like the Students for Democratic Society (SDS) and the Student Non-violent Coordinating Committee set the university campuses of America alight with protest and believed that the political system held the key for societal change. The years 1968 and 1969 are remembered for their violence and demonstrations: in 1968 the protests against the assassination of Dr Martin Luther King Junior and Robert Kennedy along with the riotous protests at Columbia University and the Democratic National Convention stand out as the more memorable ones. In 1969, sit-ins and student protests at universities occurred in rapid succession. Heightened anxiety levels spilled over into numerous anti-Vietnam war protests; the most notable being the Moratorium, staged on the November 15, 1969, on the Mall in Washington DC,

43. Yablonski, *Hippie Trip*, 36; "Hippies," 18.

44. Moses, "Runaway Youth Act," 229. The FBI only began keeping records on runaways in 1964.

which gathered a crowd of more than 250,000.[45] On May 4, 1970, mounting tensions also led to the tragedy at Kent State University, in which four students were killed and nine others wounded as the Ohio National Guard opened fire on a students' rally.[46] Groups like the SDS, The Yippies, The Weathermen, and The Black Panthers sparked the sharper political overtones in these activities. Doug Rossinow highlights that these groups, far smaller in number, shared the hippies' culture of dissent, but criticized the hippies' political aloofness as middle class escapism.[47]

The hippies, on the other hand, rejected the New Left's notion that the establishment held the keys to change and believed instead that the American establishment existed solely to maintain itself and the status quo. They declared war on the establishment through long hair, music, drama, and psychedelic spirituality. Their political response was to build an alternative, utopian society, parallel to and in contrast against the established American institutions. What the university campus meant to the New Left as a place for demonstration, the commune meant to the hippies as a place for building a new, alternative world; one that valued a communal life of shared possessions, sexual liberty, drugs, religious pursuits, love, and peace instead of war.

Entheogenic and Psychedelic Religion

The hippie movement was a religious movement and every thread of its fabric was colored with eastern and American Indian religions. A majority of hippies, being true to their existential nature, were content with a cursory familiarity of the historical and theological teachings of Hinduism and Buddhism. Instead, they preferred to experience and to practice them. Religions of the east were mystical and novel alternatives to the conventional Christianity and Judaism most hippies were accustomed to from their childhood socialization. Many hippies also took an interest in American Indian shamanism, including the use of Peyote as an entheogen, as popularized in Carlos Castaneda's controversial book *The Teachings of Don Juan* (1968). Drug induced, religious hallucinations were believed to be the path to personal transformation. A solipsistic journey and discovery of the inner self was thought to be found in altered states of consciousness and was expected to produce a more spiritually connected, tranquil, and loving individual. As esoteric as these religions were, their outcomes were pragmatically focused on individual self-improvement.

45. Leen, "Vietnam Protests," A1.
46. May Fourth Task Force, "President's Commission on Campus Unrest."
47. Rossinow, "Revolution," 99–102, 109.

Being a religious movement, it was the antithesis of skeptical atheism or agnosticism. Lawrence Swaim humorously commented, an "occasional hippie will tell you that God does exist, that he saw him sitting in a tree."[48] From the Human Be-In that featured Allen Ginsberg chanting "Om," to the blessing performed by Sri Swami Satchidananda at the opening of Woodstock—the "Aquarian Exposition"—spirituality featured so extensively in hippie symbols, words, dress, gestures, art, and music that Timothy Miller claimed "religion was as lively a center of the action as any."[49] Robert Ellwood paralleled it to the colonial Great Awakening, the frontier revivals, and the Spiritualists' movement of the 1850s, saying, "I propose that the story of religion, and religious consciousness, in that decade offers an indispensable key to understanding changes wrought by the Sixties in society as a whole."[50] Hippie gatherings included spontaneous yantric dance, and hip Haight Street shops marketed bangles, incense, crystals, and books that taught the concepts of karma and dharma. Advertisements on posters and images in underground newspapers included hippie visionaries dressed in kurta pyjamas, reverently folding their hands in a typical Hindu greeting, sadhus donning the third eye of Shiva, and new age art. In August 1967, the Beatles met with Maharishi Mahesh Yogi and embraced his Transcendental Meditation teaching, a decision that in turn influenced many thousands of young hippies to follow suit.[51] Some of the songs from the Beatles' *The White Album* were written during visits to Maharishi's ashram in Rishikesh, and a portion of the sixteen-word, Maha Mantra of ISKCON also made its way into George Harrison's familiar song "My Sweet Lord."

Anti-Established Church

With all the interest in eastern religions, it might be assumed that Jesus Christ did not fare too well in the counterculture. However, the massive success of plays like *Jesus Christ Superstar* (1971) and *Godspell* (1971) show that He was quite popular, albeit as a Jesus recreated in hippie likeness. Jesus even worked his way into many hippie songs like The Byrds and The Doobie Brothers cover versions of Arthur Reynolds' 1966 gospel hit "Jesus is Just Alright," Simon and Garfunkel's "Mrs. Robinson," and James Taylor's "Fire and Rain." Hippies may have felt that Jesus was "just alright" but they were less endearing towards established Christianity as they were seen to be "self-righteous centers of

48. Swaim, "Hippies," 17.
49. T. Miller, *60s Communes*, 92.
50. Ellwood, *Sixties*, 10, 19.
51. "Maharishi Mahesh Yogi."

hypocrisy, stations for the blessing of the establishment, wealthy organizations mainly interested in preserving themselves, havens for the narrow-minded, anachronisms utterly irrelevant to modern life."[52]

Communal Utopia

The hippie movement was a communal movement that, according to Timothy Miller, quickly became the largest in American history, out-communing all preceding movements combined.[53] Many have attempted to estimate the number of hippie communes, but Miller states that these are mere "wild guesses" and the "the quotations of the wild guesses of others."[54] Communes ranged in size from small to large and were located in urban areas as "crash pads" as well as in rural areas with extensive housing complexes. While they could be found all across America, Miller argues for three main areas of hippie communal activity centered in California, New Mexico, and from New England to Virginia.[55] And although communalism was part of the hippie movement from its inception in 1965, the year 1968 marked the point at which "the communal stream became a torrent."[56]

A paradox can be observed in the hippie movement that was best exemplified in their communes. On one hand the hippies shared a similar pessimism with their Beat Generation forefathers expressed in anti-establishment rhetoric and counterculture dissent. But on the other hand, they were optimistic and believed that they could construct a utopian society and this was a point of departure from the Beats' darker, cynical, and almost purely deconstructionist ideology.[57] The hippies believed their new world could be attained. But, like a flash in the pan, hippie communalism almost completely disappeared by the end of the seventies with a few remnants like Stephen Gaskin's "The Farm" in Summertown, Tennessee, remaining to date.

Anti-Vietnam War

The single most unifying characteristic of the many diverse groups that made up the American counterculture movement was the dissent against

52. T. Miller, *Hippies*, 18.
53. T. Miller, *60s Communes*, xiii.
54. Ibid., xviii.
55. Ibid., 41.
56. Ibid., 15.
57. Albright, *Visuals*, 354.

the Vietnam War. From the earliest days of the hippie movement, discontentment over the war inspired the responses of peace and love that were expressed in their symbols, poetry, and music. Many of the youth of the 1960s were unconvinced that the war was necessary and, according to Braunstein and Doyle, felt that the war was nothing more than another extension of Post WWII American triumphalism.[58] However, the sparks that ignited the powder keg of youthful discontentment were President Lyndon Johnson's decision to escalate the war in 1965 and the "Tet Offensive" of 1968. In order to increase the number of troops in Southeast Asia, the US Government drafted enormous numbers of young people into its military service, bolstering the US troop levels in Vietnam from 1,000 in 1961 to 537,000 in 1968; the highest level during the war.[59] The draft brought home the horrors of an inevitable destiny with death for many young American men and it was not long before soldiers returned home in coffins by the thousands. The number of American dead in the Vietnam War reached a total of 40,024 by yearend 1969.[60] Sandi Stein, a hippie from the sixties remembers, "When somebody was killed in Vietnam they would put a flag in the window. And there was not a block that you could walk in that working class, middle class neighborhood that you didn't see flags in the windows."[61] Young people retaliated by draft dodging, public draft card burnings, and protests against the US Government's decision to go to war; acts that were considered unthinkably unpatriotic by older generations. Although the hippies were less engaged in the political protests, their bitter, anti-Vietnam rhetoric served as an important recruiting tool for the movement.

Hippie Identity

The Beats were poets and novelists, but the hippies were musicians and the story of their music is one of the evolutionary transition from blues, jazz, folk, and short pop songs to folk-rock and electric (or acid) rock, including long instrumental solos at loud volume levels. Hippie themes are replete in their song titles, such as in Bob Dylan's "The Times They are a Changin'" and The Who's "My Generation" that celebrated the generation gap. Others like "Light My Fire" by The Doors flaunted free love while "Purple Haze" by Jimi Hendricks and "White Rabbit" by Jefferson Airplane sung about psychedelic trips. The songs not only became famously identified with the

58. Braunstein and Doyle, "Historicizing," 8.

59. Kane, "Global U.S. Troop."

60. Addington, *America's War in Vietnam*, 130.

61. "The American Experience."

counterculture, but the musicians also became iconic celebrities. And it was not long before the underground music movement emerged into a profitable commercial market. From 1967, the music of the Haight amalgamated with the British Invasion bringing on board bands like the Beatles, The Rolling Stones, The Animals, and The Who. An example of this merger can be seen in the Beatles *Red Album* a compilation of their pre-hippie hits from 1962 to 1966, and their *Blue Album,* their hippie hits from 1967 to 1970. Along side the burgeoning commercial market for hippie music were the outdoor festivals, where hippie music was sung as large celebration gatherings.

Music was the primary medium for the rapid spread and assimilation of hippie values to the under thirty generation. In his analysis of the lyrics of the top twenty songs of 1963–1972, Gary Burns summarized the values as the "protagonists [who] now could not find utopia within the context of Establishment society."[62] He states that the common values in the lyrics of counterculture music were "sensory gratification, escape from society, nurturance, universal love, bright future and war."[63] The fact that what had been called an alternative, subversive, and countercultural form of music could, within a few short years, be classed as a genre of American pop music, indicates how effective a medium the music was for rapidly diffusing hippie values to the American mainstream.

Through their clothing the hippies erected symbolic boundaries to indicate who was "in" and who was "out" of the movement. For the men it included homemade fashions such as long, unkempt hair, beards and moustaches, headbands, fringed leather vests, wide leather belts, and denim jeans. The girls' accessories included headbands, pseudo American Indian pieces of kit, halter-tops, miniskirts, hip-hugger and bellbottom jeans, a peasant frock with fine, floral patterns, go-go boots, and a flower in the hair. Both genders could be found wearing tie-dye shirts, a necklace of beads, the peace symbol either as a necklace or a belt buckle, and sandals or bare feet. The colorful display of costumes identified who the hippies were and created many photo opportunities that have left a memorable impression to this day. Although hippie styles have died off, their casual fashion has become acceptable in American mainstream culture.

In addition to music and fashion the hippies used the mediums of art, dialect, underground newspapers, and street drama to express themselves and to spread their movement. The most pervasive feature in hippie art, often called psychedelic art, was the kaleidoscope patterns intended to visualize the experience of LSD. Wavy patterns were splashed across album

---

62. Burns, "Trends in Lyrics," 134.

63. Ibid., 140.

covers, posters, and underground newspapers as an artistic statement of how acid had inspired every element of the movement. The hippies were fascinated with the American Indians and through their art and clothing made them an emblem of their own movement. Philip Deloria calls this "playing Indian."[64] He points out that while the hippies never took up the political causes of the American Indians, their portrayal of Indians in their art, changing their names to Indian names, and wearing Indian clothing were superficial ways of equating their movement with the struggle and op-pression of the American Indians. As for their jargon, the hippies spoke in a vocabulary of unique words, colloquialisms, and idioms so numerous that one book, *The Hippie Dictionary* (2004), contains over 6,000 entries.

Perhaps there was no place that hippie art and language was more prev-alent than in the myriad of "underground newspapers," whose widespread circulation on the streets of the Haight acted as a networking tool in the community and fostered the movement's growing ethos. All across America underground newspapers seemed as ubiquitous as hippies themselves, the most iconic one being *The San Francisco Oracle (The Oracle)*. Founded by Allen Cohen in 1966, *The Oracle* often included articles that narrated and interpreted LSD hallucinations, and at its peak in 1967, claimed to have had a circulation of 500,000.[65] Hippies also regularly performed free street dramas in parks and other public gatherings that communicated and rein-forced the culture of dissent and the optimism of utopia building. Two of the most famous street theatre companies were The San Francisco Mime Troupe and the Diggers; the latter sought to dramatize a vision of society free from private property and from all forms of buying and selling. The music, fashion, art, dialect, and street dramas all served as symbolic bound-aries that facilitated the globalization of hippiedom through the heyday of the movement and into the late seventies.

The Decline of the Hippie Movement

Several notable factors contributed to hippiedom's demise after the mid sev-enties. First, the American media played a pivotal role in popularizing, re-shaping, and normalizing the movement's values. From the Summer of Love in 1967 to Woodstock in 1969, the stories published in the news media both loathed and loved the flower children. While it is commonly thought that the movement continued to grow in numbers until 1972 or 1975, the visible pinnacle of the hippie movement was the Woodstock Music and Art Fair in

64. Deloria, "Counterculture Indians," 179–80.
65. "Allen Cohen on the San Francisco Oracle."

the 1960s and the hippies   23

August 1969. However, a series of horrifying events in 1969 and 1970 seemed to sour the overall tone in media reports. That is, in July 1969, John Sinclair, the leader of the White Panthers was sentenced to nine years in prison for his third marijuana offense. In August of 1969, Charles Manson was charged with the murders of Sharon Tate and Leo and Rosemary LaBianca. In December 1969, an incident at a Rolling Stones' concert at Altamont Speedway resulted in the stabbing death of Meredith Hunter by a member of the Hell's Angels. Then the deaths of hippie legends Jimi Hendrix, in September 1970, and Janis Joplin, in October 1970, from drug overdose seemed to bring the merriment to an end. The media portrayed these as the dour and dark underworld of the hippies. In contrast to these images, TV programs and films presented a domesticated and acceptable hippie movement to the mainstream American culture. As Bodroghkozy (*Groove Tube*) argued, these films and programs co-opted large portions of counterculture youth into a TV generated hippiedom. Kenneth Bindas and Kenneth Heindman similarly claimed that "the dominant society legitimized the countercultural ideas of youth, and that the mass media popularized the idea of a generation gap, depicting it as a phenomenon of ideological difference."[66]

Second, due to factors beyond the media's influence, hippie values amalgamated with and conformed to mainstream American cultural norms. As they did, the distinctive ethos separating the counterculture from the established culture diminished. From the early seventies, hippiedom's identity became increasingly less autonomous, less sensational, less aberrant, and more recognizable as a normal part of American culture. Not only were American values being challenged and shaped by hippie values, but hippie values were being compromised in the bartering process. As Koch et al. ("Body Art") have argued, deviant behavior is a necessary tool in a subculture's effort to maintain distance from the dominant culture. The price of legitimization and acceptability was the sacrifice of the subversive deviance and the social distance necessary to maintain the hippie identity as something separate from the majority culture.

Third, from the mid-sixties and into the early seventies, Vietnam War protests were an integral part of the hippies' and the New Left's ontology. Paradoxically, while the anti-war dissent had succeeded in bringing an end to the Vietnam War, it had also succeeded in removing an essential reason for being. Disarmed of its primary social lever, the counterculture quickly dissipated and splintered into numerous movements with diverse agendas. Fourth, as the hippie youth grew older, many completed their education, married, and began to look for employment. The establishment

66. Bindas and Heinman, "Image Is Everything?," 22.

they bemoaned, was now the system that would help them settle and succeed. And as Steve Gillon pointed out, the US economy in the 1970s slowed under the strain of absorbing nearly two million workers every year, one million of those being Baby Boomer, university graduates.[67] Competition for jobs contributed toward high levels of unemployment and coupled with inflation in the early 1970s, a generation accustomed to ever increasing prosperity encountered, for the first time, economic recession. With poor economic conditions threatening the prospects of building utopian, communal societies, optimism gave way to pessimism and many saw the hippie dream slipping beyond reach and reason. Not only did the end of the war and economics play a part, but hippie music and fashion were also superseded by the sounds and fashion of disco. According to Mary Stibal, by 1976, disco had already grossed $4 billion as an industry and witnessed the opening of 10,000 disco clubs nationwide.[68] Also, according to Frank Gillian, disco gained a gay stigma, setting it at odds with the rock loving, heterosexual hippies. The growth of disco reinforced the impression that the counterculture had ended and that America was moving on. The times, they were again changing.[69]

Evaluation and Conclusion

Over the years, an abundance of theories have been forwarded that attempt to explain why the marginal movements fomented into revolution in the 1960s. Probably the most famous are the proposals from two academics, Theodore Roszak's *The Making of the Counterculture* (1968) and Charles Reich's New York Times Best seller *The Greening of America* (1970). Roszak's optimistic speculation saw the counterculture as a youthful revolt against the modernist hegemonies that he called "technocracy" and he predicted that the clash would spell the supremacy of man over technology. Irrespective of its outdated modernization/secularization theoretical framework, the book remains one of the most helpful introductions to the counterculture. Reich was also optimistic about the destiny of the counterculture and envisioned America morphing through three stages of consciousness: from the values of the small business and agrarian lifestyle of the nineteenth century, to the values of the organizational society in the first half of the twentieth century, to the values of the new countercultural generation that esteemed the self-actualization of the individual. Reich wrote his analysis as an apologist and

67. Gillon, *Boomer Nation*, 21–22.
68. Stibal, "Disco," 82.
69. Gillian, "Discophobia," 276–307.

prophet, contending that through changing every individual conscience, the counterculture would conquer the entire establishment.

Many in the American counterculture shared Roszak and Reich's optimistic tone of triumphalism, believing they were ushering in the dawning of a new era. This mood brings to light the paradoxical tension between pessimism and optimism within the movement mentioned before. On one hand, negative sentiments bubbled over into passionate dissent and fierce protest against the establishment and was, in part, causal of their self-interpreted identity as a suppressed, "underground" revolution. This despairing mood frequently surfaces in the lyrics of hippie songs like Jefferson Airplane's "Somebody to Love." On the other hand, the counterculture emitted a positive disposition that cheerfully and naïvely anticipated an imminent victory over the mainstream establishment. Many participants believed that their mission of change would succeed, as Paul Berman in *The Tale of Two Utopias* (1996) remembers. For example, in 1967, Timothy Leary predicted that within fifteen years the US Supreme Court would be smoking marijuana.[70] Joan Baez triumphantly led the Woodstock crowd in the song "We Shall Overcome," symbolically linking the hippie struggle with the victories of the Civil Rights movement.[71] And the *Hair* anthem "Aquarius" awaited the sudden, foreordained, and irrepressible shift in the astrological ages from Pisces to Aquarius that was to be felt among men; a cosmic victory for counterculture as the gods were presumably on their side.[72]

Another paradox lies in assessing the accuracy of the predictions of the counterculture's long-term effects. On one hand the decline of the movement by the mid-seventies quickly deflated any lofty notions of the counterculture overthrowing the American establishment. Or for example, Roszak's prediction that the counterculture heyday would not decline until about 1984 had obviously missed the mark.[73] On the other hand, his predictions that the counterculture would have aftereffects on American culture for years to come were accurate. And Reich's concept of a third conscience—an era of self-actualization—is worthy of consideration. Paradoxes aside, if the counterculture were considered as broadly inclusive of the Civil Rights movement, the New Left, the Hippies movement, Environmentalism, the sexual revolution, the Women's Liberation, and the LGBT movement, it can be maintained that the values associated with these movements were no longer marginal by the eighties and nineties. Locating American Pentecostalism

---

70. Roszak, *Making of a Counterculture*, 168.

71. Wadleigh, "Woodstock."

72. The 5th Dimension, "Aquarius/Let the Sunshine In."

73. Roszak, *Making of a Counterculture*, 40.

as a similar movement that, alongside these other movements, also gained mainstream acceptability in the 1960s, makes it an integral part of the cultural revolution of this era. While these movements did not succeed in establishing a new hegemony, they did legitimized themselves as viable competitors for shaping the values of American mainstream culture. Hence it is plausible to say that a conversation can be framed around a pre-sixties and post-sixties American culture. The following chapters explore the historical, sociological, and theological nature of the JPM and its place as another marginal phenomenon that gained mainstream acceptability during the sixties and seventies.

Chapter 2

A Historical Overview

A Brief Overview of the Jesus People Movement

BY JANUARY 1967, HAIGHT-ASHBURY had already been buzzing with underground, psychedelic developments for a couple of years. The nation's media and the American public were transfixed by the swarms of youth arriving on the streets of San Francisco over the spring and summer of 1967 and were completely unaware that hippiedom had birthed another unconventional offspring, the Jesus People Movement. The first two years of its existence, this new phenomenon was comprised of young bohemians who once pursued the hippie vision but claimed instead to have found love, peace, and joy through a personal encounter with Jesus Christ. To them the hippiedom's utopian promise had proved elusive, empty, and even destructive. Jesus, on the other hand, had allegedly appeared in dramatic visions, instantaneously healed from drug addiction, delivered from demons, and given new spiritual birth.

Still flower children in their dress and general outlook on life, many of these original JP had abandoned the hippies' ethics of sexual liberty, drugs, and eastern religions and etched out a separate but similar identity to the hippies. In much the same way, the JP embraced Pentecostal spirituality, but rejected many classical Pentecostal conventions, resulting in a separate but similar identity within American Pentecostalism. The experience orientation of Pentecostalism and the person of Jesus Christ offered a replacement for the psychedelic experimentation pursued in hippiedom.[1] The JP shared the anti-Vietnam War sentiment of the hippies, but believed that only Jesus could bring real peace and love. The counterculture's dissent against the establishment and Christendom was almost completely adopted into the ethos of the early days of the JPM. And the hippies' optimistic expectation

1. Jacob, *Pop Goes Jesus*, 25.

27

of ushering in a new Aquarian age of utopia was jettisoned in exchange for Pentecostal's premillennial utopia and the soon appearing kingdom of Jesus Christ. To the bewilderment and consternation of both hippies and Christians, their message and identity was successful in converting and recruiting large numbers of youth.

News spread quickly that the psychedelic youth were holding Bible studies, conducting all night prayer meetings, speaking in tongues, experiencing healings and demonic exorcisms, courageously preaching the gospel of Jesus, and conducting public beach baptisms. The JP adopted and redeemed the long hair, fashion, music, outdoor festivals, cafés, communal homes, newspapers, and art of the hippies and eventually emerged as a burgeoning hybrid manifestation of American Pentecostalism. As the sixties progressed into the seventies, the JPM inveigled large numbers of church youth who never were hippies, but empathized with elements of hippiedom's ideologies and the generation gap. In some churches, large numbers of career professionals were also drawn to the movement.[2] The JPM also baited the curiosity of many sociologists and the national and local news media. And although peaking sometime in the mid-1970s and dissipating as a visible movement by the end of the 1970s, the institutions and offshoots of the JPM have continued to grow and to profoundly impact American Christianity into the twenty-first century. Historian Mark Noll commented, "The short-lived prominence of the Jesus People should not blind us to their wide-ranging significance."[3]

When examining the entire movement as a single phenomenon, it must be kept in mind that the JPM was an extremely vast and heterogeneous collection of movements, or a family of movements. It did not have a founder and did not emanate from a single geographical location. In fact, the JPM was a clustering of a myriad of independent communities each one led by one individual and while these communities most often shared common features, they also had developed their own hybrid peculiarities. Independent groups like the Children of God, The Jesus People Army, Gospel Outreach, The Love Inn, Calvary Chapel, are all examples of JP communities that are clustered under the single umbrella of the JPM. Each community was aware of each other and they were aware that they were associated with the JPM, quite a few even claimed to be the leader or originator of the JPM. The leaders never sought to join together as a single expression as Charismatics did in Kansas City in 1975 or to bargain at the table of ecumenicalism as Classical Pentecostals did at the formation of the

---

2. Balmer and Todd, "Calvary Chapel," 667.
3. Noll, "Where We Are," 6.

NAE in 1942. Instead, most were preoccupied with carving out their own independent identity and have remained obscure and excluded figures from American Pentecostalism's historical accounts.

This collection of movements that was loosely drawn together and classified under one broad umbrella known as the JPM, cross-pollinated with nearly every denomination of Christianity in America. In fact, if an inventory were made of the churches and ministries that did not participate in the JPM or were not affected, it would form a rather short list. The JPM's vastness and diversity quickly unravels any theories of singularity of cause, frustrates the notion that there was a founder or a single geographical place of origin, and severally complicates anecdotal conclusions. The remainder of this chapter attempts to enter this labyrinth and to rediscover some of the general qualities of this missing player in the history of American Pentecostalism.

Demographics and General Characteristics

Accounts unanimously agreed that the JP were mostly white youth, aged between 13 to 30. This could be expected since they were drawn from the ranks of the hippies. For example, the Salvation Army ran "The Answer" café in Greenwich Village and reported the average age of the hippies visiting the outreach in 1967 to have been between 14 and 22 years old.[4] One minister claimed it was not uncommon to find runaway kids as young as 11–13 years of age at meetings and many church leaders remembered the joy of reuniting youth with their distraught families.[5] It was also noted that men as young as 17–19 years old had been appointed as "elders" of communal homes.[6]

It was also frequently stated that the JP were from middle-class, educated, or wealthy families.[7] However, there never was a broad quantitative survey of the JP that sought answers to these questions and like other quantitative claims, they tended to be guesses. A few limited surveys were conducted of individual communities, like that of Simmonds et al., but these cannot be assumed to be representative of the entire JPM.[8] Although class was not the primary interest of this research, the JP interviewed in this study represented a very diverse range of family backgrounds. And the

---

4. "Salvation Army is 'Groovy,'" 18a.

5. Enroth et al., *Story*, 99.

6. Richardson et al., *Organized Miracles*, 8.

7. For example, see Jorstad, *That New Time Religion*, 62; Peterson and Mauss, *Cross*, 267.

8. Simmonds et al., "Organizational Aspects," 273.

accounts recorded in newspapers and books include JP from both wealthy and lower income families as well as those from educated and uneducated family backgrounds. Since the movement is now over, more exact statistics on class are probably beyond searching out. But, given the heterogeneity of the phenomenon, it would not be implausible to see the JP as representing a broad spectrum of class. One of the rather unusual marks of the JPM was that the majority of its participants, especially in the early days, were single males.[9] This rather unique quality distinguishes the JPM from other movements in American Pentecostalism as most were often a female majority.

The numbers of participants recorded in books and magazines were also little more than guesses that should be taken with a grain of salt. For example, Edward Plowman wrote, "Perhaps a tenth or more of the entire student body at the University of California at Irvine . . . joined the Jesus Movement in the 1970–71 school year."[10] On the back cover of *Back to Jesus*, Peter Michelmore claimed that over half a million young people were involved in the JPM. Or a *Time* article stated there were probably 10,000 JP in Holland.[11] Accuracy aside, these comments accentuate the authors' sense of astonishment at the numbers of participants and, while they may not be quantitatively reliable, they must not be immediately dismissed as mere sensationalism. Walter Hollenweger summarized the wide variance of estimations that he found as those ranging between "a kernel of several thousand to three million members."[12]

Two insightful pieces of quantitative information that indicate something of the size of the JPM are the numbers of people that attended Explo '72 and the numbers of youth baptisms in the Southern Baptist Convention (SBC) also in 1972. Held in Dallas, Texas from June 12–17 and sponsored by Campus Crusade for Christ (CCC), Explo '72 was the largest single gathering of JP with around 80,000 attending daily and approximately 200,000 showing up on the final day.[13] And according to Alvin Reid the JPM caused the youth baptisms in the SBC to peak at 137,667 in 1972, the highest ever recorded among the SBC. Reid's quantitative research is one of a kind. Yet, as impressive as these numbers are, they are limited to the SBC and a single event, Explo '72, and it is impossible to project anything concrete from these figures across the entire JPM.[14]

---

9. Richardson and Reidy, "Form and Fluidity," 189.

10. Plowman, *Jesus Movement*, 76.

11. "Jesus Evolution."

12. Hollenweger, *Pentecost Between Black and White*, 99–100.

13. Eshelman, *Explo Story*, 86.

14. Reid, "Impact," 36–37.

Although generally accepting of all races, only small numbers of Latinos, Asians, and African Americans were found among their ranks and
the JP made little effort to engage in the African American struggle for civil
rights. In the interest of inclusion there were occasional and awkward references to a "black evangelist," to highlight "black" participation.[15] In spite
of CCC's offer of $50,000 in scholarships to recruit African Americans for
Explo '72, only 3,000 were estimated to have attended.[16] Bill Bright, CCC
founder, believed the reason to be that "Blacks are not as affluent and thus as
free to leave jobs as whites."[17] Dr. Thomas Kilgore gave a different explanation for low levels of African American participation in the JPM. He said,
"The reason according to a leading Negro clergyman here is that they aren't
going to be 'sidetracked' into the white, middle-class movement because
'they've found reality in their thrust for basic human rights.' The black youth
thing is 'still in their own bag.' Young people are coming back in greater
numbers to churches in the black community."[18]

It is widely accepted that the phrase "Jesus Movement" first appeared
in an article written by Brian Vachon in *Life* Magazine in 1971, and was
coined by Jack and Betty Cheetham. The origin of the sobriquet "Jesus
People," however, was rather evolutionary and impossible to pin down to
one person. The JP were first called "Jesus Freaks," "Hippie Christians,"
"Street Christians," "street people," and "Evangelical Hippies"; names with
intentionally pejorative overtones.[19] These early nicknames indicate how
observers originally interpreted the phenomenon as a mélange of hippiedom and Evangelicalism. Pat King wrote about a group of converted hippies from Carmel Valley, California who, in 1966, called themselves "The
Fellowship of Freaks." These were the first Jesus Freaks she was aware of.[20]
Edward Plowman first heard the name "Jesus Freak" at an anti-war protest
in Golden Gate Park in April 1969, where it was applied to the Christian
World Liberation Front (CWLF).[21]

Duane Pederson, founder of the *Hollywood Free Paper* (*HFP*), claimed
to have coined the name "Jesus People" and, according to Lowell Streiker,
later registered it as a trademark.[22] Despite Pederson's claim, Plowman said

15. "Skinner Gets Them Together," 45.

16. Plowman, "Explo '72," 31.

17. Ibid.

18. "Few Blacks Seen," 25.

19. See "Street Christians"; and Mellis, *Committed*, 73.

20. P. King, *Jesus People*, 6.

21. Plowman, *Jesus Movement*, 73.

22. Streiker, *Jesus Trip*, 12.

that he first read the name "Jesus People" in a tract published in 1969 by a San Francisco based group.[23] And the first time the phrase "Jesus People" appeared in a print was in February 1967, when the Rev. Malcolm Boyd, the "espresso priest," used it to describe an "underground church" in which there was a "religious revolution" that was largely unknown to the organized church.[24] He had been aware of the movement since August 1966 and claimed that it was spreading across the country, it cut through denominational lines, and it constituted a variety of people who were concerned with poverty and peace.[25] He said, "They are 'Jesus People' and they include many Jews."[26] Pederson may have popularized the name Jesus People by publishing it in the *HFP*, but the examples of Boyd and Plowman present evidence that the phrase was already in circulation from the earliest days of the JPM and cast doubt on his claim to originality.

In dress, hair, and fashion the JP were indistinguishable from the hippies and maintaining their outward appearance facilitated their outreach to other hippies. As one JP said, "A Christian, like Paul said, has to become all things to all men. I really believe that a Christian has to dress or act or groom himself according to the type of people he witnesses to."[27] Although it built a bridge with their fellow hippies, their appearance also meant ostracism from established churches, as this JP complained, "Church people have twisted my arm trying to make me conform to their life-style, but Jesus never told me to cut my hair."[28]

The JP successfully adopted the hippies' and Beats' coffeehouses into their movement and frequented them as places to associate with people of like mind. They were often the initial point of contact between the JP and the hippies, offering free food and coffee as well as prayer and Bible discussions, known as "raps." Often operating on shoe string budgets and from very rudimentary facilities, the average JP coffeehouse bore no resemblance to the upscale, high street cafés. However, these humble coffeehouses played a vital role in the birth of Jesus Music as bands were regularly offered a chance to play, often for little or no money. One of the more famous coffeehouses was The Salt Company, sponsored by Hollywood Presbyterian Church and according to Plowman the largest coffeehouse was called The Catacombs.[29]

23. Plowman, *Jesus Movement*, 73–74.

24. "'Underground Church' Spreads In U.S.," 25.

25. Ibid.

26. Ibid.

27. Ortega, *Jesus People*, 85.

28. Halliday, *Spaced out*, 38.

29. Plowman, *Jesus Movement*, 63.

Located in Seattle and operated by Linda Meissner's Jesus People Army, by 1971 The Catacombs reportedly drew as many as 400 young people on a single evening and claimed weekly attendances of 2000.[30]

Communal living was such a prominent feature of the JPM that according to Timothy Miller the JP may have out-communed the hippies. Miller wrote, "Indeed, so many of them erupted that the Jesus communes may have been in terms of sheer numbers of communes and of members, the largest identifiable communal type during the 1960s era."[31] He estimates that the number of JP communes ran into the thousands and that any estimation at the exact number is only a "wild guess."[32] He also observed that most were urban, and mostly situated in California.[33]

Although communal living was a borrowed hippie practice, the JP interpreted it to be a biblical practice as found in Acts 2:42–47. One JP said, "I don't know what the Socialists are but the Bible talks about communal living as it's called; living together, sharing all of the things that you have. This is the way the Bible preaches it."[34] JP communes varied from urban to rural and from tightly to loosely structured. All offered a combination of practical housing needs for transient youth as well as a place for teaching and Christian friendships. A majority of the communes received financial sponsorship from sympathetic Christians while others sought to be self-supporting. The JP communes also proved to be extremely temporary and by the late seventies had nearly completely vanished from the stage of American history.

Borrowing the idea of the hippies' "underground press," the JP also printed and distributed their own "underground newspapers" called Jesus newspapers. Like the numbers of participants and the numbers of communes, estimates at the numbers of Jesus newspapers would only be wild guesses. Most emerged from local JP communities and could be found from New York, as in the paper *Credence* on Columbia University campus, to small towns like Atchison, Kansas with its *The Born Again Free Paper*. In 1974, there was a meeting planned by Craig Yoe, the editor of *Jesus Loves You*, in Akron, Ohio to coordinate and network Jesus newspaper efforts in the region.[35] But this sort of effort was rare as most JP made little effort to collaborate with other local Jesus newspapers.

30. Ibid.
31. T. Miller, *60s Communes*, xxiv.
32. Ibid., xviii.
33. Ibid., 94.
34. Ortega, *Jesus People*, 90.
35. "Jesus Newspapers," 56.

The largest and most famed Jesus newspaper was the *HFP*. Founded by former Assemblies of God (AG) minister Duane Pederson and funded by Hollywood Presbyterian Church, the *HFP* allegedly attained a peak circulation of 500,000 and was distributed as far as Europe and Scandinavia.[36] Enroth berated the *HFP* for what he saw as a tragically amateurish style of writing and a rather shallow content compared to higher quality Jesus newspapers like The Voice of Elijah's *Truth* and the CWLF's *Right On* (now *Radix*).[37] The *Post-American* was an unusual newspaper published by a community of politically liberal JP who eventually moved to Washington DC and changed their name and publication to *Sojourners*.[38] Most Jesus newspapers were short lived, only producing a couple volumes, and like the communes and long hair, nearly all died out along with the heyday of the phenomenon.

One enduring offshoot of the JPM was its musical expression, a hybrid known as Jesus Music that mixed the rock and folk sounds of the hippies' music with Christian lyrical content. Like the Jesus communes and Jesus newspapers, the Jesus Music bands were so prolific, and in many cases short lived, that no one seems to have ventured a guess at their number. The more famous bands included names like Larry Norman, Agape, Love Song, Children of the Day, the Second Chapter of Acts, Wilson McKinley, the Resurrection Band, and Sheep, to mention only a very few. In most cases JP bands were associated with the community from which they arose and while some, like Love Song, relied on that community for their sustenance others, like Wilson McKinley, contributed to the needs of the community through concert and record proceeds. Jesus Music, in the early days, was controversial with both Christian and non-Christian music markets and consequently ended up birthing its own recording and distribution markets. And although it was controversial, from the earliest days JP bands travelled the globe and were loved by many. For example, Larry Norman travelled to Australia, Love Song to the Philippines, Andraé Crouch to Vietnam, and Sheep to Scandinavia and Europe.

Jesus Music served as an initial catalyst for four distinguishable and interdependent streams in recent American Christian history: the Contemporary Christian Music (CCM) industry, Christian alternative radio stations, contemporary worship music, and outdoor Christian music festivals. Although there were other factors contributing to the birth and growth of the CCM, according to William Romanowski ("Rock'n'religion") the CCM industry emerged primarily because of Jesus Music. The CCM quickly

---

36. "Duane's Interview with Josh Tinley."

37. Enroth et al., *Story*, 74–77, 111, 124, 125.

38. "The Sojourner's."

burgeoned into a large industry consisting of several distinct genres and, according to Heather Hendershot, by 1998 had total industry sales in the USA that surpassed classical and jazz combined.[39] Second, groundbreaking Christian Radio programs like Scott Ross' *Tell It Like It Is,* adopted an alternative format that gave airplay to Jesus Music and interviews with the JP band members.[40] In interviews, some JP who felt distanced from established Christianity said that radio programs like Ross' provided a source of Christian teaching and guidance. The third stream is often referred to as contemporary Christian worship and has evolved out of early Jesus Music manifestations like Maranatha Praise music and later ones like Vineyard Music. Maranatha Praise and Vineyard Worship, along with contributions from Graham Kendrick of Ichthus Christian Fellowship and Integrity Media, played foundational roles in the birth and transformation of modern worship music. This invention and spin-off of the JPM has been arguably one of its most influential contributions to global Christianity.

Finally, borrowing the hippies' idea of the Trips Festival, Jesus Music featured in large concerts that were held in farm fields, in auditoriums like the Hollywood Palladium, and in outdoor parks like Knott's Berry Farm. In May 1971, the Love Song Festival at Knott's Berry Farm, the first Jesus concert at the park, reportedly drew the largest crowds in the theme parks' history.[41] Festivals too numerous to catalogue featured in many states and drew crowds in excess of 20,000; as in the Fishnet Festival in Virginia or the Agape Farm that hosted 15,000 at the original Jesus '73 Festival in Lancaster, Pennsylvania.[42] Travelling JP evangelistic teams took their Jesus Music with them and hosted concerts in Scandinavia, Asia, and Europe leaving a legacy of festivals in other countries like the Greenbelt Festival in the England. Today, Christian Music festivals in the USA are so numerous that network organizations like the Christian Festival Association exist to help direct festival seekers to the event of their choosing. The largest single festival is LifeLight in Sioux Falls, South Dakota that claims attendances of over 300,000.[43]

There are a number of independent churches and church movements whose roots are in the JPM. Donald Miller (*Reinventing American Protestantism*) famously examined three: Hope Chapel, Calvary Chapel, and the Association Vineyard of Churches. While conducting the research for this

39. Hendershot, *Shaking the World*, 56.

40. Sherrill and Sherrill, *Scott Free*, 90.

41. Baker, *Why Should the Devil*, 148.

42. "Fishnet Ministries"; Zidock Jr., "Jesus People Gather in Paradise," 12.

43. Montgomery, "Lifelight Still Growing." This is not to suggest that the organizers of LifeLight are JP, but to say that LifeLight lies in a trajectory of outdoor, Christian music festivals continuing from the JPM.

book, several others were uncovered including, but not limited to, Potter's House Christian Fellowship (PHCF), Gospel Outreach (GO), Dove Christian Fellowship International (DCFI), Maranatha Campus Ministries (MCM), Praise Chapel, and Church of the Open Door in San Francisco. Almost all of these churches have spin off churches or have inspired established, denominational churches to adapt some of their countercultural accouterments. Most of these churches and church movements have continued to grow and flourish into the present day and demonstrate the diversity and flexibility within Pentecostalism.

Participants, authors, journalists, and scholars alike unanimously confirmed that the vast majority of JP could be classified as part of American Pentecostalism. Stephen Hunt's recent conclusion that "the movement proved to be a hybrid form of Pentecostalism" is repeatedly confirmed in the popular and scholarly literature of the day.[44] For example, Ruben Ortega wrote, "If the Jesus Movement could be tagged with a denominational label, without doubt, it would have to fall under the category of Pentecostal— those who seek to be baptized with the Holy Spirit."[45] Enroth noted, "One of the most distinctive hallmarks of the Jesus Movement is its involvement in the Pentecostal scene."[46] Roger Palms, formerly the editor of *Decision*, observed that, "Another teaching which is strongly emphasized to the Jesus kids is the charismatic gift of speaking in tongues."[47]

The religious editor of the *Washington Star*, William F. Willoughby, ventured a guess at the percentage of charismatic participation when he commented that "a minimum of 70% and as high as 85% of the Jesus people movement is charismatic, with most of these having the experience of glossolalia and, in many cases, other gifts of the Spirit."[48] Richardson proposed that as many as 90 percent of the JP spoke in tongues.[49] Rex Davis wrote, "What struck me again and again in worship meetings or times of prayer with different groups associated with the Jesus movement was the easy acceptance of praying in tongues and exclamations of praise . . . but on the other hand, it was seldom made into a big issue. Asked about praying in tongues, a young man once said to me, in a rather surprised voice: 'What, don't all Christians pray like this?'"[50]

---

44. S. Hunt, "Were the Jesus People Pentecostals?," 27.

45. Ortega, *Jesus People*, 95.

46. Enroth et al., *Story*, 95.

47. Palms, *Jesus Kids*, 80.

48. Hills, "New Charismatics 1973," 33.

49. Richardson, *From Cult to Sect*, 54.

50. Davis, *Locusts*, 37. The following two paragraphs were adapted from Bustraan, "Jesus People," 30–31.

The JP believed they were living in the last days and were part of a large movement that was the work of the Holy Spirit, an outpouring intended to bring in a harvest of souls before Jesus would descend to earth to set up His kingdom. They believed they were restoring the church to its original beliefs and practices as found in the book of Acts and anticipated Jesus' return at any moment. In 1970, Hal Lindsey, who was also part of the JPM, wrote what became one of the best selling nonfiction books of the seventies, *The Late Great Planet Earth (LGPE)*. The book popularized biblical eschatology by interpreting current events like the formation of the State of Israel in 1948, the Six Day War of 1967, and the Cold War to be the prophetic signs that the end of the world was near and Jesus' return was imminent. The *LGPE* articulated what many JP probably already believed and since it was, according to Eskridge and Di Sabatino ("Remembering"), the second most widely read book among the JP it also served to harmonize and globalize their commonly held dispensational theology.

The Birth—1967 to the Summer of 1968

It is not possible to establish the exact time that the movement started, but by and large the timeline of the JPM shadowed the ebb and flow of the hippie movement and the counterculture. Beginning in 1967, as a response to the popular hippie movement, many sympathetic individuals and church members around America opened rather humble outreaches and went onto the streets to talk to hippies about faith in Jesus Christ. What they lacked in sophistication and budgeting they made up for in inventiveness and concern for the hippies. Rudimentary shop fronts and church halls functioned as makeshift coffeehouses where young people were offered free sandwiches, drinks, and, if needed, a place to stay. Bible studies would run late into the night and prayers were made for healing as well as for personal salvation through Jesus Christ. Almost as soon as hippies experienced conversion they took over the front lines of outreach, as they were more adept than traditional church members at reaching their own. However, hippy conversions brought parishioners as much chagrin as joy since they did not cut their long hair, they kept their disdain for the establishment, and dissent against the Vietnam War. Because hippie converts felt unwelcomed in churches and traditional Christians felt a sense of trespass in hippie enclaves, the street outreaches functioned as a buffer zone between the two. During the first several years, it was commonly observed that the youth on the streets were deeply disenchanted with established Christianity, but were exceptionally receptive to the message of Jesus Christ, to the Bible, to prayer, and to experiences in the Holy Spirit.

At this juncture it is important to make two statements about the origins and spread of the JPM from 1967 into the middle of 1968. First, there never was an original Jesus freak or an originating community of freaks that founded the JPM and became the prototype that inspired the entire movement. Second, statements like Vinson Synan's that "the 'Jesus People' revolution . . . began in California and spread rapidly across the nation" are simply not true.[51] Admittedly, the prominence of Southern California, especially Orange County, had a homogenizing effect on the entire ethos of the JPM. And certainly this California-centric influence attracted many curious visitors, journalists, and ministers who wanted to learn and imitate countercultural outreach methods. However, Southern California's homogenizing influence was exerted much later, picking up with the years 1969 or perhaps 1970 and running through 1973. And it came mostly through the agencies of the media, Jesus Music, and the famed hippie churches like Calvary Chapel at a time when the movement was more self-aware. The failure to make this distinction has fostered the false notion that the movement began on the West Coast and moved state by state like a wave until it reached the east coast.

During this early stage, however, such a highly developed level of organization, imitation, or self-awareness did not exist. When the evidence is examined, it is impossible to establish the links that show the JPM spreading from a single prototypical commune or from California to the east. In fact what does emerge is a very different story; one that shows the independent initiation of many unassociated and disconnected outreaches all across America and Canada. They did not arise by imitating a California phenomenon, and they were not diachronically connected to what was occurring in California or any other city around the continent. Instead, these many individuals and churches pioneered outreaches as a response to what they witnessed taking place among young people in their own local context. The following random examples are presented to clarify these claims about the origins of the JPM.

In the very few historical accounts that record the early days of the JPM, San Francisco features prominently and especially the work of the Living Room café outreach in Haight-Ashbury. In part, this is because two of the JPM's main chroniclers, John MacDonald and Edward Plowman, were also part founders of Evangelical Concerns; an organization created by Bay Area American Baptists to give financial support and oversight to the Living Room

---

51. Synan, *Holiness Pentecostal*, 255–56.

and its workers. Consequently, Ted Wise and the Living Room quickly gained regional notoriety and acceptability among the American Baptists, the SBC, and even further afield.[52] In subsequent years Plowman's very popular *The Jesus Movement* (1972) and his numerous articles for *CT* gained him the reputation as "the historian of the movement" and more than likely drew further attention to The Living Room even many years after its closure.[53]

However, from early in 1967 and even before, the streets of San Francisco were bustling with evangelistic activity from all varieties of Christians. There were numerous works in Haight-Ashbury that predated the Living Room such as the Pentecostal styled Clayton House operated by AG minister Dick Keys and the "experimental street ministry" of South San Francisco's Immanuel Baptist Church that was opened in November 1966 by Ron Willis.[54] In February 1967, Kent Philpott launched the Soul Inn that was operated out of Lincoln Park Baptist Church and Oliver Heath founded the Veg Hut and Harvest House.[55] Philpott's and Heath's connection with Golden Gate Baptist Seminary resulted in teams of Seminary students taking mission trips into Haight-Ashbury and onto the campus of the University of California Berkeley in the summer of 1967.[56] As early as February 1967, mainline churches like Father Harris' All Saints Episcopal, Howard Presbyterian, Hamilton Methodist, and St Agnes Roman Catholic Church also opened their doors to hippies creating a formidable storm of controversy among their parishioners.[57] From 1967, Glide Memorial Church welcomed hippies into its meetings. And in January 1968, hippies disrupted Glide's services and demanded that the church open its doors 24 hours a day to run a café outreach.[58] Afterwards the same group was found singing hymns with church members in the basement.[59]

Further south in Orange County, Tony and Susan Alamo had arrived in Hollywood by 1966 and founded the "Music Square Church," a Pentecostal ministry that reached out to street youth, drug addicts, and prostitutes.[60] In 1967, Chuck Smith made his first connections with the hippies through John Higgins and in 1968 Arthur Blessitt opened "His Place" as a "Christian

---

52. "Church Delegate From The Haight," 2. Also see "Parley Faces Major Issues," 2.

53. "The Alternative Jesus."

54. For Dick Keys, see Plowman, *Jesus Movement*, 68; "Ron Willis Named," 1.

55. Philpott, *Awakenings*, 77; For Oliver Heath, see Enroth et al., *Story*, 218–19.

56. "Golden Gate Seminary," 36.

57. Kinsolving, "Rector, a Church," 667–68.

58. "Hip Heckling," 5.

59. Ibid.

60. Lammers and Lewis, "Tony Alamo Materials (MC 1673)."

night club" on the Sunset Strip.[61] To the north in Seattle, by May 1965 Linda Meissner, in cooperation with David Wilkerson, had established Teen Harvest Headquarters as a drug rehabilitation center for youth.[62] Between the years 1965 to 1967 her work partnered with local charismatic and classical Pentecostal churches to experience small numbers of hippies converting through visions and healings from addiction.[63] However, it was in 1967 that a greater receptivity by the hippies was reported in her ministry.

In August 1966, a newspaper article reported on a communal, drug rehabilitation house that was operated by Chicago's Faith Tabernacle in a small, rural town named Plano, Illinois. The article featured a resident named Ron, "a hippie from New York's Spanish Harlem," who, along with others, was "trying to kick their habit 'through Jesus.'"[64] The Rev Walterman of Faith Tabernacle stated, "For those who place their faith in God, God takes the place of the drug."[65] Further west in Rock City, Illinois, in 1968, Lester Anderson founded an eclectic counterculture and charismatic commune called Salem Acres.[66]

By the middle of 1967, in New York City, a famous radio DJ named Scott Ross had claimed a miraculous deliverance from drug addiction and joined the staff of Pat Robertson's 700 Club.[67] New Milford Church of the Nazarene in New Jersey, pastored by Paul Moore, gained the self-acclaimed notoriety as the beginning point of the JPM on the east coast.[68] Although an overstatement, the church's noteworthy success began in 1968 with the help of a young, hippie rock n' roller named Charles Rizzo. Their coffeehouse, recording studio, and church flourished and, according to Peter Michelmore, influenced the growth of the JPM in New York, New Jersey, and Connecticut.[69]

In February 1967, The Salvation Army opened a café in Greenwich Village called "The Answer" that was operated by two men in their early twenties named Brian Figueroa and Ed Hertzberg.[70] In March 1967, also in Greenwich Village, a Catholic Priest known as Father Bendetto, or

61. Fromm, "Textual Communities," 172.

62. "1000 Attracted," 5; and Barnes, "Teen-Agers Aided," 5.

63. P. King, *Jesus People*, 3–7.

64. "Junkies Get Help From Rustic Home," 2.

65. Ibid.

66. Melton, "Salem Acres," 612.

67. Sherrill and Sherrill, *Scott Free*, 73–75.

68. Moore and Musser, *Shepherd*, 33–34.

69. Michelmore, *Back to Jesus*, 184–89.

70. "Salvation Army Is 'Groovy,'" 18a.

"Father B," went onto the streets to talk to young hippies. In an attempt to meet more youth, he ran ads in local weekly newspapers that promised, "no sermonizing."[71] There is ample evidence from numerous newspaper articles to suggest that Greenwich Village and its environs were hotspots for Christian outreaches to hippies in the opening months of 1967. The following comment by Sam Levenson sheds some light on the nature of the Jesus Freaks in New York's East Village by May 1967. He said, "Others believe that they are the twentieth-century early Christians. Many of these profess to follow the pre-establishment Jesus, comparing their East Village pads with catacombs."[72]

Jerry Halliday wrote about a group of young people that gave him Christian literature in Hampton, Virginia, in 1967 while he was still a devout hippie who "preached Timothy Leary."[73] Plowman wrote about a hippie named Danny Flanders who claimed to have been converted through a Christian witness while in Washington, DC, in 1967.[74] By 1971 he lead a JP group called Maranatha that conducted public baptisms in the reflecting pool at Lincoln Memorial.[75] In July 1967, members of a SBC Student Union and a musical group called the Lively Ones travelled to Dayton, Ohio to conduct evangelism among the cities hippies.[76] And according to Di Sabatino, one of the earliest known Jesus Music records, *Till the Whole World Knows,* was released in 1968 by the Sons of Thunder, a band from Bethseda, Maryland that formed sometime in 1967.[77]

In addition to this there were accounts of hippies starting their own churches, like Benjamin Osterberg who, in December 1967, opened a local branch of the Neo-American Church in Pensacola, Florida.[78] He renamed his house "The All Night Harmonica Shop," published a newspaper called *The Mouth Organ,* and had aspirations of becoming America's first "psychedelic chaplain."[79] In 1968, Kent Philpott, Oliver Heath, and Paul Bryant travelled in a Volkswagen from San Francisco to several southeastern states. There they discovered many Christians engaging in street outreach, distributing alternative Christian literature, and starting coffeehouses similar

71. "Village Priest Offers," 12.

72. Flowers, "So I'm Square," 8. Also see "Flower-Pelting Hippies," 25.

73. Halliday, *Spaced out,* 21.

74. Plowman, *Jesus Movement,* 67.

75. Ibid.

76. "1181 Decisions Reported," 1.

77. Di Sabatino, *Jesus People Movement,* 136.

78. "Army Wants No Hippie Chaplain," 1.

79. Ibid.

to what was being done in Haight-Ashbury, yet without any connection to what was taking place in California.[80]

According to Di Sabatino, the House of the Mandarin Door that opened in 1966 in Montreal, Canada, and was operated by Dave Ward, preceded many other works in the USA.[81] Also in Montreal, around June 1967, Rev Father Burke opened an outreach to young hippies out of St John the Evangelist Church.[82] However, in January 1968, an overly zealous police chief named Captain Bernard shut down the outreach and arrested one hundred young people aged 14–21, under suspicion of drug possession.[83] As early as October 1967, at a three day "Centennial Crusade" in Saskatoon, Leighton Ford was urging Christians to consider the potential of the hippies saying, "Hippies could be a tremendous force if they would turn all the way to Christ."[84]

These examples show that there were churches and individuals all across North America that made contact with hippies and established hippie outreaches, without any connection to the people and ministries in California. All this activity took place from late 1966 to mid 1968, before the name Jesus People existed and before there was a large-scale, socio-religious, California influenced phenomenon, called the Jesus People Movement that could be imitated. These examples also indicate a broad range of methodology from those that heavily adopted counterculture ways to those that did not. While there has never been a shortage of claimed leaders and centers for the JPM, there simply was not. In the same way that Allan Anderson described early American Pentecostalism as "polynucleated and variegated," the evidence strongly suggests that the origins of the JPM were both "polynucleated and variegated."[85] Eskridge, who elaborates with a different list of ministries from around the USA, Plowman, and Philpott also make similar claims about the origins of the JPM.[86]

The Groundswell—the Summer of 1968 to the End of 1969

Between the summer of 1968 and the end of 1969 untold multitudes of churches and individuals took note that the hippies were extremely

---

80. Philpott, *Awakenings*, 97–98.

81. Di Sabatino, "Jesus People Movement," 27.

82. "Church hall raid nets drug users," 4.

83. Ibid.

84. "Leighton Ford speaks out," 4.

85. A. Anderson, *Spreading Fires*, 4.

86. Eskridge, "God's Forever," 178–79; Plowman, *Jesus Movement*; and Philpott, *Awakenings*, 77.

receptive to the gospel and they threw themselves into evangelistic over-drive. Those involved in the outreaches at this stage frequently remarked with a bewildered but delighted tone at the openness of the hippies and their readiness to believe in Jesus. It was not uncommon to read accounts or to hear testimonies of outreaches on the streets and in high schools that would reportedly yield scores of conversions. Many believed that there could only be one explanation; that a movement of God had been birthed. For example, Kent Philpott wrote, "One hippie, after hearing only one word spoken, simply fell to his knees in the middle of the side walk and started praying loudly to Jesus. This would happen on the street, in stores, on Hippie Hill, or on the way to that place, and crowds would sometimes gather to listen to our preaching."[87] Ray Rempt said, "All you had to do is walk down the street and clear your throat and 10 people would be saved."[88] Jim Palosaari remarked, "The Spirit was huge."[89] Rex Davis penned this observation of Los Angeles. "Many groups have claimed some patent on the title Jesus movement, but most agree that in the summer of 1968 there erupted in coffee halls and through beach missions in and around Los Angeles something quite distinctive."[90] What Rex Davis saw in LA was also true in many locations around the USA. For example, in the east coast city of Aiken, South Carolina, the "Destination" coffeehouse, operated by the Salvation Army, reported as many as 300 teens sitting on the floor to hear local Christian bands.[91]

The shear volume of "underground" Jesus newspapers, coffeehouses, music bands, and communes that proliferated during this time makes it nearly impossible to give any kind of accounting. The more famous JP cafés, newspapers, musicians, and communes also made their entry during this time. For example, Hollywood Presbyterian Church's Salt Company Coffeehouse, Duane Pederson's *HFP*, and the CWLF at UC Berkeley trace their beginnings to 1968 and 1969. The nascent Jesus Music took huge steps forward with the release of what has become known as the first popular Jesus Rock album, *Upon This Rock*, by Larry Norman.[92]

Several California based ministries began to branch out either by default or by design. For example, after the closure of the Living Room, Lonnie Frisbee moved to Orange County in May 1968 to work with Calvary Chapel

---

87. Philpott, *Awakenings,* 85.

88. Ray Rempt, interview with author, June 14, 2011.

89. Jim Palosaari, interview with author, March 24, 2009.

90. Davis, *Locusts,* 35–36.

91. "Coffee House for Teens," 3.

92. Norman, *Upon This Rock.*

Costa Mesa. Calvary Chapel's successful communal network in Orange County was moved to Oregon, renamed as the Shiloh Youth Revival Centre (SYRC), and, under the leadership of John Higgins, began to spread across the nation. David Berg's The Children of God (COG) communal network also spread form Orange County into several other states. In 1969, David Hoyt moved from the Soul Inn in San Francisco to establish a thriving JP work in Atlanta and "Diane and Mickey" moved from the Living Room in San Francisco to establish the IXOYE House in Denver.[93] In October 1968, Arthur Blessitt could be found "urging" the SBC to reach out to hippies, and inspiring future JP leaders like Sammy Tippit.[94] With the exception of the Baptists, who published at least 62 articles between 1968 and 1969, the lack of newspaper and television coverage suggests that the Christian and secular media were completely unaware of the magnitude of this burgeoning groundswell.[95] But in December 1969, when Arthur Blessitt made his ceremonious exodus from Hollywood by walking from Los Angeles to Washington DC carrying a cross he had taken from the wall of His Place, the media began to take note. Previously, Blessitt had drawn local media attention by holding a forty-day fast while chained to a cross. And he had been featured on a local TV show called *Ralph Story's Los Angeles*.[96] There were many other factors at work beyond Blessitt's cross-country walk and this should not be seen as some sort of single, trigger event. However, the slow drama of this 3500 mile journey, which lasted into July of 1970, attracted national media interest in Blessitt's story and in what was taking place among the hippies on the streets of Southern California.[97]

The Heyday—1970 to 1973

What marks this period as distinctly different was the extraordinarily high rate that JP communes, coffeehouses, Jesus marches, Jesus Music, Jesus Festivals, and Jesus newspapers proliferated across the USA and in several other countries. The news media was now publishing a steady flow of accounts and popularizing the phenomenon. The JPM became visible and even tangible to the American public because it had blossomed in nearly every small town and big city. Articles in newspapers and magazines would repeatedly list several brief samples of JP and their cafés or music from

93. For IXOYE, see MacDonald, *House of Acts*, 93–95.
94. Lee, "'Gut-Level Witnessing,'" 4–6.
95. Reid, "Impact," 216–44.
96. Blessitt, *Turned on*, 134.
97. Eggebroten, "Rally Round the Cross," 42.

around the country to illustrate a single point; the movement was prodigious and ubiquitous. For example, ABC Radio Broadcaster Paul Harvey wrote a syndicated article in 1971 that gave a sample of the smorgasbord of activity around the country. Besides some of America's big cities, it included JP performing evangelism on Ft. Lauderdale beaches at Spring Break, youth singing praises on the beach in St. Petersburg, Florida, 300 youth street preaching in Owensboro, Kentucky, and twenty JP entering a police station to hand over their supply of hashish and LSD in Hot Springs, Arkansas.[98]

By 1973, the JPM had spread internationally with some type of JP presence in Canada, Norway, Finland, Sweden, Germany, Netherlands, Belgium, France, Italy, the United Kingdom, Central Europe, New Zealand, Australia, Philippines, Singapore, South Africa, and Mexico.[99] The movement spread during this time, in part, as a result of the travels of JP, many of who were quite transient. Some were known to have hitchhiked across the country to share the gospel. Perhaps the most common form of travel was through evangelistic missions, sponsored by non-denominational organizations like the FGBMFI, YWAM, Operation Mobilization, and Campus Crusade for Christ.[100] Another channel for the spread of the movement was the Jesus Music. What began as simple songs sung by hippie Christians was evolving into a music industry and JP bands were making national and international travelling tours to perform in front of thousands of people.

Another characteristic that demarcates this period was the exponential increase in media attention. From the major national news magazines to the local small town newspapers, media interest, previously nonexistent, began to pick up in 1970, mushroomed in the years 1971 and 1972, quickly declined in 1973, and was almost nonexistent from 1974 on. This four-year season of media interest spun a rather positive interpretation of the JP by featuring stories of young people that claimed to be freed from drug addiction and other vices. A very consistent message to emerge from the testimonies recorded in these media accounts were statements of unabashed allegiance to Jesus as a revolutionary who was on the side of the hippies and soon to come back to earth. The American public was exposed to images of hippies in their hundreds being baptized at Calvary Chapel's Pacific Ocean services, of Bethel Tabernacle's dramatic Pentecostal church meetings, of 200,000 who gathered for the final night of Explo '72, and of the bearded, Jesus-looking, hippie Christian named Lonnie Frisbee. In 1971, full feature articles on the JPM ran in American national news magazines *Life, Time,*

98. Harvey, "Jesus Freaks," 4.
99. Balswick, "The Jesus People Movement," 23–42.
100. Edward E. Plowman, "Report from Europe," 18–21, 24–25.

and *Newsweek* and the June 21, 1971 front cover of *Time* magazine declared it to be "The Jesus Revolution."[101] According to Di Sabatino, the JPM had been chosen by *Time* magazine as the third most popular religious story of the year in 1971.[102] The movement became so popular that Jesus freaks appeared in the most unlikely of places, like the 1971 song, "Tiny Dancer," by Elton John.[103] The media helped to raise public awareness and to solidify the JP's identity as a youth movement with a foot in hippiedom and in Christianity.

Although the movement was permeating every corner of the nation, by this time Orange County, California had become a large center and attracted the lion's share of media attention. In this region a journalist or researcher could make an abundance of interviews and photographs of the phenomenon in one single location, and indeed many did. The voluminous pictures and stories to emerge from Orange County throughout these years helped foster a California centric ethos over the entire movement. Consequently, by 1971, groups of people were travelling from around the country and from as far as England, Switzerland, and Philippines to see what was happening in Southern California, not realizing they could have witnessed the same phenomenon in almost every city in America.[104]

Examining local newspaper articles is especially intriguing, as they report small town happenings alongside editorials with opinions from common people that range from supportive to cynical. Some authors ambiguously applied the name JP to describe any kind of church youth meeting. The most common question to arise in the local newspapers was whether or not the movement was only a passing youth fad.[105] In addition to local and national media coverage, there were a small number of documentary films and a smattering of very brief accounts published in small books. Most of these were rather simplistic publications produced by Christians whose two-pronged aim was to chastise the JP and to legitimize the JPM to mainstream Evangelicalism and Pentecostalism. Throughout the years 1970 to 1973 Baptist denominational publications continued to chronicle the JPM and the AG's *Pentecostal Evangel* churned out approximately sixty-three articles.

Finally, during this era several successful JP churches began to multiply and spread. For a number of these churches, these years would prove to be a formational season from which they would later emerge as thriving

---

101. "Alternative Jesus."

102. Di Sabatino, *Jesus People Movement*, 13.

103. John and Taupin, *Tiny Dancer*.

104. Smith and Steven, *Reproducers*, 9.

105. For example, see L. Thompson, "'FAD' in 2000th Year," 4.

alternative church movements, bearing the distinguishable JP traits of the American counterculture and American Pentecostalism.

Continued Growth—1974 to 1975

As quickly as the media's interest was aroused it also abated, with the exception of *CT*, which continued to publish articles on the JP through 1976. This trend is reflected across the entire media spectrum from the national media magazines to the local newspapers, and including Christian magazines and books; all offered fewer stories in 1973 and had become virtually silent by 1974. An analysis of the movement's rise and fall based on media interest creates the illusion that the movement had fizzled out by 1973 or 1974. However, there is ample evidence to suggest that the JPM was still flourishing through this period. As a couple brief examples, in 1974 Calvary Chapel Costa Mesa opened its 2300 seat auditorium and within five weeks needed triple services to accommodate the growth.[106] In addition to Costa Mesa's growth, Chuck Smith was also commissioning many of his protégés to begin Calvary Chapel church plants, including Kenn Gulliksen, who in 1974 launched his successful Vineyard outreaches. In 1974, through Kenn Gulliksen's Bible study, Keith Green experienced Christian conversion and one year later launched Last Days Ministries.[107] And in 1975 Gospel Outreach (GO), centered in Northern California, had just entered a new stage of growth, intentionally reproducing their communal church models across the country. The media may have grown apathetic and disinterested, but the movement remained in full swing and continued to grow.

Devolution—1976 to 1979

As the decade of the 1970s neared its end, the JPM could be divided into two rather distinct streams. First, there was a stream that was fading away with the counterculture or had dissolved due to internal conflicts. For example, by 1968, The Living Room in San Francisco had already closed and in 1971, Linda Meissner had left Jesus People Army of Seattle to join the COG. Peter Michelmore wrote his observations of Haight-Ashbury in 1972 stating, "The Haight-Ashbury district of San Francisco has been deserted by everyone . . . In any event they [the Jesus People] had moved on."[108] On the

106. Chuck Smith, "History," 9.

107. Thomas, "Keith Green Story."

108. Michelmore, *Back to Jesus*, 174.

campus of UC Berkeley the CWLF had dissolved by 1975, as did Resurrection City by 1978. Harry Hewat commented that many of the hitchhikers in Northern California during the early and mid-seventies had been spiritually minded seekers, but by the late 1970s they were more "needy" and less idealistic; a sign to him that the times had changed and the heyday of the movement had passed.[109] The large communal ministry of The Voice of Elijah and the even larger SYRC closed in 1979. SYRC's closure not only ended its eleven-year run as the largest single communal collective in the JPM, but also seemed to symbolically represent the ending of the JP communal era. By the end of the decade, with the closure of many organizations whose identity was tied to the glory years of the JPM, and with the counterculture considered passé, there was little disagreement that the visible religious phenomenon called the JPM was over.

However, there was a second stream that consisted of groups that have continued to grow, reproduce, institutionalize, and create new spin offs beyond the end of the twentieth century. For example, in 1976, Mike Neville, after a few years with Wayman Mitchell, founded Praise Chapel, a church movement that claims to have 200 churches in its fold. John Wimber, from 1975 to 1977, joined Calvary Chapel and launched the famous Calvary Chapel Yorba Linda. Regarding the JPM's direction from 1975, parallel conclusions can be drawn to those of the counterculture and American culture. That is, although by the late 1970s, the JPM as a visible movement, had passed from the scene in America, its aftermath has continued to flourish and influence American Pentecostalism and American Christianity until the present day.

The Aftermath—1980 to the Present

By the 1980s many JP, now several years older, had married, found jobs, entered university, or had entered into Christian ministry. Some JP dropped out on Christianity, but many settled into new JP churches or into the classical Pentecostal, Charismatic, Protestant, and Catholic churches they had attended during the heyday of the JPM. The Jesus Music had burgeoned into the CCM musical industry and had diversified and solidified its recording, marketing, and distribution channels. Some JP became more involved in the political process, and aligned with the revival in conservative politics of the early 1980s. Established JP churches like Calvary Chapel and GO continued to grow and multiply. Also during the 1980s, Larry Lea launched Church on the Rock, John Wimber the Association of Vineyard Churches,

109. Harry Hewat, interview with author, December 12, 2008.

Wayman Mitchell went independent of the ICFG, and Larry Kreider formed Dove Christian Fellowship International (DCFI). While the JPM as a large socio-religious phenomenon had passed with the 1970s, the music and the new church networks were emerging as features that would endure through the end of the century.

The Short-term Transnational Globalization

The next few paragraphs attempt to give a broad sweeping analysis of the international spread of the JPM by differentiating its more immediate spread from its ensuing after-effects over the course of forty years. Turning first to the immediate spread, it should be noted that by 1971 the positive, extensive coverage in the secular and Christian media in America combined with the international travels of JP music groups and leaders like Arthur Blessitt, Jim Palosaari, Duane Pederson, Sammy Tippit, Carl Parks, Bob Weiner, and Lonnie Frisbee heightened the awareness in other countries that there was a spiritual revival among the youth in America. In some countries a very small portion of Christian youth and church leaders were imitative of the American JPM—its music, fashion, Pentecostalism, and outreach to young drug addicts. In other countries there were reports of street preaching, coffeehouses, outreach centers for drug addicts, musical festivals, and in some cases, Jesus newspapers.

The JPM in Canada so extensively paralleled what took place in the USA that there are too many ministries and JP leaders to be covered here.[110] The United Kingdom, Germany, the Netherlands, and Australia were also popular locations for JP outreaches, but with the exception of Canada, Scandinavia seemed to top the list. The following report from Duane Pederson in 1972 recorded that, "Crowds as large as 10,000 swarmed into tents across Scandinavia to hear about Jesus and this new movement. 3,000 people accepted Christ on the street and in festivals."[111] Later he wrote, "Norway's first-ever Jesus festival in Hamar brought over 4,000 Jesus People together from all over Norway. Soon after, Denmark's first Jesus festival was standing-room-only in Copenhagen."[112] Swedish Pentecostal leader, Lewi Pethrus was very supportive of the JPM and was partially responsible for helping it flourish in Sweden. In 1972, he invited a group of JP to the Swedish Pentecostal's Annual Conference at Nyhem.[113] According to Tommy

110. See Di Sabatino, "Jesus People Movement."
111. "Victory for Jesus."
112. "World Revival."
113. Davidsson, "Lewi Pethrus," 205.

Davidsson, Pethrus defended the JP's hesitance to work with established churches in Sweden referencing Revelation 2:5 for support. He said, "There are perhaps churches even today from which he [Jesus] needs to remove the lampstand. If he desires to move it to the amusement parks among sinners and publicans, which he did in the past, who dares to blame him for doing so."[114]

Immediately after the emergence of the Jesus Music, bands and singers were invited to play large, international tours abroad. Bands like Sheep featured in Scandinavia and Europe and Love Song visited countries throughout Europe and Asia. In the Philippines, Love Song's music was aired on national radio stations, making the band famous before they arrived. The US military personnel living abroad were affected by the JPM through singers like Andraé Crouch who toured Vietnam. In Germany, JP within the military converted unused munitions storage facilities into "One Way" coffeehouse outreaches under the approving eye of their commanders.[115] By 1972 in New Zealand, Jesus marches were held in eleven locations around the country with the largest, single march totaling 15–20,000. The cumulative total for all eleven marches was estimated at 85,000.[116] Australia was another stopping point for Jesus Music bands and JP leaders including Jack Sparks, Barry McGuire, and Larry Norman.[117] In addition, reports from South Africa to Russia tell of JP styled ministries that were either imported by traveling American JP or were initiated by locals mimicking what they read was taking place in California. Peter Chao's Eagles Communications in Singapore, for example, incorporated the "One Way" symbol into its ministry in the 1970s.[118]

On first glance these reports give the appearance that the movement was spreading into and impacting many countries. However, several necessary considerations complicate such an assumption and highlight how elusive the definition of a "revival" or religious movement can be as it moves across cultural and linguistic boundaries. In fact, given the difference in the character and extent of the phenomenon in each country, a nation-by-nation analysis, as Kevin Smith ("Origins") does with Australia, would be a more appropriate way to assess the impact in each country. As a first observation, the JPM received much of its impetus from the American counterculture

114. Ibid.

115. Trott, "Hanau GI," 9; Godec, "They're High on Jesus," 10; and Hart, "Top Army Chaplain," 9.

116. "10,000 March for Jesus," 45.

117. K. Smith, "Origins, Nature," 322.

118. "Eagles Communications."

and hippie movement. Since this was predominantly a North American phenomenon, the JPM was more readily accepted in countries where American countercultural themes had at least a negligible degree of currency. It is for this reason that it was most successful in Scandinavia, Germany, the United Kingdom, and Australia. Second, while not wanting to slight anyone's effort, it is important to note that a group of JP, or a JP leader holding a concert, opening a coffeehouse, or conducting an outreach in a "foreign" country, no matter how successful the venture, could hardly qualify as a large socio-religious phenomenon that paralleled what took place in America.

Third, the American interpretation of events "abroad" was optimistic and differed considerably from reports written by a more cynical British and German press. In many cases, misunderstandings in the foreign media resulted from a lack of differentiation that lumped the mainstream JP, the COG, the hippies, and *Jesus Christ Superstar* into one category.[119] Also the connotations associated with the American hippies were not always the same as in America and this colored the interpretations and acceptability of the JP abroad. Coupled with this, local Christian leaders in foreign countries were in some cases more selective about those with whom they would partner.[120] Some leaders expressed their frustration with travelling American evangelists who had little appreciation for local culture and in other cases leaders shunned the use of American JP idioms like "Jesus is the best trip."[121] Most often, the American based phenomenon did not transfer cross-culturally without serious impediment and distortion.

Finally, it is necessary, if possible, to tease out of some reports what was indeed JP activity and what was not. For example, an article written by Edward Plowman for *CT* covered the spread of the JP "revolution" throughout Scandinavia, Eastern, and Western Europe. In some cases he reported on the work of Youth for Christ, Navigators, CCC, YWAM, TC, and Operation Mobilization as though it was the JPM in Europe. But most of these organizations' endeavors in Europe predated the JPM. For example, he wrote, "The Christian developments there [Netherlands] approximates developments in the American youth scene of the past few years."[122] Much of Plowman's report on the Netherlands was Operation Mobilization's (OM) "mobilizing" mission that had begun to take off in Europe in 1963.[123] It was

119. "Curse of the Hallelujah Chorus," 7; Chippindale, "Jesus People," 5; and "Gott Sein."

120. K. Smith, "Origins, Nature" 322–24.

121. Plowman, "Report from Europe," 21; Munstra, "Evangelism among Hippies," 800–805.

122. Plowman, "Report from Europe," 21.

123. Ibid., 18–21, 24–25.

true that OM had, like other organizations, taken on some JP elements like the "One Way" symbol, long hair, and praise choruses emerging from the USA. But attributing the European activity of OM to the international spread of the JPM overstates its impact in Europe.

Having said this, it was also true that several non-denominational mission organizations used the momentum of the JPM to gain recruits and to increase their own territories in Europe and elsewhere. To illustrate this, during the JPM, Campus Crusade for Christ (CCC) pursued aggressive campus strategies in the USA to reach university students and to organize Explo '72. As a result of their participation in the JPM, between the years 1970 and 1978, CCC experienced a very sharp rise in the numbers of new applicants seeking to join the organization.[124] Encouraged by the 200,000 JP in attendance at Explo '72, CCC took intentional steps to "explode" the growth of their existing international work in South Korea through Explo '74 in Seoul; an even that attracted 300,000.[125] Or for example, the attendance at InterVarsity Christian Fellowship's (IVCF) Urbana conference increased from 7,000 in 1965 to 14,000 in 1973 and the organization experienced a swell in the numbers of students participating in campus chapters.[126] While the JPM may have caused some growth within IVCF, according to Ned Hale, IVCF's growth during this period of time was more directly attributable to the changes and restructuring of the organization under Dr. John Alexander, leader of IVCF from 1965 to 1981.[127]

YWAM also grew as a result of a large influx of JP coming from the USA and from Europe and the 1972 Summer Olympics in Munich proved pivotal in this relationship. Two thousand youth, many of whom were JP, travelled to Munich for the Olympic outreach that featured coffeehouses, tent meetings, testimonies, Jesus Music, and a Jesus newspaper.[128] A journalist covering the Olympics wrote, "sports had failed as a medium of world unity but that the Jesus people were proving Jesus to be the answer."[129] YWAM recruited 1000 young people for the event and although the organization was in existence since 1960, according to Ray Rempt, it was YWAM's "first big splash."[130] After the Olympics, and with the help of new JP recruits,

124. Rainey, "Campus Ministry," 8. The spike in recruitment statistics was interpreted by CCC leadership to be the result of the JPM. CCC leadership email correspondence with author.

125. CCC leadership email correspondence with author, July 6, 2009.

126. Winter, "Is a Big New Student,"12; and Plowman, "Urbana '73," 41–42.

127. Ned Hale, email correspondence with author, December 6, 2010.

128. Plowman, "2,000 Christian Youth," 42–43.

129. Ibid. 43.

130. Ray Rempt, interview with author, June 14, 2011.

YWAM went on to establish large and enduring works among drug addicts in Denmark in 1972 and in the Netherlands in 1973.[131] Founded in 1974, YWAM's very popular Discipleship Training Program (DTS), the invention of Leland Paris, was initiated in response to the JPM. YWAM's website states, "Leland Paris, noticed that many YWAM students had no Christian background, having only recently come to Christ through the 'Jesus Movement' of the 1970's. 'I remember asking a student about his religious background,' recalls Leland. 'He said, "Drugs."'"[132] The growth of YWAM from 40 fulltime staff in 1970 to 1800 in 1980 gives some indication of the impact of the JPM on the missionary organization.

Beyond the non-denominational missionary organizations, there were independent missionaries and mission organizations that also arose from the JPM. For example, GO sent missionaries into Guatemala in 1974 and established an influential church and school there. In Norway, American James MacInnes arrived in 1971 and remained on for thirty years, impacting the growth of the JPM and in the work in the Methodist church there.[133] Large and enduring, indigenous works were also initiated as a direct result of the JPM as in Theos Youth Ministries, the House of the New World, and the God Squad Christian Motorcycle Club in Australia, Ron Munstra's ministry to drug addicts in the Netherlands, Belgium, and Germany, and Volkhard Spitzer's church and coffeehouse in Berlin.[134] Numerous other independent missionaries have been found in Asia, Latin America, and Europe as a result of the JPM.

In summary, there were cases in which the JPM bolstered the work of previously existing mission organizations, campus outreaches, and local Pentecostal churches. There were also cases of indigenous JP groups that arose for a season and in some cases have endured into the present day as a direct result of the JPM. However, excluding Canada, and with a minor exception given to Scandinavia, the United Kingdom, Australia, and New Zealand, the immediate effects of the JPM outside the USA did not result in a similar, large-scale, religious phenomenon that paralleled what took place in America. And again, perhaps excepting Canada and Scandinavia, whether or not there were any notable changes in the Pentecostalism of any other country attributable to the transnationalization of the JPM, has not been examined. And given the JPM's American counterculture trappings,

131. "YWAM Denmark." "YWAM Netherlands."

132. "YWAM History."

133. "Fisherman's Net Revival Center."

134. For Australian works, see K. Smith, "Origins, Nature." For Ron Munstra's work see both Munstra, "Evangelism among Hippies," 800–805; and "Jesus People." For Volkhard Spitzer, see "Jesus-Revolution Im Nächsten Jahr?"

the Central Asian states, the Arab world, northern and sub-Saharan Africa, and probably much of Asia, remained unaffected by and perhaps, completely unaware of the JPM.

Having said this, given the lack of access to denominational records and the limitations of time, the AG, CG, and the ICFG have not been examined to see if there are any trends in missionary recruits that paralleled what Alvin Reid discovered among the SBC. Also, there remains a need for individual regions and countries to be researched to see what links can be established with the American JP. There are resources materials in other countries—mostly people links and the newspaper archives—that need to be researched before stronger statements can be made on the JPM's transnational impact.

Long-term Transnational Globalization

Finally, it is suggested that the following four areas offer the best instruments upon which a plausible appraisal of the long term, international impact of the JPM might be gauged. First, there are a multitude of active organizations like Christ is the Answer and the God Squad Christian Motorcycle Club that trace their roots to the JPM and whose original counterculture ethos remains somewhat intact. While their fame and individual influence may not always be far reaching, they continue to make an impact in the country they live and in some cases they maintain their own transnational missionary network. Second, there are many American missionaries living abroad who trace their entrance into "foreign missions" to their experience in the JPM. Some serve under denominational and independent missionary organizations, some have formed their own mission, while others work as independent self-supporting missionaries.

Third, Jesus Music as a unique genre may have died off by the late seventies, but it should not be dismissed as a trivial, ephemeral expression of the JP. Instead it was the harbinger of the transformation in Christian worship music that subsequently permeated Christian churches around the globe and the seed out of which the CCM industry blossomed. The unbroken chain of continuity that can be traced from Jesus Music to Maranatha, Vineyard Music and to many other worship music derivatives of the present day shows this short lived genre to be one of the most enduring and influential contributions to global Christianity from the JPM. Fourth, JP communalism was more than a temporary and charming feature of the movement's heyday, as communal collectives from the JPM thrived in the UK, Europe, Scandinavia, and Australia. With the exception of Canada, none of these paralleled the JP's communalism in America and in most cases, also died off by the end of the seventies. However, this research has discovered individuals who lived in JP communes abroad or were raised as children of JP in communal collectives in other countries who believe the experience has shaped their perspective of Pentecostalism and of Christianity.

Fifth, the Messianic movement has blossomed and flourished since the 1970s and there are a number of JP who are either involved in it or who ideologically support it. Quite a few JP churches not only continue with premillennial theologies but also support Messianic Christianity and have emphasized teaching pilgrimages to the Holy Land. While some non-charismatic Jewish outreaches like Jews for Jesus have arisen from the JPM, there is a continuity of Pentecostalism in the Messianic Movement that was initiated in large part by the JPM.

Finally, with the exception of Gospel Outreach, the church movements stemming from the JPM continue to expand transnationally and export their own hybrid of Pentecostalism wherever they embed locally. And in addition to the multiplication of their own global church networks, each one of these church movements has spawned countless local ministries, has had breakaway church movements, and has sent and supported their own missionaries and those of other mission organizations. Also to be considered is the knock-on effect of what is commonly referred to as "Vineyard influenced" churches or the thousands of churches that unofficially affiliate with the Calvary Chapel in Asia.[135] For example, the "Toronto Blessing" arose out of the Toronto Airport Vineyard Church and has influenced many other churches globally. The church subsequently broke away and changed its name to Catch the Fire. Also, the numbers of unaffiliated Calvary Chapels in China and India allegedly exceeds twenty thousand. While the Calvary Chapel Association believes these numbers are often exaggerated and does not include them in their official listings of churches, it does show that there are unaccounted for, transnational influences of JP church. It would be safe to say that the JPM churches and their offshoots have been the best vehicles for preserving and spreading the JP's counterculture version of Pentecostal spirituality.

Summary

What began with simple Christian concern for hippies and as very humble, rudimentary cafés, gospel track distribution, prayers for healing, and street preaching, resulted in a large socio-religious phenomenon that significantly

---

135. Calvary Chapel Association, email correspondence with author, October 21, 2009. Also see Richardson, "Mergers, 'Marriages,'" 206.

impacted American Christianity, and in some cases global Christianity for years to come. Many of those involved in the initial outreaches had no idea that such a movement was about to occur. Others, however, claimed that God had revealed in advance through prophetic words and visions that there would be a large scale, end times harvest and that they would be a leader in this movement. Classical Pentecostal churches that prayed for and anticipated another great, end times revival found themselves embroiled in and perplexed by the controversy over the hippies sharing in the Pentecostal spirituality. The CM, so often assumed to be a separate and segregated stream of Pentecostalism, would also find itself fully involved in the JPM and being transformed by the Jesus Freaks. This overview has not attempted an encyclopedic list of names and ministries. But having introduced the timeline and broad characteristics of the JPM, it is now time to more carefully analyze its historical links to and its qualities of Pentecostalism.

Chapter 3

A Story of American Pentecostalism

PEERING BELOW THE SURFACE of the broad storyline unveils a vast array of individuals and communities, all with stories of their own. This chapter features vignettes of selected people and churches involved in the JPM so that their connection with Pentecostalism might be elucidated. Chosen due of the availability of information and their prominence in the movement, then categorized based on their location in Pentecostalism, the following biographical snapshots are intended to add some depth and color to the narrative of the JPM. These are very abridged stories, but they should demonstrate that the JPM cross-pollinated with nearly every denomination and every movement of Pentecostalism in the 1960s and 1970s, hence its heterogeneity and ubiquity. It is also the aim of this section to dispel any wrongful notions that the JP were merely passive recipients of a Pentecostal experience. For once they were animated with Pentecostal spirituality they engaged reciprocally in shaping new hybrid variations of Pentecostalism, and they contributed to the numerical growth and transformation of the churches that decided to open their doors to them.

Young Jesus People Leaders

The first group represents a random selection of eleven young JP who, at the time, fell into the average age band of 13 to 30 year olds. Some entered the JPM from the heart of hippiedom, while others joined from a Christian background. Some are still alive, while others have passed away. All helped shape the movement and demonstrate the normal variety of Pentecostal experience in the JPM.

Mario Murillo—Resurrection City

When the story of the JPM on the campus of the University of California Berkeley is told it often centers on the CWLF. But a large Pentecostal ministry led by Mario Murillo also flourished there. In 1969, Murillo, nineteen years old, made his way back to his native San Francisco to open Resurrection City out of facilities that he rented on campus. Claiming Amiee Semple McPherson as his mentor, his methodology for outreach resembled that of the healing evangelists of the 1950s.[1] He began with student meetings held at Resurrection City, but his ministry quickly grew to include large healing and evangelistic gatherings hosted in the Pauley Ballroom at UC Berkeley. After outgrowing Pauley Ballroom he moved to the Berkeley Community Centre and eventually to the Oakland Theatre where he claimed, "we saw awesome miracles for eight years."[2] Throughout his time at UC Berkeley Murillo regularly travelled to Melodyland in Anaheim to conduct evangelistic meetings. He also shared the Resurrection City facilities with an AG church-planting venture from First Church Oakland, with a national AG campus ministry called Chi Alpha, and the CWLF.[3]

After ten years, Murillo closed Resurrection City and launched an international evangelistic and healing ministry from an outreach in San Jose. One newspaper dubbed the meetings "an Azusa Street-type visitation" as they had to be extended from the four days initially planned to six months and reached an alleged 250,000 people.[4] Murillo would be best located as a minister with roots in the JPM, in the CM, and in classical Pentecostalism who, after his beginnings in the JPM, has maintained relationships with the AG, the ICFG, and other independent Pentecostal and Charismatic churches.

Bob Weiner—Maranatha Campus Ministries

Bob Weiner, the founder of Maranatha Campus Ministries (MCM), also called Maranatha Christian Churches, made his initial entry into Christian ministry through the JPM. Brought up in the Elim Evangelical Free Church, Weiner received his Christian training at Trinity College and his baptism in the Holy Spirit (BHS) when Albie Pearson laid hands on him.[5] Weiner claimed the experience was accompanied by ecstatic feelings, stating, "for the

1. "Mario Murillo."
2. Ibid.
3. "Chapel of Jesus," 28.
4. "Mario Murillo Featured Speaker," 14.
5. Weiner, *Take Dominion*, 24.

next two hours I spoke in tongues and had the most glorious experience of my life."[6] Weiner's involvement in the JPM began in San Bernardino, in 1970, when he and Bob Cording formed Sound Mind Productions; a company that produced a Jesus newspaper called *Sound Mind* and promoted Jesus Music concerts that included bands like Andraé Crouch and the Disciples and Love Song.[7] In 1971, the two men adventurously drove a 1919 Nash from Chicago to California, giving away 100,000 copies of *Sound Mind*, and preaching to hippies on university campuses along the way. After this, Weiner spent one year at First Assembly Long Beach as a minister of youth under Wesley Steelberg, organizing Jesus Marches in Long Beach and Hollywood. As an AG minister, Steelberg looked favorably on the JPM and encouraged Weiner to "channel some of the Jesus Movement into the local churches."[8]

In 1972, Weiner and his wife moved to Paducah, Kentucky and, from a week of successful youth meetings at Broadway Methodist Church, founded MCM as a Christian center for teaching young believers. Later that year, at the invitation of the Swedish Pentecostal leader Lewi Pethrus, Weiner, accompanied by a group of 200 other JP, went to Scandinavia where it is claimed that as many as 10,000 young people gathered for tent meetings.[9] Upon returning to Paducah, Weiner's ministry quickly spread to university campuses in Kentucky and Tennessee. From 1972 to 1989, MCM grew to become a ministry of 300 full time workers in twenty nations that operated a satellite TV network and a training school that drew visiting teachers like J. Rodman Williams, Larry Tomczak, Winkie Pratney, and Albie Pearson. After its peak in the late 1980s, Weiner left MCM to found Weiner Ministries International and Christian Youth International. The former works toward a goal of recruiting youth to reach one billion people with the gospel and the latter was a Moscow based ministry with an estimated 370 cell churches in former Soviet Union nations.[10]

Ted Wise—The Living Room and The House of Acts

Moving away from university campuses, Larry Eskridge wrote that as early as 1965 bohemian converts gathered at First Baptist Church of Mill Valley where John MacDonald was the pastor.[11] Among them was a former sail maker

---

6. "Weiner Ministries."
7. Weiner, *Take Dominion*, 41.
8. Ibid., 47–48.
9. "Victory in for Jesus."
10. Strang, "Weiner," 1186–87.
11. Eskridge, "Jesus People," 28.

named Ted Wise who had recently been converted through prayers and coax-
ing of his wife, Liz. Mill Valley's close proximity to Haight-Ashbury allowed
the Wises to frequent the area, maintain their links with the community, and
share their new faith with fellow hippies. Before long the Wises' efforts yielded
results in the conversion of Steve and Sandi Heefner, Jim and Judy Doop, and
Dan and Sandi Sands.[12] Ted would return from Haight-Ashbury with stories
so intriguing that Pastor MacDonald decided to accompany the Wises to their
flat to see what was taking place among the hippies.

Ted Wise brought his counterculture friends into MacDonald's
church, but not without controversy. MacDonald (*House of Acts*) wrote
very candidly of the mounting tensions he faced in his role as mediator
between Ted Wise, a counterculture convert, and the traditional church
members he oversaw. Instead of integrating the hippies into the church,
they established Evangelical Concerns, a para-church organization whose
aim it was to financially support the Wises in a venture called the Living
Room coffeehouse in Haight Ashbury.[13] Alongside the Living Room, which
was established in 1967, the Wises, Heefners, Doops, and Sands sold their
personal possessions and acquired a home in Novato that they called "The
House of Acts" where they lived communally.

Where traditional church people felt out of place, the hippie converts
felt at home, navigating comfortably among their own people. Like many
other church outreaches to hippies, Evangelical Concerns recognized that
to succeed in their mission, a generous level of trust had to be extended to
the ex-bohemians so they could operate with freedom in an environment
that was familiar to them. The Living Room's counterculture identity gave it
credibility with hippie organizations like the Diggers and it is estimated that
many thousands of hippies came through its doors to talk about the Bible;
including the singer Janis Joplin, the actor Robin Williams, and even the
infamous Charles Manson.[14]

The extension of trust also permitted the Wises and their associates
to be creative and fluid in their belief and praxis and it was to the Book of
Acts that they looked for their pattern. Ted Wise said, "A few of us agreed
on one thing: that we ought to live out a portion of the Bible called the Book
of Acts, as though it were a script."[15] Consequently, Pentecostal activity occurred in the Baptist outreach. MacDonald wrote, "God did move indeed in
a supernatural way. And while some of my theological friends might demur

12. Riss, *A Survey*, 151.

13. MacDonald, *House of Acts*, 59–68.

14. Vachon, *Time*, 6.

15. Cronn, "Jason Questions."

at the suggestion that the gifts of the Holy Spirit as evident in the record of the early church could be operational today, yet both my Christian hippie friends and I could produce evidence that would be hard to refute."[16]

Another visitor to the Living Room, Victor Paul Vierwille, founder of The Way International, also influenced their Pentecostalism.[17] In spite of being met with strong opposition regarding his non-Trinitarian views, according to Plowman, before his departure he successfully recruited Steve Heefner to coordinate The Way East in Rye, New York and Jim Doop to lead the Way West in Mill Valley, California.[18] Within a year and a half the Living Room had closed and the Wises subsequently associated with Ray Stedman's Peninsula Bible Church.

Lonnie Frisbee (1949–1993)

Arriving in San Francisco to study art and needing a place to stay, Lonnie Frisbee met the Wises at the Living Room in 1967 and moved into the House of Acts. It seems that as a child he had been exposed to classical Pentecostalism through his grandmother and by 19 years of age, Frisbee's own Pentecostalism, and his general understanding of Christianity were in a formative stage. Only weeks before arriving in Haight-Ashbury he had experienced what he claimed was an electrifying Christophany in Tahquiz Canyon, in which Jesus told him that he would be used to bring many to faith.[19] According to Di Sabatio, Frisbee was known for rather unusual dramatics like wearing a deerskin cape on which he had painted an image of Jesus and which he would use as a mantle to put on people when he prayed for the Holy Spirit to come upon them.[20] Ted Wise explained that his first meeting with Frisbee involved listening to rather confusing stories about Jesus appearing from another planet in a flying saucer.[21]

In May 1968, Frisbee, accompanied by his new wife Connie, moved to Calvary Chapel Costa Mesa to begin a ministry with John Higgins under Chuck Smith. It was during his time at Calvary Chapel that he became known as the famous hippie evangelist who featured in *Look* (1971) and *Time* (1971) and in accounts of Calvary Chapel's early history. Under Smith, Frisbee was a youth leader, an elder in the House of Miracles, and teacher

16. MacDonald, *House of Acts,* 90.

17. Kent Philpott, email correspondence, August 11, 2009.

18. Plowman, *Jesus Movement,* 45–46.

19. Cording and Hardenbrook, "Son Worshippers."

20. Di Sabatino, "Frisbee."

21. Ibid.

at Wednesday night Bible studies. Frisbee's evangelism and Pentecostalism from 1968 to 1971 was a factor in Calvary Chapel's remarkable growth and according to Vachon, he was personally "responsible for tens of thousands of new converts in the southern California area."[22] However, his aggressive Pentecostalism clashed with what Balmer and Todd called Smith's "soft Pentecostalism"—"an accommodation to mainstream, middle-class sensibilities."[23] Enroth wrote that "Frisbee seems more preoccupied than the other pastors with charismatic manifestations, and one gets the distinct impression that he is more or less 'kept in line' by the older staff members."[24]

Due to a troubled marriage and a clash in Pentecostalism, Frisbee departed from Calvary Chapel in the autumn of 1971. After a brief stay with Bob Mumford in Ft. Lauderdale, a visit to several countries abroad and some time in Santa Cruz, he eventually returned to Calvary Chapel in 1976. Over the course of the next four years his presence in Calvary Chapel was rather obscure, until he was invited by John Wimber to speak at Calvary Chapel Yorba Linda on Mother's Day 1980. The service was a tipping point in John Wimber's subsequent break from Calvary Chapel and foundational in the Pentecostalism that emerged out of Vineyard Fellowships. By 1983, Frisbee had parted company with Vineyard and after a ten year season of relative obscurity, died in 1993.[25]

John Higgins—Shiloh Youth Revival Centers

Central to the story of Calvary Chapel Costa Mesa's communal outreaches in Orange County and the Shiloh Youth Revival Centers was a young hippie named John Higgins. Higgins, according to Chuck Fromm, was Chuck Smith's original connection to the hippies.[26] He first met Smith at a Bible study in 1967 and soon afterward received the BHS. Inspired by the House of Acts in Novato, Calvary Chapel rented a home on 19th Street in Costa Mesa as a communal outreach project where John Higgins, Lonnie Frisbee, and their wives lived together and reached out to hippies.[27] By opening the communal homes, the young duo of Higgins and Frisbee had a place to daily gather hippies and within weeks the home was heaving with young bohemians that were claiming a new faith in Jesus. Over the next year a

22. Vachon, *Time*, 90.

23. Balmer and Todd, "Calvary Chapel," 684.

24. Enroth et al., *Story*, 93.

25. Di Sabatino, "Frisbee."

26. Fromm, "Textual Communities," 172.

27. Chuck Smith, "The History," 6.

network of 19 communal homes was opened in Southern California and through them over 500 young people converted.[28]

In April 1969, Higgins and a group of leaders from the House of Miracles moved north to Dexter, Oregon where, being directed by a dream, they secured a 90 acre plot of land as a base for their new communal movement. They took the name Shiloh Youth Revival Centers (SYRC) from Genesis 49:10 as they believed they were accomplishing an end time work of God before the coming of Jesus. At its peak in 1978, SYRC's communal network included 75 homes that stretched from Fairbanks, Alaska to the Virgin Islands.[29] Between 1969 and 1979 they maintained a core of 5000 committed members and saw an estimated 100,000 young people pass through their doors.[30]

Based on the numbers of participants and full time members, SYRC was larger than the highly publicized Children of God (COG) and their sources of income were very diverse; including private donations, a working farm, apple picking, tree planting, and construction crews.[31] With greater attention being given to pre-millennial and pre-tribulational themes Higgins' emphasis on Pentecostalism in SYRC gradually diminished. SYRC's sudden collapse in 1978 also meant the sudden closure of most of its communal homes; a few of which formed into Calvary Chapels and a few went independent. Higgins himself later founded Calvary Chapel Tri-City in Tempe, Arizona, where he ministers to the present day.[32]

Kenn Gulliksen—Vineyard Outreaches

One of Chuck Smith's young protégés to rise out of Calvary Chapel Costa Mesa was Kenn Gulliksen; a man that Smith called "the pastor of love."[33] From West Los Angeles in 1974, Gulliksen launched a Calvary Chapel Bible study that incorporated the intimate worship songs played at the Costa Mesa's weeknight services with the Sunday morning Bible study, since up to that point in time Smith had continued to sing hymns on Sunday mornings.[34] Between 1974 and 1979, Gulliksen built and oversaw eight similar styled fellowships in Southern California under the name Vineyard. His

28. Richardson et al., *Organized*, 8.

29. Stewart and Richardson, "Mundane," 827.

30. Goldman, "Continuity," 342.

31. Richardson, "New Religious Movements," 87; and Stewart and Richarson, "Mundane," 842.

32. "Calvary Chapel Tri-City."

33. A. Hunter, "Kenn Gulliksen."

34. Fromm, "Textual Communities," 258.

Pentecostalism lacked the sharper edge of Frisbee's and maintained the "softer" style of Smith's with an emphasis on love. Gulliksen's Vineyard's attracted creative musicians and celebrities including the likes of Bob Dylan and Bernie Leadon of The Eagles, both of whom confessed a conversion to Christianity. It was also at Gulliksen's meetings in 1974 that twenty-one year old Keith Green confessed faith in Jesus.[35] In 1982, Gulliksen joined John Wimber in his exodus from the Calvary Chapel movement and, feeling weary from ministry, turned his eight Vineyards over to the leadership of Wimber. Gulliksen continued to plant churches through 2001, when, due to poor health, he moved to San Juan Capistrano, California, where he now teaches Bible studies.[36]

Keith Green (1953–1982)—Last Days Ministries

From the time of his conversion at Gulliksen's study, Keith Green and his wife Melody immediately began to open their homes to anyone who needed a place to stay. As a result from 1975 to 1979, the Greens formed their own communal network of seventy people in seven neighboring homes in San Bernardino.[37] Green quickly became a famous JP musician noted for his bold style of confrontational singing and preaching and for causing his record producers contractual concerns when he insisted on giving away his music to those who could not afford to buy it. In 1977 Green named their group Last Days Ministries and in 1979, relocated with twenty-five others to a 140 acre site in Garden Valley, Texas.[38] Built off an ever growing, personal mailing list, Green published a Jesus newspaper called *Last Days Newsletter* that by the mid-1980s was mailed to 500,000 people around the world.[39] The newsletter later became the *Last Days Magazine*, which the ministry claims to have distributed 16 million copies worldwide.[40] The Green's mixed freely with classical Pentecostals, Charismatics, and Evangelicals and personally practiced what was an amalgamation of hippiedom and Pentecostalism common in the JPM. Towards the latter years of his life, his music and ministry became more thematically focused on world missions. Since Green's sudden demise in a plane crash in 1982, Last Days Ministries has

---

35. Green and Hazard, *No Compromise*, 147–50.
36. A. Hunter, "Kenn Gulliksen."
37. Thomas, "Keith Green Story."
38. Green and Hazard, *No Compromise*, 323–27.
39. "Last Days Ministries."
40. Ibid.

associated with YWAM and Melody Green went on to become a noted pro-Life campaigner.

Scott Ross—The Love Inn and Tell It Like It Is

One of the early accounts of the JPM on the east coast began with the story of a New York City radio DJ named Scott Ross; a young man well connected with many famous musicians of the hippie movement like the Beatles. Ross' parents, the Pentecostal minister at his mother's church, and Pat Robertson were influential in the formation of his faith and his Pentecostal spirituality. Ross says that it was out of desperation that he called out to Jesus one day while on a "trip" and experienced a miraculous deliverance from drug abuse.[41] Although Ross said he confessed a personal faith in Jesus at the age of five, this experience of healing was to him a significant turning point at which God was changing the course of his life. Soon after his healing, Pat Robertson invited Ross to work as a host of a program on his 700 Club. But Ross's show proved to be hugely controversial among the staff since he had been offering prayers for Martin Luther King Jr., dressed like a hippie, and invited "unconverted" hippies as guests onto his program. After being confronted by fundamentalist pastors and threatened with the withdrawal of financial pledges, Robertson himself took a stand with Ross. He told his staff, "The day this building becomes more important than these people, I will personally burn the building to the ground."[42]

With the encouragement of Pat Robertson, Ross began to broadcast the first Christian Rock 'n' Roll radio program called *Tell It Like It Is* from Freeville, New York on January 1, 1969. The show quickly blossomed into a popular syndicated program that was carried by over 150 stations around the USA and received responses from listeners who reportedly claimed that they "were finding Jesus, or breaking destructive habits, or receiving the BHS all while listening to the show."[43] Ross also founded a community in Freeville called The Love Inn, a Jesus newspaper called *Free Love*, and a record label called New Song that featured talents like Phil Keaggy.[44] At its peak the community grew to about 270 people and included a coffee-house ministry and a school through the eighth grade.[45] Ross's Love Inn

41. "Scott Ross Interview."
42. Ibid.
43. Sherrill, *Scott Free*, 90–91, back cover.
44. Ibid., 145.
45. Jackson, *Coming Together*, 183.

Community is now defunct but he has maintained a close relationship with Pat Robertson and regularly features on CBN.

Jim (1939–2011) and Sue Palosaari

Jim and Sue Palosaari were converted under Linda Meissner's ministry at a classical Pentecostal styled tent meeting in a rural town called Cathcart, Washington. They served alongside Meissner, Russell Griggs, and other as leaders in the Jesus People Army (JPA). Jim recalled his conversion experience saying that he and Sue were the only non-church members in the tent, but after hearing the message he stood to his feet, grabbed the main post supporting the tent, and began to tremble. As a result the entire tent began to shake and the church members' were excited by the fact that their only hippies in attendance had just believed the gospel.[46]

In 1971, before the breakup of the JPA, Linda Meissner travelled together with Jim and Sue Palosaari to Milwaukee and organized a large meeting that resulted in the birth of the Jesus People Milwaukee. The Palosaari's remained in Milwaukee and within one and a half years the outreach grew to become an urban ministry with 150 fulltime workers living in a formerly abandoned, 315 bed hospital that they rented for $1000 per month.[47] The Jesus People Milwaukee was short lived and at its demise divided into four factions. Jim Palosaari, accompanied by a group of 30 young people and the rock band called Sheep, travelled to Scandinavia, Europe, and England under the name The Jesus Family. From the Jesus People Milwaukee also came the Jesus People USA (JPUSA)—still based in Chicago to the present day—and Bill Lowery's travelling tent ministry known as Christ is the Answer (CITA). Palosaari's group of thirty journeyed to Scandinavia under the financial sponsorship of the FGBMFI and reportedly saw large numbers of young people respond to their gospel message. With his Swedish heritage giving him some measure of credibility, churches warmly welcomed them, giving them the nickname "Jesus hippits," (Jesus hippies) and even furnished a train to transport them from town to town to preach and sing.[48]

After their time in Scandinavia, they hitchhiked through Lautzenhausen and Berlin, Germany, and the Netherlands, preaching and praying along the way. They slept on church floors, in church basements, and in abandoned brothels, living on less than meager finances. While in the Netherlands, Russell Griggs invited them to come to England under the financial

---

46. Jim Palosaari, interview with author, March 24, 2009.

47. Ibid.

48. Ibid., and Lynn Marie Malmberg, interview with author, September 16, 2010.

sponsorship of a Christian philanthropist Kenneth Frampton to preach and to "rescue" Frampton's sons from the COG. Once in London they started the Living Room Coffee House and two communes in Bromley, and the entire group, including the band Sheep, toured the UK in a double-decker bus performing a rock opera called Lonesome Stone.[49] Before leaving, Palosaari helped found the UK's Greenbelt Christian music festival in 1974.[50]

Back in the USA, Palosaari was a key leader in a new communal experiment called the Highway Missionary Society that formed out of the large Jesus Northwest music festival in 1976. After moving from San Francisco to Oregon, the Highway Missionary Society finally settled in Cincinnati, Ohio, where the tragic death of Palosaari's son in 1981 brought the group to an abrupt end.[51] Palosaari characterized his own Pentecostalism as a belief and praxis that had shifted over time away from his original, and rather aggressive, classical Pentecostal praxis in the days of the JPA. He attributed this change to his exposure to various strands of charismatic and non-charismatic Christianity.[52]

Jim and Dawn Herrin—Jesus People USA (JPUSA)

In 1972, after Palosaari's departure for Europe, Jim and Dawn Herrin left Milwaukee with thirty others and made their way to Chicago to form JPUSA.[53] They initiated urban outreaches that included communal living, youth meetings, street drama, the Resurrection Band (Rez Band), and a Jesus newspaper called *Cornerstone*. Several businesses were also initiated in the areas of construction, music recording, and graphic design to provide financial support for the ministry. From 1976 to 1989 JPUSA was associated with a small Pentecostal denomination called the Full Gospel Church in Christ, but since 1989 has been affiliated with the Evangelical Covenant Church.[54] With a community of 500 members in residence, a variety of ongoing ministries, the Rez Band, and the Cornerstone Festival still vibrantly operational, the JPUSA has endured as one of the most iconic and intact examples a JPM communal church.[55]

49. Corey, *Jesus Bubble*, 28–30.

50. Northup, "Turning Thirty," 3.

51. Stewart and Richardson, "Mundane," 828–29.

52. Jim Palosaari, interview with author, March 24, 2009.

53. "JPUSA."

54. Ibid. Also see Bozeman, "Jesus People USA," 309.

55. "JPUSA."

Bill Lowery—Christ Is the Answer (CITA)

Fifty other members of the JP Milwaukee group followed a young AG tent evangelist named Bill Lowery and formed a ministry called CITA. Moving from city to city, CITA pursued a rigorous daily schedule of street preaching and street drama during the day and big tent meetings during the evening. From 1971 to 1974, CITA grew to become a communal caravan of lorries, buses, campers, and 250 workers travelling the USA. CITA has since moved its base of operations to El Paso, Texas and has expanded internationally to Finland, Italy, Spain, Portugal, Mexico, Philippines, El Salvador, Honduras, Ukraine, and India.[56] Although today the ministry is a scaled down version of what it was in the seventies, it has not altered its tent styled evangelistic emphasis. From the earliest days CITA's praxis included evangelism, tongues, and healing, but according to Bozeman (1990) it has shifted from the standard AG position and tongues are limited to a private prayer language.

Links With Classical Pentecostalism

In the few discussions that exist on the JPM, it is often assumed that it was occurring "outside" of any established churches and that this is what made it unique. While it is true that new streams were birthed and grew "outside" of existing church structures, the JPM also thrived within existing churches and this includes classical Pentecostal churches.

David Wilkerson (1931–2011)—Teen Challenge and TCTS

If the AG had to rank their twentieth leaders according to influence and acclaim, David Wilkerson would be near the top. Wilkerson founded a ministry called Teen Challenge (TC) in 1958 as an outreach to gangs and drug addicts in New York City and from the outset his story aroused the curiosity of the nation. The narrative of the young, country preacher who had fearlessly moved to New York City to stand face to face with gang leaders and confront them with the love of Jesus Christ was published in the book *The Cross and the Switchblade* (*TCTS*). The book recorded Wilkerson's encounter with one particularly ornery drug addict and a gang leader named Nicky Cruz. What seemed to intrigue readers was how the experience of the BHS could subdue such a wild man like Cruz, instantly free him from drug addiction, and transform him into a bold Christian witness. His experience tacitly implied

56. "Christ is the Answer."

that readers with drug addiction, depression, or almost any felt need could invoke the BHS and await similar results. A best seller in the 1960s, a popular Christian film in 1970, a comic book in 1972, and perhaps the third most widely read book among the JP, *TCTS* became the primary vehicle to carry this unmediated offer of Pentecostal power to many in the JPM.[57]

Alongside Wilkerson's book, new Teen Challenge Centers (TCC) were opened all across the country at a fast rate, reaching as far as Southern California by at least 1964.[58] TC had tapped into a deep current of concern within the American public over drug use and drug addiction among young people and boasted an instantaneous remedy available to all. The pragmatic benefit of drug rehabilitation and the alleged success rates at TCC were so intriguing to the American public that the means of rehabilitation, which lay in the experience of the BHS, also became increasingly appealing. A study carried out by the US Department of Health, Education, and Welfare seemed to confirm TC's claim of a 70 percent "cure rate'" from drug addiction; this compared to 1–15 percent "cure rate" of other programs.[59] In addition to the healing from drug addiction, an AG report also claimed 9,000 Christian conversions through TCCs by the end of the 1960s.[60] The growing TC ministry was eventually handed over to the US Missions Department of the AG denomination in 1971 and Wilkerson founded a new ministry called World Challenge.[61] By 2007, TC had been welcomed into almost sixty countries around the world as a successful drug rehabilitative program that was beneficial for youth.

Early on, Wilkerson seemed to be aware of his prominence and potential influence upon the youthful drug culture in America and his contact with the West Coast hippie youth and the JPM can be traced back to 1965 in Seattle and 1967 in San Francisco.[62] With his opinion of the JP vacillating between wildly antagonistic to reluctantly affirming, but never fully supportive, Wilkerson personified the tension between classical Pentecostals and the JP. His main frustration lay in his inability to see anything redeemable in hippiedom and therefore nothing healthy in its union with Pentecostalism. Wilkerson published an aggressive polemic against early JP outreaches in a book called *Purple-Violet-Squish* and in a thirty minute, 16mm color film

57. Eskridge and Di Sabatino, "Remembering." Third most widely read book.

58. "Teen Challenge Centers Merge," 31.

59. Hess, "National Institute."

60. "Executive Reviews," 28.

61. "World Challenge."

62. In Seattle, see Barnes, "Teen-Agers Aided," 5. In San Francisco, see MacDonald, *House of Acts*, 83.

called *The Runaway Generation*. Both of these misrepresented the Living Room in Haight-Ashbury as a seedy place where hippies and staff surreptitiously used hallucinogens and marijuana to enhance their Bible studies.[63] In an attempt to warn as many as possible of the dangers in the JPM, the film aired on San Francisco TV, was advertised in local newspapers from coast to coast, and screened at AG churches around the country from March 1968 through April 1970.[64] Wilkerson continued his vociferous attack in a series of articles published in the *PE* that seemed to be intent on contrasting the virtues of TCCs with the vices of the JPM.

In spite of his dislike for mingling hippiedom and classical Pentecostalism, some TCCs went ahead and adopted a more sympathetic approach to the hippies. For example, in Atlanta a TCC was established in the hippie district—Piedmont Park—with a coffeehouse, a halfway house, and borrowed hippie idioms like praise-ins and study-ins for its prayer and Bible studies.[65] In Muskegon, Michigan AG Pastor Phil McClain opened a new TCC where the members of a recently converted rock band called Living Waters led singing, praise, and Bible raps.[66] In Nashville, Tennessee a TCC took the name The Open Door and shifted its emphasis from urban drug addicts and gangs to students from the University of Vanderbilt.[67] In 1970, a TCC in St. Louis, Missouri attended a hippie rock festival called The Festival of Life, gave away Christian literature, and preached.[68] In 1968, David Berg, founder of the COG, transformed the TCC in Huntington Beach into the countercultural Light Club; something Wilkerson was very disapprovingly aware of.[69] Wilkerson was not hands on involved in street level outreach to the JP and he never led a local JP group, but his influence was wielded through *TCTS* and TCCs. His relationship with the JPM was paradoxical. On one hand, his book *TCTS* was one of the primary vehicles to infuse Pentecostal spirituality into the JPM and on the other hand he never really participated in or sympathized with the JP. Given his prominence in the AG, it is plausible to assume the AG denomination as a whole may have been more favorably disposed to the JP, had he adopted a more affirming posture.

---

63. D. Wilkerson, *Purple*, 23, 42; MacDonald, *House of Acts*, 83.

64. MacDonald, *House of Acts*, 83. The *House of Acts* is, in part, a rebuttal to *Purple-Violet-Squish*.

65. "Teen Challenge," 21.

66. "New Michigan Teen Challenge." 20–21.

67. "Coffeehouse Ministers," 20.

68. Bush, "Christian Witness," 18.

69. D. Wilkerson, *Purple*, 51–61.

The Assemblies of God

The AG denomination was far less flexible in its interaction with the JPM than the International Church of the Foursquare Gospel (ICFG). Articles published in the *PE* show that AG churches were reticent to swap the 1950s jargon of "youth rallies" for the JP idioms like "Bible raps" and "Jesus festivals." Some conversion accounts emphasized hippies getting a haircut and a bath, implying that a credible salvation experience must also comprise an abstersion from the counterculture.[70] Pictures show AG ministers awkwardly placed in coffeehouses and outdoor meetings with crew-cuts, horn rimmed glasses, and suits and ties alongside young JP with long hair, jeans, and tee shirts. Some youth workers, apparently trying to please both the youth and the AG establishment, grew beards and long hair while wearing a suit and tie; a few went completely native and took on hippie attire. Editorials in the *PE* reflect a full range of opinions from the supportive to prophetic warnings. For example, in a single issue, one person thanked God for the JPM, while another wrote, "I have been profoundly disturbed by the fact that many believers have been duped into believing that God, rather than Satan, is behind the thrust of Jesus rock."[71] Reflecting back after many years, one AG pastor in California lamented his antipathy towards the JPM as the worst decisions in his entire ministry.[72]

In contrast however, many small town newspapers, some books, and the *PE* are peppered with stories of independent AG churches and evangelistic organizations that reached out to the hippies and experienced transformation and numerical growth. The earliest AG involvement could be traced to the first days of Linda Meissner's ministry in Spokane, Washington. Newspaper articles record the names of AG churches and ministers like Glad Tidings, Calvary Temple, and the reverend Jim Nicholson that supported her outreaches and helped organize her meetings.[73] According to Edward Plowman, the first Christian outreach in Haight-Ashbury was probably Clayton House; a coffeehouse and commune operated by AG minister Dick Keys.[74] Roger Palms records that Keys was well supported by area AG churches and that his ministry also included a fleet of cars and a syndicated radio program.[75] Although located in the heart of the Haight,

70. Brotzman, "Deaf Hippie," 17.

71. Thomas, letter to editor, "Thanks for the 'Jesus Movement,'" 24. "Rock and the Church," 27.

72. George Thomas, email correspondence with author, October 12, 2009.

73. "1000 Attracted," 5; Barnes, "Teen-Agers Aided," 5; "Coffee House Operator," 6.

74. Plowman, *Jesus Movement*, 68.

75. Palms, *Jesus Kids*, 55.

his communes forbade beards and long hair.[76] Clayton House followed the short life cycle common among the early communes in Haight-Ashbury, opening in 1967 and closing by 1969 or 1970. In October 1971, Keys moved to Ft. Lauderdale to join Bob Mumford in the Shepherding Movement.[77] In addition, local newspapers were filled with accounts of AG churches initiating JP styled outreaches as, in August 1971, when The Evangel Temple in Redlands, California sponsored a Jesus People Festival in the Redlands Bowl. It was a weekend long event that included a lineup of Jesus musicians, speakers like Duane Pederson, and Jesus marches.[78]

In 1971, Watson Argue Jr., pastor of First Assembly in Santa Rosa, California, permitted Youth Pastor Jim Boehner to open the church's Tuesday night Bible studies to local hippies. They claimed that within two weeks the attendance increased from 120 to over 700, that prayer meetings lasted until after midnight, that many were saved, and as many as 35 hippies received the BHS in a single night.[79] In that same year at Bethel Temple in Sacramento, Youth Pastor Dick Eastman helped organize mountain prayer retreats where he claimed that intercession was often so intense that the young JP were unable to move from the place of prayer. At one such prayer meeting he wrote that after midnight the Holy Spirit settled on fifty youth and "in moments teens were slain prostrate everywhere."[80] According to Eastman, the young people, motivated by the belief that Jesus could return at any moment, left the meetings and returned to their schools with a "revolutionary fervor to witness."[81] It was from these meetings that some of the first mentions are made of Tony Salerno and the musical group Agape Force, who became influential among AG youth for many years to follow.[82] In 1976, Eastman moved from Bethel Temple to lead the ministry of Every Home for Christ.[83]

In 1973, in Houston Texas, Pastor Austin Wilkerson reported that his Evangelistic Temple, "has had a phenomenal growth over six years. It has quadrupled in attendance, and there have been an average of 300 water baptisms per year over the past four years. More than 3,000 teenagers

76. Ibid., 55.

77. D. Moore, *Shepherding Movement*, 50–51.

78. "Jesus People Festival," 20.

79. Eastman, "Prayer Power," 22.

80. Ibid.

81. Ibid.

82. Harrel, "Awakening in Reedley," 9. Also see "Building Kid's Character."

83. "Every Home for Christ."

were converted in one year."[84] The minister of youth, Buddy Hicks, took controversial steps to open the church up to the hippies and Wilkerson, in agreement, wrote that "our congregation found it necessary to sacrifice if we were going to minister to this new congregation."[85] During an initial, short-lived season it was reported that hippies sat on the floor instead of in pews and flooded the front of the church by the hundreds at the end of services to pray for salvation. After meetings, new converts would often surrender cigarettes, pipes, needles, marijuana, and pill bottles and discuss the Bible into the early morning hours. They claimed that without instruction or pastoral mediation, new believers would often break out into spontaneous praise and speak in tongues.

This break from convention was not without incidence. Wilkerson wrote that the church was praying, "'God, send a revival; fill our altars with penitent sinners; use us to win the lost.' But when it began to happen, some were saying, 'It's stones, serpents, scorpions! We are not sure this is what we were seeking.'"[86] One member complained to Wilkerson, "Pastor, I am broken hearted because I had never thought our altars would be desecrated by dirty feet."[87] Following his years at Evangelistic Temple and his work among the JP, Buddy Hicks became a popular youth minister founding Youthquake ministries and later Buddy Hicks Ministries.[88]

In 1972, First Assembly Binghampton, New York opened a coffee-house outreach called Turning Point, complete with black lights, candles, and a separate room for prayer and counseling. To operate the ministry, the church financially supported fulltime workers named Bob and Jeanetta Reed and recruited volunteers from their own church, from a TC, and from a local charismatic prayer meeting.[89] Turning Point produced its own Jesus paper *The Word of Peace* with a circulation of 30,000 and sponsored two Jesus concerts that drew in excess of 4,500 youth.[90] The church made no issue of hair and clothing styles and incorporated Jesus choruses and scripture songs into their Sunday evening services. In 1974, Reed appealed to other AG churches to imitate their model since many within the denomination still resisted countercultural methods of outreach.

84. A. Wilkerson, "Jesus Movement," 16.

85. Ibid., 18.

86. Ibid., 19.

87. Ibid., 18.

88. "Rallies Planned," 5.

89. "Church Sponsors Outreach," 25.

90. Ibid.

While it is difficult to find even the slightest mention of the JPM in AG academic works or denominational publications, both Edith Blumhofer and Margaret Poloma have admitted that the AG grew numerically from the 1970s to the mid-1980s and that the source of this growth was renewal movements outside the AG denomination.[91] Poloma also wrote that the AG's normal posture has been to resist renewal movements that occur outside their own denomination, and this is true of the JPM.[92] While, the JPM did not originate with AG people or with the AG denomination, their ministers were involved in the earliest outreaches and all throughout the heyday. It would be inaccurate to draw hard and fast lines that imagine the JPM occurring only outside the AG denomination and that a quantitative or qualitative spill over trickled into AG churches. The JPM also took place within the AG and the relationship between the growth mentioned by Blumhofer and Poloma in the 1970s and 1980s and the JPM needs to be examined. The parallel dates are not coincidental. In 2001 Thomas E. Trask, AG Superintendent from 1993–2007, candidly admitted that AG churches were well aware of the JPM and were divided in their opinions over it. Yet, he also said that the "churches that welcomed the Jesus people had the joy of seeing a great harvest. Today, many of these former Jesus people are adults in our churches, and some are even pastors."[93] While many resisted the JPM, just as many in the AG participated in it, reciprocally infusing the movement with Pentecostal spirituality and also being revitalized by it.

The Foursquare Church—ICFG

Compared to the AG, the ICFG experienced a greater amount of reciprocal interchange, both by shaping the JPM and being shaped by the JPM. Not only were many JP leaders active or former ICFG ministers, but from the early 1970s many ICFG churches experienced numerical growth and transformation as a consequence of their involvement in the JPM. Several ICFG ministers, exemplified for "setting patterns for explosive growth and renewal" during the 1970s and the 1980s, were involved in JPM.[94] For example, Jack Hayford's Church on the Way in Van Nuys grew from a small congregation to many thousands, in part, as a result of the JPM. Hayford never identified himself as a JP leader or his church as a JP church. But the

91. Blumhofer, *Assemblies of God*, 139–41, 166; Poloma, "Charisma and Structure," 2n1.

92. "Charisma and Structure," 2n1.

93. Goodall, "Ask the Superintendent."

94. "ICFG History."

famous JP band The 2nd Chapter of Acts began to attend Hayford's church when it was less than one hundred members and was part of the story of its rapid growth. The band members saw Hayford as one the most influential people in their life.[95] For twenty-nine years Church on the Way was also home to Christian celebrity Pat Boone.[96] Boone not only identified himself as a JP, but he opened a center to aid JP, established Lion and Lamb Records in order to promote Jesus Music, and, in JP style, baptized as many as 250 people in his swimming pool in 1971.[97] The church's growth and Pentecostalism was affected by the presence of these prominent JP, but Hayford reciprocally impacted them.

While there were many individual ICFG churches like Hayford's, another peculiar hybrid also arose within the ICFG as a result of the JPM. In these cases there were distinctly identifiable clusters of churches that were started by and flourished under one ICFG leader. While these clusters of churches remained underneath the ICFG denominational umbrella, they also functioned with a degree of autonomy under the leader and with a distinct counterculture identity. Two such examples are given here: Ralph Moore's Hope Chapel and Roy Hicks Junior's Eugene Faith Center.

In August 1971, Ralph Moore claimed that God had commanded him to go to Manhattan Beach to pastor a failing ICFG fellowship. As he recalled, God interrupted his mocking jokes about the church with a single word, "GO!"[98] Upon his arrival he was confronted with a crisis decision of permitting the hippies into the meetings or maintaining a "straight" congregation. One irate member expressed her discontent to Moore in an attempt to persuade him not to accommodate the counterculture youth, but her complaints only served to strengthen his resolve to side with the hippies. He wrote, "That one lady, however, catalyzed my decision. I chose to pastor hurting people, as Jesus had said, 'It is the sick who need a physician.'"[99] Only three weeks into his new role as pastor and Moore decided to swap his formal attire for a more casual one as a means of identifying with the menagerie of marines, bikers, and former topless dancers entering his congregation.[100]

In the first year of Moore's ministry he engaged the church in an ambitious outreach plan to give away 20,000 copies of *TCTS*, paid for with

95. "2nd Chapter of Acts."

96. Gilbreath, "Why Pat Boone," 5.

97. "Pat Boone Baptizes in His Swimming Pool," 40. Tiegel, "Pat Boone Opens Center," 3, 59; and D. Lynch, "Pat Boone," 1170.

98. R. Moore, *Let Go of the Ring*, 36.

99. Ibid., 58. For a full discussion, see ibid., 52–57.

100. "History of Hope Chapel."

a donation of $5,000 from a Christian philanthropist named W. Clement Stone.[101] To give people a means to respond, a red sticker reading, "Need Help? Call Hope Chapel," was attached to the book. The outreach was successful and the church grew to the extent that by 1976 an abandoned bowling alley was purchased and converted into a church facility to make room for the 2,500 that attended services on the weekend. In 1983, Moore moved to Hawaii where he founded Hope Chapel Kaneohe, out of which another twenty Hope Chapels were established.[102] By 1997, there were a total of 30 Hope Chapels.[103]

Hope Chapels have also succeeded at forging a separate, collective identity while still functioning under the ICFG denominational umbrella. Ralph Moore has admitted his appreciation for aspects of Jack Hayford's Church on the Way, Chuck Smith's Calvary Chapel, and Ralph Wilkerson's Melodyland Christian Center, yet has also said, "I couldn't substitute either man for the Holy Spirit."[104] Hope Chapel stands as an example of a distinct, ICFG group of churches whose growth and ethos has been affected by counterculture values.

Operating out of Eugene, Oregon in a similar vein to Ralph Moore was another ICFG minister named Roy Hicks Jr. (1944–1994). Having arrived in 1968 to take the leadership of a small struggling ICFG church called the Eugene Faith Center (EFC), the twenty-six year old was confronted with the same crisis of blending the "straight" congregation with the growing number of hippies at his meetings. Hicks never adopted counterculture apparel, grew his hair long, or spoke in hip jargon. Yet he did believe that there were valuable and redeemable qualities in hippiedom and he willingly incorporated them into the ethos of EFC. This accommodating posture gained EFC a reputation in the region as an oasis for hippie seekers to understand the Bible, to pray, and to be around other counterculture people. In addition, JP from area communes like SYRC—also in Eugene—regularly attended EFC meetings and by the early 1970s the church had a majority of hippie seekers and JP in attendance. Under Hicks' leadership from 1969–1988, EFC grew from 50 to 5,000 members, planted seven other ICFG churches, and another fifty daughter churches in the Northwest.[105] This amounted to twice the number of Moore's Hope Chapels and in half the time. In 1994, at the age of 50, Hicks life and ministry were curtailed when he died in a plane crash. At

101. R. Moore, *Let Go of the Ring*, 59–60.

102. "History of Hope Chapel."

103. D. Miller, *Reinventing*, 42.

104. R. Moore, *Let Go of the Ring*, 77.

105. Mortenson, "Thousands Bid Pastor Farewell," 6A.

his funeral was attended by over 5,000 people that he had influenced over his twenty-six years of ministry.[106]

Bethel Tabernacle

In addition to the denominations, there were untold numbers of independent, classical Pentecostal churches that participated in the JPM. One such church was Bethel Tabernacle, a "squat white church with a brown-linoleum floor and old movie theatre seats" located "in a slum of North Redondo Beach, California."[107] The "solid blue collar," Pentecostal church began in 1949 and in the late sixties was led by a "transplanted Midwesterner" named Lyle Steenis.[108] However, in 1968, the church entered a different era when a tall, ex-hippie named Breck Stevens, who had recently been converted and healed from drug addiction at David Berg's TCC in Huntington Beach, began to bring his hippie friends into the meetings.[109] Soon afterward, a major controversy erupted among the older members who disapproved of the long hair and clothing of Stevens' friends. Steenis decided to open the church to the hippies; a decision that resulted in many of the older members leaving and a flood of hippies entering. Over the next two years Steenis claimed that over 15,000 youth had passed through the church and 4,000 had stopped using drugs as a result of the Holy Spirit's healing power.[110] In 1971, national attention was drawn to the dramatic events at the little church when *Look* magazine published a cover story on the JPM that featured Bethel Tabernacle. Steenis claimed that as a result of the media coverage the number youth that had passed through their doors rose from 15,000 to 60,000.[111]

Reading the literature and watching film clips recorded at Bethel during the JPM, leaves a strong impression that the hippies entering Bethel were rough, hard-core users, something akin to the early days in Seattle and San Francisco. Although Steenis and Stephens warmly welcomed the hippies, they also preached a strong message of repentance and enforced strict regulations upon the members which consisted of a dress code and prohibitions against watching TV and listening to rock n' roll—especially Jesus Rock. The more serious among the members at Bethel joined the "one hundred percenters"—a group expected to attend meetings on Tuesday,

106. Ibid., 1.
107. Vachon, "Jesus Movement," 19–20.
108. Ibid.
109. Enroth et al., *Story*, 95.
110. Vachon, "Jesus Movement," 20.
111. Vachon, *Time to Be Born*, 46.

Wednesday, Friday, Saturday nights, twice on Sundays, and to go into the streets to preach on their days off. Stevens famously claimed that the BHS resulted in a thirty-second cure from drugs and Steenis stressed the practice of nine gifts of the Holy Spirit.[112] A clip from a Bethel Tabernacle service recorded in the film *Jesus People* shows scenes reminiscent of any classical Pentecostal meeting, complete with singing, testimonies, hand clapping, dancing, speaking in tongues, and shouts of hallelujah.[113] Although famous in JP historical accounts, the church never grew beyond 200 members and has been defunct for a number of years.

Links to People Coming Out of Classical Pentecostalism

Migration of people from one branch of Christianity to another is not uncommon and here the term "coming-outers" is used to describe those who do so.[114] Turning now from classical Pentecostal churches the following set of examples draws attention to the largest category of Pentecostal influencers within the JPM: people whose spiritual formation and training occurred within classical Pentecostalism but who made a departure from classical Pentecostal institutions and practices. These individuals launched new independent churches and outreach initiatives that manifested an array of hybrid Pentecostalisms, each one as a consequence of incorporating elements of hippiedom.

Linda Meissner—The Jesus People Army

Linda Meissner, christened the "Joan of Arc of The Jesus People's Army," (JPA) was an AG minister who first appeared on the pages of *TCTS* working alongside David Wilkerson as a teenager in the formative years of New York City's TC in 1960.[115] While praying on a rooftop in New York, Meissner claimed to have seen a vision of an army of kids marching through Seattle with Bibles in hand.[116] Arriving in Spokane in May of 1965, she established Teen Harvest Headquarters and spent the next two years ministering under the TC theme of drug rehabilitation through Christian conversion and

---

112. Enroth, et al., *Story,* 95–97.

113. Adams, "Jesus People."

114. Edith Blumhofer first used "coming-outism." Blumhofer, *Assemblies of God,* 1:19.

115. Enroth et al., *Story,* 117. D. Wilkerson, *Cross,* 132–37.

116. P. King, *Jesus People,* 7.

BHS. While traveling in Hong Kong she claimed that Jesus spoke to her, saying, "[C]ome back to Seattle, Washington, and by yourself . . . be obedient to what I tell you. I will raise up a mighty army of young people and you'll go forth and speak the words of life, and he said they'll go forth and bring healing to the people."[117] Returning to Seattle in 1967, she traversed the city preaching in churches and schools but with minimal success. During this season she crossed paths and networked with many AG ministers, a Church of God minister named Wendell Wallace, Dennis Bennett, and Catholic priests Father Fulton and Father Jerry Brown; people who were all beginning to experience church growth through an influx of JP.[118]

The rapid growth of the JPA, however, began in 1969 after Meissner jettisoned her "straight" looks and methods in exchange for countercultural dress and means of outreach. According to Preston Shires, it was John and Diana Breithaupt, a couple who operated a Christian commune in Seattle called the House of Zacchaeus, that convinced Meissner to make this change.[119] Jim and Sue Palosaari, Meissner's first hippie converts, worked alongside her to shape the JPA into a hippie styled outreach. Meissner, however, never altered her insistence upon evidential tongues and healing and she continued to use elements of TC's methodology for the JPA's organizational structure.

Over the next two years, the JPA grew very rapidly and began to influence the charismatic ethos of the JPM in the Pacific Northwest. Beginning at Lincoln High School, a school troubled with drug problems, the JPA was able to reach many teens, claiming dramatic conversions and instant healings through the BHS. Meissner stated that in one instance 250 were baptized in a river and on another occasion seventy-five to one hundred youth received the BHS at the same time.[120] The students were organized into campus Bible studies and coffeehouses were opened with names like the Ark, the Eleventh Hour, and the Catacombs. With her communal homes sprouting up in neighboring states and across the Canadian border, Meissner envisioned the JPA becoming an umbrella network for all "street Christians" in the Pacific Northwest.[121] The JPA published a newspaper called *Agape*, and in a memorable stunt, released the first ten thousand copies from an airplane over crowds attending a pop festival at Golden Creek

117. "Evangelist to Speak," 2. For Hong Kong, see Enroth et al., *The Story*, 118.

118. P. King, *Jesus People*, 7–29.

119. Shires, *Hippies*, 105.

120. Runge, "Jesus People Rally Here," 3. For BHS, see Enroth et al., *Story*, 119.

121. Plowman, *Jesus Movement*, 52.

Park. Under the leadership of young people like Russell Griggs, Meissner's JPA spread throughout Northwest Canada and Alaska.[122]

The two years of rapid growth of the JPA came to a dramatic halt in 1971, when Meissner left her husband John Salveson and the JPA to join David Berg's COG.[123] Overnight the massive JPA network collapsed and split into three directions. First, according to Enroth, a committee of twenty or thirty charismatic pastors was formed in an attempt to bring stability to the leaderless JPA.[124] This proved unsuccessful and most of the followers assimilated into local churches or walked away from the JPM. A second group followed Jim and Sue Palosaari, moving east to start the Jesus People Milwaukee. Third, Spokane based neighbor Carl Parks, and his communal based ministry, the Voice of Elijah (VoE), picked up a large portion of young people from the JPA. Meissner served in the publishing arm of the COG and led works in Israel and Algeria under the alias of Esther, before exiting the organization in the late 1970s.[125] After living in obscurity for many years in the hippie enclave of Christiania she now intends to publish her autobiography.

Carl Parks—Voice of Elijah

Another example of a coming outer was Carl Parks, who in 1970, founded the Voice of Elijah (VoE) in Spokane, Washington. Raised in a classical Pentecostal home by a mother who was an evangelist, Parks was influenced by Pentecostalism from an early age. At the age of 33, however, after spending three weeks locked away in isolation to read his Bible and pray, Parks claimed that God had called him to minister to the street people of Spokane.[126] He immediately responded by preaching to the youth who gathered in Shadle Park and High Bridge Park.

Among the youth who gathered to listen were the members of a rock band named Wilson McKinley. After believing Parks' message they decided to abandon the band and join Parks in his ministry on the streets. However, the band members resurrected Wilson McKinley at Parks' request, being convinced by him that they would be effective at reaching young people with

---

122. "Jesus People's Army Meets," 5.

123. "Children of God Seen Two Ways," 22.

124. Enroth et al., *Story*, 122.

125. Balmer, "Linda Meissner," 371. For Israel and Algeria, see Michelmore, *Back to Jesus*, 59.

126. "Man with the Plan," 9.

their music.[127] While en route to Lewiston, Idaho to pick up a band member, the newly formed Christian group was praying in the car when, according to Mike Messer, they felt the presence of the Holy Spirit overpowering them.[128] After this experience of Spirit empowerment, the band noticed a large increase in the numbers of conversions at their concerts and in the growth of membership in the VoE. For a number of years Wilson McKinley travelled extensively increasing the popularity of VoE and becoming famous among the bands of the nascent Jesus Music of the early seventies.

The VoE had a ten year life cycle that, at its peak in 1975, included a Jesus newspaper called *Truth* with a circulation of 250,000 and a staff of over one hundred that lived in a series of communal houses in Coeur D'Alene, Idaho and Yakima, Walla Walla, and Spokane, Washington.[129] With a large financial donation Parks was able to purchase 260 acres of land, which they called The Farm, as a base for the ministry.[130] Although Parks was from a classical Pentecostal home, his Pentecostalism was notably more measured than Meissner's, especially in the absence of evidential tongues, placing an equal emphasis upon prophesy, healing, miraculous provisions, and Bible teaching. Just before the ministry closed in 1979, Parks changed the name from VoE to Carl Parks and Associates. Like other closures, many members were disappointed and either filtered into local churches and other ministries or stopped going to church altogether.

Jim Durkin (1925–1996)—Gospel Outreach

The JPM story of Northern California centers on Jim Durkin, the leader of what became a collective of independent communes that associated under the name Gospel Outreach (GO). Durkin's personal journey began at Portland Bible Temple, a classical Pentecostal church, where he served on staff under Dick Iverson until a divorce cost him his position. Durkin claimed that from a very low point of despair, while he was alone and praying to God in a log cabin, Jesus spoke directly to him, telling him to remarry his wife Dacie and to go "Practice the Word."[131] From there he moved on to pastor twelve elderly people at a church called Soul's Harbour. During a church

127. "Tanignak Productions."
128. Mike Messer, interview with author, September 24, 2010.
129. "Alternative Jesus."
130. "Jesus Evolution."
131. Durkin et al., *Coming World Crisis*, 8.

prayer meeting in 1970, a woman at Soul's Harbour had a vision that the whole place would be filled with barefoot hippies worshipping God.[132]

The remote and rural nature of Northern California differed from San Francisco and Southern California. As such it became the migratory destination for many "back-to-the-land hippies" who sought to restore the original hippie vision of pre-1967 Haight-Ashbury. Hippies purchased lands collectively, wealthy individuals donated properties, and religious organizations bought massive plots of land. And from 1967 to 1977 large numbers of youth journeyed to northern California to pursue what they believed would be a peaceful, and spiritual, utopian lifestyle in a commune.

In 1968, one such story began with German born Sabine Bell, who purchased 150 acres of land in Albion, California—simply dubbed "the Land"—as a commune for hippies to pursue their spiritual interests. In 1970, a visit to the Land by a Christian couple resulted in a few conversions and much controversy among the communards. Over the subsequent months more communards, including Bell, also converted, the commune changed its name to "The Lord's Land," and came under Durkin's leadership.[133] Durkin found himself being approached by other communes in the region that had, in a similar way, experienced mass conversions and were seeking Christian teaching and leadership. In 1971, Durkin and about 30 others moved to a donated property just south of Eureka that housed an abandoned coast guard lighthouse.[134] Renamed as the Lighthouse Ranch, this property became the base of GO's operations, which at its height housed 320 people.[135]

Durkin maintained a strong emphasis on Pentecostal spirituality, yet like many others who led outreaches to the hippies, he negotiated with the counterculture converts to forge a hybrid Pentecostalism. For example, Wednesday night chapel services at the Lighthouse were quiet times of reflection in which no talking or "vain babbling" was permitted. Communards were expected to wait on the Lord in silence while praying or reading the Bible. Or as James Jankowiak explained, "We practiced all the gifts of the Spirit, but we were not Pentecostals. The tendency of traditional Pentecostals in those days was to shout into microphones and holler, 'Jeeesssusss.' And we were not having any of that."[136]

Durkin believed that the communes needed to be financially self-sufficient, so GO communes engaged in small businesses from leather making

132. Michelmore, *Back to Jesus,* 70–71.

133. "The Lord's Land;" and Michelmore, *Back to Jesus,* 79–85.

134. Jackson, *Coming Together,* 169.

135. Ibid.

136. James Jankowiak, interview with author, May 18, 2008.

to a donut shop, and the operation of a free advertising newspaper in Eureka called the *Tri-City Advertiser*.[137] Also Living Waters Reforestation was founded by GO to gain reforestation contracts with the U.S. Department of Forestry and private companies throughout the Pacific Northwest. Radiance Ministries was set up to promote Durkin's teachings by duplicating and distributing cassette recordings and by purchasing time on Christian radio to air his Practice the Word program. Between 1972 and 1977, GO communal churches were established throughout California, Washington, Oregon, Alaska, Chicago, New York, Germany, England, and Guatemala. With the exception of a thriving work in Guatemala that functions under the name Verbo, much of GO is defunct and what remains in Eureka has taken on the name Gospel Outreach Reformational Church.[138]

Chuck Smith (1927–2013)—Calvary Chapel

While Ralph Moore and Roy Hicks created hybrid churches under the ICFG denominational umbrella, others came out from the ICFG denomination and formed new church movements. One such story is that of Chuck Smith, pastor of Calvary Chapel, a church which has grown from a single congregation of twenty-five members in 1965 to a network of affiliates that numbers over 1500 churches worldwide.[139] Smith was raised in the ICFG and was dedicated by his mother to Christian ministry from a very young age.[140] After graduating from L.I.F.E. Bible College he served for seventeen years as an ICFG evangelist, beginning in Prescott, Arizona and then in various locations throughout Southern California.[141] Dissatisfied with what he felt was an overemphasis on gimmicky church growth contests, charismatic practices that were out of order, and a lack of thorough Bible teaching, Smith admitted that he did not fit into the ICFG.[142] Consequently, he left the ICFG in 1964 to begin an independent church plant called Corona Christian Fellowship.[143] In 1965 Smith moved to a small church called Calvary Chapel in Costa Mesa, California and instituted several changes in the church's ecclesiology; hoping to establish what he believed to me a more orderly praxis of Pentecostalism than that he had previously experienced.

137. Michelmore, *Back to Jesus,* 72–73.

138. "GO Alumni."

139. "Calvary Chapel Association."

140. Macintosh and Ries, "Venture of Faith."

141. Smith and Steven, *Reproducers,* 13–14.

142. Chuck Smith, *Charisma vs. Charismania,* 7–10.

143. Smith and Steven, *Reproducers,* 14–15.

Smith explained the birth and growth of Calvary Chapel as a fulfillment of two prophecies.[144] The first stated that the church would outgrow its present facility and that his teaching would be put on radio; the second that he would be a shepherd of many flocks.[145] Shortly after these, in 1967 and 1968 hippies began to swarm the beaches of Orange County and Smith, influenced by his wife's compassion for the young people, began to pray that the church could have an inroad into the hippies' lives. Around April 1968 Chuck Smith met Lonnie Frisbee, a young hippie who had been part of the House of Acts in San Francisco, and invited him and his wife Connie to Southern California to lead outreach for Calvary Chapel. Lonnie Frisbee began to bring young people into the church, to baptize them in swimming pools, and to pray for them to receive the BHS.

Smith soon faced the same resistance and disdain from church members as other ministers had and on one occasion an older member placed a placard in the church lawn that read, "No bare feet allowed in the church."[146] Smith resolved to stand with the young people and responded, "If because of our plush carpeting we have to close the door to one young person who has bare feet, then I'm in favor of ripping out all the carpeting and having bare concrete floors."[147] The church continued to experience phenomenal growth with both "straights" and hippies worshipping side by side. By 1969, the 330 seat church was holding two Sunday services and 500 additional seats were set up outside the building to accommodate the overflow.[148] By 1971, Calvary Chapel had purchased a plot of land for a new building but had to erect a tent as a temporary facility for the 12,000 to 15,000 who were attending each week.[149] During a two year period of time in the early seventies there were an estimated 20,000 conversions with 8,000 baptisms being recorded in 1971 alone; 1000 of which were on a single day.[150] L. E. Romaine was among those who baptized that day and he remarked, "I've never run into anything like that in my life. Four of us were baptizing people, and it took us two-and-a-half hours to baptize everyone who wanted to be baptized. I was stupefied, I couldn't see straight."[151]

144. Macintosh, "Venture of Faith."

145. Chuck Smith, "History of Calvary Chapel," 5.

146. Smith and Steven, *Reproducers*, 60.

147. Ibid., 61.

148. Smith and Brooke, "Harvest," 7.

149. Fromm, "Textual Communities," 195–96.

150. Ibid., 6; and "1,000 'Jesus People' Baptized," 26. The date of the baptism is April 17, 1971.

151. Balmer, *Mine Eyes*," 23.

Among the numerous ministries to emerge from Calvary Chapel, there are four that should be noted as stemming from the early years of the church. First, in the early 1970s Ed Plummer began to record and to duplicate Smith's teaching onto cassette tapes so that they might be distributed and played at Bible studies. By 1981, 20,000 cassettes were posted each month around the USA and to places like Russia, China, Scandinavia, and Europe. Smith's teaching was also aired on 100 radio stations across America.[152] The teaching ministry eventually developed into The Word for Today ministry and the Calvary Satellite Network of radio stations that by 2007 reached an estimated 22 million listeners in forty-five states.[153]

Second, as people gathered for Bible studies around Orange County to listen to Smith's teachings on cassette, requests came to Smith asking him to send people to lead Bible studies and start churches. Smith sent young men like Greg Laurie, Jeff Johnson, Steve Mays, and Mike MacIntosh to fulfill these requests and many of them watched their Bible studies grow into large churches. For example, at the age of twenty-two, Greg Laurie, who had converted through Lonnie Frisbee at Newport Harbor High School, was given the leadership of a Bible study in Riverside that was attended by eighty people. By 1974, Laurie's Bible study, known as Riverside Calvary Chapel, was holding multiple services in a 1500 seat civic center.[154] Laurie still pastors the church of 15,000, now known as Harvest Christian Fellowship, and has also launched Harvest Crusades—Billy Graham styled evangelistic meetings held in stadiums around the world. Laurie's church is only one example, but these new Bible studies and churches launched in the 1970s were the beginning of what would become the global network of Bible colleges and Calvary Chapel churches that operate under Calvary Chapel Association.

Third, by 1970, a plethora of new musical groups had formed and many wanted to play their music at Calvary Chapel's weeknight meetings. In response, the church spent $3500 and opened a four-track recording studio that they called Maranatha Music.[155] The first recording, produced in June 1971, was entitled *Everlastin' Living Music Concert,* and since that release, Maranatha Music has blossomed into a multi-million dollar company that has sponsored many artists. In connection with Maranatha Music were the Everlasting Living Waters rock concerts, where bands like Love Song and Children of the Day were utterly significant in creating a new stage for Christian Rock and outdoor concerts. The recorded music and live concerts

152. Chuck Smith, "History of Calvary Chapel," 10.

153. Goffard, "God's Word."

154. Smith and Brooke, "Harvest," 31.

155. Chuck Smith, "History of Calvary Chapel," 10.

not only bolstered Calvary Chapel's growth, but were a significant key to the success of the nascent Jesus Music and the transformation of Christian worship in America. Fourth, to assist in living accommodations and Bible training for new hippie converts, Calvary Chapel initiated a communal home network in Orange County in May 1968 called the House of Miracles. As already mentioned, within the following year this network would be moved to Oregon and under the leadership of John Higgins became SYRC. Although short lived in Orange County, because SYRC was connected with Calvary Chapel, a number of Calvary Chapels were formed at the closure of SYRC in 1979.

Commenting on the reasons for Calvary Chapel's phenomenal growth, Enroth attributed it to the coverage in *Look* and *Time* magazines that created a "tourist attraction for the Evangelical subculture."[156] Di Sabatino (2005) credits Lonnie Frisbee's charisma while Chuck Fromm (2006) recognizes several factors, the primary one being the popularity of the band Love Song. Certainly Chuck Smith's openness to the hippies and his Bible teaching were also instrumental and the success of Calvary Chapel is best understood in a combination of these above mentioned factors. Also, it must be noted that while Calvary Chapel was hugely responsible for shaping the Southern California ethos of the JPM, its prominence has been at times been overstated; as in Vinson Synan calling Chuck Smith the leader of the JPM.[157] The church did, however, become a place to which many made pilgrimages with the intention of evaluating and perhaps mimicking the practices found there. For example, Calvary Chapel's dove symbol was noticed by east coast JP in the early 1970s and in 1971, Church of God pastor Floyd McClung journeyed to Calvary Chapel from Cleveland, Tennessee to make an assessment of his own.[158] New church initiatives patterned their methods on Calvary Chapel. So did mainline denominational churches like Ft Boulevard Methodist and St Paul's Methodist Church in El Paso, Texas, that welcomed the blend of charismatic and counterculture practice. At these churches hundreds of hippies and JP gathered for meetings, afterglows, and mass baptisms in the Rio Grand River all led by a couple of very young men from Calvary Chapel.[159] By the early 1970s Dane Claussen rightfully placed Calvary Chapel as "the spiritual hot spot" in the JPM.[160]

156. Enroth et al., *Story*, 85–86.

157. Synan, *Century*, 378–79.

158. McClung, "I Visited, 8–9.

159. Little, "Jesus People," 1.

160. Claussen, *Promise Keepers*, 22.

Wayman Mitchell—Potter's House Christian Fellowship

Another JP leader who came out of the ICFG was Wayman Mitchell, founder of the Potter's House Christian Fellowship (PHCF) in Prescott, Arizona. Mitchell was converted and received the BHS through the ICFG and later completed a degree from L.I.F.E. Bible College to become an ICFG minister. His first exposure to hippies came during a brief stint of pastoring the EFC just before the arrival of Roy Hicks Jr.[161] However, it was a visit to Calvary Chapel and a coffeehouse in La Habra that first inspired him to use counterculture means to reach out to hippies.[162] Upon returning to his church in Prescott, Mitchell began to welcome hippies into meetings, to sponsor music outreaches, and to hold talks about drug addiction. He "overlooked what the people looked like and smelt like, and saw the potential in each person to be strong Christians."[163]

Out of his growing Prescott church, many other hippies launched their own churches and continued to look to Mitchell as their leader. According to Mitchell, tensions mounted between himself and the ICFG denomination once his new church plants began to expand beyond the borders of Arizona. Since the men looked to Mitchell for guidance they tended to be careless about filing reports to the denominational headquarters. Besides, the hippie pastors lacked respect for the denominational leaders and this aggravated their strained relationship. Mitchell stated, "It became almost humorous to watch appointed denominational leaders that had never had a hundred people in their churches trying to force pastors running hundreds to make all their decisions through them."[164] However, Mitchell's main contention lay in his philosophy that valued the local church as the place for training leaders. The men under his leadership were neither denominationally trained nor ordained; consequently the ICFG did not approve of them. In January 1985, Mitchell separated from the ICFG and claims that he has since seen the number of churches in his PHCF grow from 100 to 1400 globally.[165]

In their own words PHCF is a "militant church with a radical approach" that disapproves of Bible colleges and of expressions of Pentecostalism like the Toronto blessing.[166] A look at the names and faces of ministers at PHCF

161. I. Wilson, *In Pursuit*, 14.

162. Ibid., 17.

163. "Wayman Mitchell." Also see I. Wilson, *In Pursuit*, 9–26.

164. Simpkins, *Open Door*, 168.

165. "Wayman Mitchell."

166. I. Wilson, *In Pursuit*, 39–48; and "Wayman Mitchell."

internationally indicates that the church is perhaps far more ethnically diverse, especially in its leadership, than the other JPM church movements. Mitchell sees the PHCF movement to be in the same stream as what took place in the early days of the Salvation Army, Methodist, Elim, or AG movements.[167] He has operated as a healing evangelist and an apostle and as a result has attracted sharp criticism regarding the church's leadership praxis.[168]

Other Minor Mentions

The JPM was causal of many AG "coming outers" across the United States. For example, in Abilene, Texas, long haired AG minister Carlton Earp, transformed two three-story houses into an independent outreach and training center that he called the Agape Inn. He collected the names and addresses of youth who converted at AG "rallies" and invited them to come live in the homes and join his one year, free, Bible training course. According to Earp, after completing the year training some went on to Bible college while others started coffeehouse outreaches, Christian rock bands, and one became an associate pastor of a church in California.[169] Or there was Pastor William Thornton who, in 1971, withdrew from the AG fellowship in San Francisco and with denominational blessing founded a church called the Christian Centre. The church took intentional steps to sympathize with the counter culture youth as Thornton stated, "you can't beat it [the gospel] down people's throats. The only way is to love them. Love to each other in our group is one of our main concerns."[170] Thornton deemphasized the standard AG position on initial evidence saying, "Those who attend the Christian Center believe in the Baptism of the Holy Spirit and all the gifts that it is supposed to bring with it, though not everyone receives the same gifts."[171] While the migration in and out of denominations and churches is not unique to the JPM, this category, those leaving classical Pentecostal denominations, may have been the largest among its leaders.

167. "Wayman Mitchell."

168. I. Wilson, *In Pursuit*, 79–86, 92. For criticisms, see Enroth (*Churches That Abuse*; *Recovering from Churches That Abuse*) and "The Potter's House."

169. D. Wilson, "Earp Has Three-Pronged Ministry," 44.

170. Mills, "Jesus People Rapping," 7.

171. Ibid.

Links With the Charismatic Renewal (CR)

As early as the 1940s, Pentecostalism began to spread among the mainline Protestant churches of America; a movement often called the Charismatic Renewal (CR). An incorrect notion underpins much of the thinking about the CR in America, one that envisions distinct boundaries lines that cordon off the CR from other CM and classical Pentecostal movements and imagines the CR thriving in isolation. While the historians of American Pentecostalism remain strangely silent over the relationship between the JP and the CR, evidence shows that from the earliest days of the JPM, churches involved in the CR opened their doors to hippies and JP. As was pointed out with classical Pentecostals, the JP were not simply passive recipients of Spirit baptism from CR churches, but they actively engaged in a relationship of reciprocity with the CR. Many of the flagship CR churches grew numerically and experienced transformation in their Pentecostalism as a result of an influx of JP. The following examples illustrate this interplay between the two.

Dennis Bennett (1917–1991)—St Luke's Seattle

Dennis Bennett, the priest at St Mark's Episcopal Church in Van Nuys, is without doubt important in the story of American Pentecostalism. However, what is not published in historical accounts is that Bennett not only knew, but also worked together with the big players in JPM, and even benefited from the JP throughout the years of his ministry. His first contact, for example, with Chuck Smith came in 1959 in Southern California and with Linda Meissner in 1965 in Seattle, Washington, before the JPM ever began. Chuck Smith acknowledged that he was the Pentecostal minister who introduced Frank Maguire to the BHS in 1959. This occurred at a Bible study he led at the home of John and Joan Baker in Pomona, California, while he was still an ICFG minister.[172] Maguire brought a number of people to Smith's church in Pomona because they were requesting to be water baptized by emersion and Smith's church had the facility to do so.[173] Bennett wrote that Maguire was the one to introduce him to the BHS; an event that famously resulted in his subsequent departure from St Mark's and his move to St Luke's Church in Seattle.[174]

From 1965, Bennett networked with Linda Meissner, classical Pentecostals, and Catholics in the Seattle area as they all expressed a growing

---

172. Chuck Smith, interview with author, August 6, 2009.

173. Ibid.

174. Bennett, *Nine O'clock*, 15–88.

concern for the increasing drug problems among young people.[175] Sometime in 1965, Bennett introduced John and Diana Breithaupt to the BHS; the couple who would subsequently convince Linda Meissner to adopt countercultural methods of outreach.[176] St. Luke's Church reached out to the hippies by financially supporting the Breithaupts and the work of local JP coffeehouses like the House of Zacchaeus and later Zac's House.[177] In 1967, Bennett was invited to a meeting hosted by a young couple named Jack and Sybil who, as local youth workers, had noticed the receptivity to the gospel among young people on the streets of Seattle.[178] This pivotal meeting inspired him to open the basement of St. Luke's to young people for a Friday and Saturday evening prayer service. At these prayer meetings, Bennett claimed that many counterculture young people experienced salvation, miracles, and received the BHS.[179] He also claimed that for a period of three years the attendance at the meetings in St Luke's basement exceeded 200 and many of these same young people also participated with Linda Meissner, a band called the New Men, and other area Christians in outreaches to local schools.[180]

That same year, Bennett and his wife also opened their home for Bible studies where they said that as many as one hundred hippies and JP would gather. According to Bennett, young people would pack into their home and recount stories of miraculous deliverance from drug addiction and other vices, often speaking in common JP idioms. Testimonies would be followed by spontaneous outbursts of praise.[181] A newspaper article written in 1973, summarized the Bennett's involvement with the CR and the JPM and the growth and vibrancy of St Luke's as a result. It stated, "The Bennetts and the Jesus People . . . speak in tongues and believe in other manifestations of God's power on earth . . . Father Bennett moved to Seattle where a bishop there encouraged him to work in a church that was about to close. Today it is one of the largest and most vital congregations in the city."[182]

175. P. King, *Jesus People*, 7–19, 21, 25–27.

176. Shires, *Hippies*, 105.

177. Bennett, *Nine O'clock*, 233.

178. Ibid., 228.

179. Ibid., 228–29.

180. Ibid., 230–31.

181. Ibid., 232.

182. Boyce, "Father Bennett's Mission," 5.

Graham Pulkingham (1926–1993)—Church of the Redeemer

Another Episcopal church that participated in the JPM was Graham Pulkingham's Church of the Redeemer in Houston, Texas. Known for its charismatic worship services that attracted people from all different denominations, by 1966 the church also had a strong communal identity with at least one house situated in the hippie district.[183] At this house, called Baldwin House, young JP would sit cross-legged on the floor for Bible study and prayer.[184] The church also launched a youth oriented coffeehouse outreach called The Way In that featured a band from the church called the Keyhole. The Keyhole, now known as the Fisherfolk, has continued to live in intentional community since the 1970s and to produce music to help pay for their living expenses.[185] Pulkingham eventually moved to Coventry, England, where he connected with the hippie styled, communal church known as The Jesus Army.[186] Stephen Hunt concludes that the Jesus Fellowship (Jesus Army) had no direct links with the California JP.[187] Yet Pulkingham's contact with the JPM in Texas and familiarity with 1960s American communalism may actually establish a stronger connection than has been previously assumed.

Ralph Wilkerson—Melodyland Christian Center

In 1969, charismatic minister Ralph Wilkerson moved his growing congregation into a facility across from Disneyland in Anaheim, California called Melodyland; later renamed the Melodyland Christian Center.[188] By the early 1970s the church held multiple Sunday services and by January 1973 had established its own ecumenical, Charismatic school of theology, headed by J. Rodman Williams.[189] While Melodyland seemed to be a prototype of what the white, middle-class CR could become, it had also opened its doors to the counterculture and experienced an enormous influx of young JP. Melodyland was the church that marketed the famous Jesus People wristwatch and inspired journalist Brian Vachon to coin the phrase "Jesus Movement."[190] It was the place where photographers Jack and Betty Cheetham ventured to

183. S. Hunt, "Radical Kingdom," 22.

184. M. Harper, *New Way*, 197.

185. Ibid., 175.

186. S. Hunt, "Radical Kingdom," 22.

187. Ibid.

188. Chandler, "Melodyland School," 42.

189. Cunningham, "Theater-in-the-Round."

190. Vachon, *Time*, 130. Vachon, "Jesus Movement," 16.

California to photograph the JPM and ended up converting and joining the movement.[191]

In his renowned article for *Life* magazine, Vachon wrote, "Anaheim California, is the home of . . . an astonishing number of young people who call the Jesus Movement their own. The physical center of the activity is Melodyland, where Ralph Wilkerson conducts the adult services, and young kids by the hundreds are witnessing to young kids by the thousands all over southern California."[192] Although it is an overstatement to call Melodyland the center of the JPM, the hive of JP activity noted in Vachon's article demonstrates that there was a very significant interplay between Melodyland and the JPM. Importantly, it also indicates that an appreciable source of the church's numerical growth and transformation came from the JPM. Louie Monteith remembered hoards of JP like himself coming to Melodyland to hear Mario Murillo, to receive the BHS through the charismatic clinics, and to undergo theological training at the Melodyland School of Theology.[193] The Melodyland ethos was mildly affected by the presence of the JP, but it never had the classical Pentecostal edge of Bethel Tabernacle or the laid-back hippie ethos that Calvary Chapel fostered. Describing the difference between Calvary Chapel and Melodyland, Monteith said, "It was like apples and oranges."[194] To him it was very different, but "it was the fruit of the Lord happening in Orange County at the time and it was all so wonderful and complemented each other like fruit on the table."[195] Soon afterward, Melodyland Christian Centre closed and its buildings were eventually demolished, leaving a shopping mall called Anaheim Garden Walk in its place.

John and Anne Gimenez—Rock Church

John Gimenez was an ex-heroin addict from the Bronx who, after his release from prison and training at an Elim Bible College, began the Rock Church in Virginia Beach with his wife Anne.[196] Under their leadership, the Rock Church grew from a small church in 1968 into a mega church that overseas a global network of 500 Rock Churches. According to Richard Peterson, the explosive growth of Gimenez's Rock Church was partially caused by a huge influx of JP during its formative years of 1968 to 1974; an influx so large that

191. Young, "Writer-Photographer Meets," 3.

192. Vachon, *Time to Be Born*, 52.

193. Louie Monteith, interview with author, August 9, 2009.

194. Ibid.

195. Ibid.

196. "John Gimenez."

the building they used for meetings became a fire hazard.[197] John Gimenez frequently shared the stage alongside other JP leaders at events like Jesus '73 in Lancaster County, Pennsylvania.[198] John and Anne Gimenez did not locate Rock Church solely in the JPM stream as Calvary Chapel did and John's leadership in the Washington for Jesus' prayer day in 1980 may have positioned him more closely with the politically conservative movement known as the religious right. However, strong countercultural and charismatic themes commonly found in other JP influenced churches remain intact in the worship styles and ethos of the Rock Churches.[199]

Howard Conatser (1926–1978)—Beverly Hills Baptist Church

Howard Conatser, the pastor of Beverly Hills Baptist Church in Dallas, Texas who was famously disfellowshipped by the SBC for his shift into Pentecostalism, also participated in the JPM and benefitted from the interplay. In his book *Bite Your Tongues* he told the story of the church's rapid numerical growth. He wrote, "In January of 1975 Beverly Hills moved its Sunday morning services from the church sanctuary jammed each week with a little over 1,000 worshippers, to the 2500 seat Bronco Bowl theatre. When the service began, the Lord had provided at least one person for each of the 2,500 seats available, doubling in one week the congregation of the church."[200]

Contributing to the growth of the church was a large influx of Jesus Freaks that claimed to have experienced conversion and healing through the ministry of a young couple named Larry and Melva Lea. In 1972, three years before the church moved into the Bronco Bowl, twenty-one year old Larry and his wife Melva were hired as youth pastors. Conatser's and Lea's relationship was reminiscent of Smith and Frisbee or Steenis and Stephens, and it was reported, "a year after his [Larry's] arrival the youth group had exploded from 40 to 1,000 . . . Melva suddenly found herself ministering to young people who were involved in the drug culture and yet searching for spiritual answers."[201] One story of conversion and healing from drug addiction was that of Lulu, the then famous star of the TV program *Hee Haw*.[202] From the Bronco Bowl, the church became a hive of JP activity by hosting and nationally televising Jesus Music concerts that included famous

197. Peterson, *Electric Sister*, 131.
198. "Great Camp Meeting in 1973," 48.
199. "Rock Church."
200. S. Martin, *Bite Your Tongues*, 155.
201. Stertzer, "Journey toward Healing."
202. S. Martin, *Bite Your Tongues*, 61–74.

JP bands like Love Song, 2nd Chapter of Acts, Hope of Glory, Daniel Amos, and Resurrection Band. In 1978, Conatser's life was cut short when he died of cancer and the leadership of the church was offered to Lea.[203] However, in 1979, Larry and Melva Lea left Beverly Hills Baptist Church to found The Church on the Rock, a church that reportedly grew from 12 to 5,000 members by the mid-1980s.[204]

"Bro" Dave Lombardi—Trinity Gospel Temple

Dave Lombardi's Trinity Gospel Temple is perhaps best known for the *Hour of Power* weekly radio broadcasts and their association with the CM through the 700 Club, now CBN.[205] However, the early success and growth of Lombardi's church was inextricably tied to the JPM. And he also reciprocally shaped the lives of JP in Canton and Akron, Ohio through his teaching and support of their outreaches. Local JP wrote about Lombardi's first encounter with counterculture Christians in the spring of 1970. "Around the room were several of these hippie-types—some sitting cross-legged on the floor, some with beards, long hair, tie-dyed T-shirts, ragged pants—and all of them had their eyes glued on him. They began their questions: 'Do you believe Jesus is coming soon?' 'Do you believe in speaking in tongues?' 'What about the Rapture?' . . . Bro Dave says, 'That began the most interesting period of my life.'"[206] The story of the JPM in Canton and Akron features the typical communal homes, outreaches into high schools, Jesus newspapers, river baptisms, and a center called the Shepherds Inn.[207]

Dotted across the country, other churches involved in the CR were touched by the JPM, as in the case of the Cathedral of St Philip in Atlanta, where Corky Alexander witnessed hundreds JP gathering for prayer, worship, and to play their music.[208] The Holy Innocents Episcopal Church in Corte Madera, California, led by Father Todd Ewald also welcomed many hippies into its charismatic meetings.[209] If there were a central figure in the JPM on the east coast it might be Pat Robertson. While he never planted a JP church like Chuck Smith or Jim Durkin, his congeniality, encouragement,

203. "Rev. Howard Conatser," 8.

204. Stertzer, "Journey."

205. "Trinity Gospel Temple."

206. "Shepherds Inn Canton Ohio Jesus People."

207. Ibid.

208. Corky Alexander, interview with author, August 2, 2010.

209. Philpott, *Awakenings*, 78.

and financial support bolstered many JP ministries; and this at a time when his own 700 Club was rapidly aggrandizing.

Carter Lindberg believed that the CR in the Lutheran Church had three stages and that the third stage, from 1970–1975, was a charismatic outbreak among Lutheran youth fuelled by the JPM.[210] Denominational leader Dave Anderson, founder of Lutheran Youth Encounter and Fellowship Ministries, also started Renewal House and Lutheran Youth Alive while ministering in Van Nuys in 1969.[211] He opened these mildly charismatic ministries to a wide range of speakers from the more conservative D. James Kennedy to classical Pentecostals like David Wilkerson.[212] Lindberg also wrote that from the early 1970s the Lutheran CR in the Netherlands predominantly thrived among the youth and that in Norway during the same time, YWAM was one of its primary contributors to Pentecostalism among Lutheran young people.[213]

In Lancaster, Pennsylvania, 2500 Mennonites gathered from around Canada and the USA for "Renewal '74"; a conference where Mennonite leaders promoted the BHS and tongues and many members allegedly experienced these gifts for the first time.[214] The JPM was one of the precursors to the charismatic renewal among the Mennonites in Lancaster, the area being a hotbed of JP activity that predated the renewal conference by a few years. Only one year earlier, the Jesus '73 music festival gathered 20,000 JP to the Lancaster area to hear speakers like Bob Mumford, Nicky Cruz, and numerous well known JP bands.[215] Mennonite Harold Zimmerman formed Agape Ministries and purchased 281 acres in nearby Huntingdon County to continue the annual Jesus Music festival—today called Creation Fest Northeast that attracts 100,000 participants each summer.[216] According to one church leader, the JPM had disappointingly caused an exodus of twenty to thirty year olds from the Mennonite church, but it had also brought a welcomed renewal. He said, "the enthusiasm generated by these young people is the greatest change that has swept our church in the last 50 years."[217]

Many similar JP stories can be found throughout Methodist, Nazarene, Baptist, Presbyterian, and reformed churches. These few accounts are

210. Lindberg, *Third Reformation*, 200.

211. "Central Lutheran Concert," 7.

212. "Dave Anderson"; and "Youth Encounter."

213. Lindberg, *Third Reformation*, 212.

214. "Mennonites Hold First," 23.

215. Zidock, "Jesus People gather in Paradise," 12.

216. J. Hunt, "'Jesus People' Are Locating in County," 1.

217. Ibid. 2.

presented to demonstrate that the iconic CR churches and CR leaders were not only aware of the JPM, but also participated in it and as a result benefited both in numerical growth and, to some degree, in the transformation of their ministry ethos.

Links With The Catholic Charismatic Renewal

The beginning of the Catholic Charismatic Renewal (CCR) is most often traced to a student prayer meeting on the campus of Duquesne University in 1967, from which it initially spread among other Catholic university students. As Killian McDonnell stated, "Beginning in 1967, the so-called Pentecostal Movement has spread among our Catholic faithful. It has attracted especially college students."[218] Like the CR, the CCR is often envisioned as a CM that flourished in isolation from other contemporary movements of Pentecostalism. But its 1967 start date and its location on university campuses were much more than coincidental points of commonality with the JPM. In the early years, the overlap between the two movements was so great that Michael Harrison believed the CCR was "one of the most vigorous sectors of the current 'Jesus movement.'"[219] Both Erling Jorstad and Charles Hummel commented that JP and CCR participants were indistinguishable on university campuses and many JP were known for frequenting CCR masses.[220] Given a similarity in age and association with the counterculture it would be difficult to detect whether a long haired, male attendee at a Catholic mass was a JP or simply a CCR participant who associated with the counterculture. And presumably these were distinctions that the individual himself may not have made.

King (*Jesus People*) named a number of Catholic priests in the Seattle area who participated in the JPM. Her book is free of distinctions between the movements and simply records Catholics, alongside Protestants, Evangelicals, and classical Pentecostals, reaching out to young hippies. Philpott wrote that he and many other hippies participated in charismatic services at a Marist seminary in San Rafael and at a local Carmelite Monastery and that priest from these centers also visited their meetings.[221] His close relationship with CCR meant that it was Catholic priest Ed Sweeney who first contacted him from Atlanta to inform him that David Hoyt had joined the

218. McDonnell, *Catholic Pentecostalism*, 43.

219. M. Harrison, "Sources of Recruitment, 50.

220. Jorstad, *That New Time*, 92; and Hummel, *Fire*, 25–27.

221. Philpott, *Awakenings*, 78–79.

COG.[222] Singer and songwriter John Michael Talbot experienced his conversion through the JPM and soon afterward entered Catholicism where he has remained as worship musician since.

All was not harmonious between the two groups, however. Considerable numbers of JP were from Catholic background and left the Catholic Church because of the JPM.[223] Some Catholic JP even spoke out in protest against the Catholic Church asking for their leaders to provide a religious experience and not to simply enforce their authority.[224] In return, some Catholic priests branded the JPM as religious hysteria on par with the political mania witnessed in Hitler or Mussolini's day.[225] On one hand, the CCR and the JPM may be considered as two recognizably distinct movements; primarily because the CCR took place within the spatial boundaries of Catholic Churches, Cathedrals, and Catholic Universities. This is especially true as the years passed and the JPM declined in the late 1970s. In contrast, the CCR, as a distinct stream of Pentecostalism, continued a steady pattern of growth at 14.6 percent per annum, from around 2 million participants in 1970 to around 120 million by the year 2000.[226] On the other hand, in the early years of both the CCR and the JPM, the cross pollination between the two movements was so extraordinary that the lines of distinction were often blurred. It is plausible to assume that the JPM contributed in some way to the birth and growth of the CCR and the CCR to the growth of the JPM; both share a number of common roots and both mutually benefited from their relationship.

Links to People Coming Out of Evangelicalism

Kent Philpott and David Hoyt

As with classical Pentecostals, there were large numbers of Evangelical people who did not consider themselves to be Charismatic or Pentecostal but, as a result of their personal experiences, entered into Pentecostalism and became prominent leaders in the JPM. Four such stories are told here. In February 1967, Kent Philpott, a twenty-four year old student at Golden Gate Baptist Seminary, was driving home from his job at J C Penney's

222. Ibid., 104.

223. Cassels, "Young Life Group," 11; Dalton, "Charismatics," 6; and C. Cox, "Jesus Movement Continues," 4.

224. Fiske, "Religious Authority," 18.

225. Coleman, "Religious Movement," 5.

226. Barrett et al., "Catholic Charismatic Renewal," 278.

when he claimed that the Holy Spirit spoke the words "go to hippies in San Francisco."[227] Philpott identified with the Beats and frequented Beat clubs like Cosmo Alley and Pandora's Box in Hollywood and was sympathetic to the early developments of hippiedom in Haight-Ashbury.[228] He believed that as early as August 1965, God had been urging him to preach the gospel to the hippies, but when he heard the song "Flowers in Your Hair," he believed God was calling him.

Upon his arrival in the Haight, he met a young man named David Hoyt, a former member of the Council for the Summer of Love, an ex-con, a hippie, and guru at ISKCON's Rhada Krishna Temple on Frederick Street. Philpott and Hoyt would discuss the Bible in the basement of the temple, but Hoyt remained unconvinced. One night, however, he had a dream in which he was "left behind when Jesus reached down and took all God's children home."[229] Then the following day, a fire in the basement of the temple burned everything but a copy of the Bible, and Hoyt, interpreting this as a sign from God, believed the gospel.[230] After Hoyt's conversion, he and his wife Victoria moved in with Kent and his wife Bobbi, and Hoyt joined Philpott in his daily routines of street preaching and handing out gospel leaflets in Hippie Park. Together they formed a new organization named United Youth Ministries and opened a series of communal homes around San Francisco: the Soul Inn, Zion's Inn for Girls, Beracah House, Home for His Glory, Upper Streams, and House of Pergamos.

Before his involvement in the JPM, Philpott had been strongly opposed to Pentecostalism, believing it to be associated with fringe Christian groups. However, his opinion changed in 1968 after witnessing what he claimed to be miracles and "demonic spirits in action" at an outreach called Anchor Rescue Mission.[231] Another experience that altered his perspective occurred in the winter of 1968 while he was asleep behind the pulpit of Lincoln Park Baptist Church. From a deep sleep he awoke speaking in tongues. Philpott claimed that immediately after this experience his ministry "took off" and they witnessed many conversions, demonic exorcisms, healings, and other types of miracles including the supply of food for running the houses.[232]

In 1969, Hoyt secured the financial backing of the FGBMFI to support a move to Atlanta, where he began a series of communal homes and

227. Kent Philpott, email correspondence with author, September 7, 2010.

228. Philpott, *Awakenings*, 80.

229. Plowman, *Jesus Movement*, 50.

230. Ibid., 50.

231. Philpott, *Awakenings*, 86–87.

232. Kent Philpott, interview with author, September 7, 2010.

coffeehouses modeled on the ones he and Philpott had opened in San Fran-cisco. By 1971, Hoyt's ministry, called the Atlanta Discipleship Training Cen-ter, featured the House of Judah for boys and the Temple of Still Waters for girls, the Bread of Life Restaurant, the Chamber Gates Lightclub, and similar homes in nine other states in the southeast. The attention gained Hoyt a spot on NBC's *First Tuesday* program and an interview on Pat Robertson's 700 Club.[233] With the administrative load proving to be too much for Hoyt, he and his wife joined the COG and relinquished the entire Atlanta ministry to them.[234] One year later Hoyt, minus his wife Victoria, exited the COG in England with the assistance of Kenneth Frampton and Jim Palosaari's travel-ling band of JP.[235] Philpott traveled to England on two occasions for extended visits re-establishing contact with Hoyt and teaching JP.

In 1972, Philpott moved to San Rafael and from the communal homes in San Francisco founded Church of the Open Door; a collective of five churches that he described as theologically Baptistic and Charismatic.[236] In 1973, John Evans, Frank Worthen, and Philpott formed Love In Action, a ministry to individuals "exiting" the homosexual lifestyle, and subsequently they became known as the "founders" of the "ex-gay movement." Contro-versy quickly erupted over the ex-gay movement when the claims made in a book Philpott had penned on homosexuality, *The Third Sex*, came under fire. In 1976, the center for the ex-gay movement shifted south to Melody-land Christian Center and operated under the name Exodus Internation-al. Throughout the course of Philpott's years he was involved in the JPM, spoke at SBC meetings, at CCR masses, joined with Charles Simpson and Bob Mumford in the Shepherding Movement, and connected with Opera-tion Mobilization in London. Since 1985, he has been the pastor of John MacDonald's Mill Valley Baptist Church, the church that supported some of the original hippie outreaches in San Francisco.

Oliver Heath—Veg Hut, Harvest House

One of Philpott's colleagues at Golden Gate Baptist Seminary, Oliver Heath, also moved into Haight-Ashbury in the early years of the JPM and opened the Veg Hut Christian health food shop and five communal homes un-der the name Harvest House. During his outreach to the hippies in San Francisco, Heath shifted his belief and practice and aligned himself with

233. "David Hoyt."

234. Plowman, *Jesus Movement,* 51.

235. Plowman, "Where Are All," 36.

236. Kent Philpott, interview with author, September 26, 2009.

Pentecostal spirituality. Enroth observed that his ministry "harbors young people who were more deeply involved in the counter-culture than most segments of the Jesus Movement."[237] In October 1970, Jewish born David Abraham, founder of *The San Francisco Oracle*, converted through the witness of Chris D'Alessandro, a minister at the Veg Hut. By the spring of 1971, *The San Francisco Oracle* was rereleased as a Jesus newspaper for Harvest House with D'Alessandro as the editor. Harvest House, like other JP communal collectives in Haight-Ashbury, was rather short lived and closed sometime in the early seventies.

John Wimber (1934–1997)—The Association of Vineyard Churches

A well known figure in the history of Pentecostalism, John Wimber, was also a man whose life story was rooted in the JPM. While Wimber was not known to have considered himself a JP during the phenomenon's heyday, his early 1960s musical career as a keyboard player in the Righteous Brothers gave him credibility with the JP. Following his conversion experience in the 1960s, he served as an ordained minister of Friends Church and by 1970, led eleven Bible studies that were reportedly attended by some 500 people.[238] His personal journey into Pentecostal spirituality was initiated by a glossolalic experience that he claimed began spontaneously while walking alongside an irrigation ditch.[239] Yet, in spite of this experience, during his days as a Friends Church minister, Wimber resisted the Pentecostalism that he observed in the JPM, and, according to Fromm, he later lamented this negative posture as one that precluded his place as a leader in the JPM.[240] In 1975, Wimber left Yorba Linda Friends Church and joined the Fuller Evangelistic Association, where for two years he led the Charles E. Fuller Institute of Evangelism and Church Growth.[241] Later, from 1981 to 1985, he would return to Fuller to teach the "Signs and Wonders and Church Growth" class, which, according to Peter Wagner, became the most popular and controversial course in the Seminary's history.[242]

During his early two year stint at Fuller, 1975–1976, he also attended Calvary Chapel Twin Peaks and was ordained as a Calvary Chapel pastor.

237. Enroth et al., *Story*, 218–19.

238. "Vineyard History."

239. C. Wimber, *John Wimber*, 74–75.

240. Fromm, "Textual Communities," 263.

241. P. Wagner, "Wimber, John," 1199.

242. Ibid., 1200.

In 1977, Wimber left his position at Fuller and returned to Yorba Linda to begin Calvary Chapel Yorba Linda, and like many other Calvary Chapels that were rapidly expanding due to the JPM, his church became a fast growing fellowship. The Yorba Linda church also gained a reputation for its Sunday morning worship music. While Chuck Smith had allowed for musical experimentation at other services, Sunday morning services at Costa Mesa had continued to sing hymns during its worship time. Perhaps most famous in Pentecostal and Charismatic circles was the May 1980 Mother's Day Service that reintroduced Lonnie Frisbee onto the Calvary Chapel stage and set Wimber on a course to depart from the Calvary Chapel fellowship.

Wimber's relationship within the growing network of Calvary Chapels was broadened by his service as a consultant at Maranatha Music from 1977 to 1982 and as the director of Calvary Chapel's Maranatha Music Development from 1978 to 1982.[243] However, his growing interest in a more expressive Pentecostal praxis and his theological penchant toward the kingdom emphasis of George Eldon Ladd clashed with Chuck Smith's post-classical Pentecostal desire for "orderliness" and Dispensationalism. Increased tensions between Smith and Wimber finally led to a church split in 1982, in which Gulliksen's eight Vineyard Fellowships and thirty-two Calvary Chapels followed Wimber to form a new denomination called Vineyard Christian Fellowship.

Today Vineyard International functions as an umbrella organization for three areas of Vineyard's ministry: a growing global movement of 1500 churches, Vineyard Resources, and the very influential Vineyard Music.[244] Like many JPM groups, it is difficult to write a précis of the Vineyard story. Vineyard Fellowship has birthed other offshoots like the Toronto Vineyard Fellowship from which emerged the so-called "Toronto Blessing." According to Stephen Hunt, Vineyard, through the Toronto Blessing and Third Wavism, has impacted the Church of England and the ethos and growth of the Alpha Course. Hunt contends that from the mid-1980s to the mid-1990s "in Britain . . . Vineyard has had more impact on the wider Charismatic movement than any other comparable organization ever since the 'Third Wave' conference held in 1984 at the Methodist Central Hall, Westminster."[245] Vineyard has also attracted the most scholarly attention of any JPM church movement or JP organization.

---

243. Fromm, "Textual Communities," 253, 264–67.

244. "Vineyard History."

245. S. Hunt, "Anglican Wimberites," 105.

Don Finto—Belmont Church

By way of brief mention, another pastor and church that came out of Evangelicalism because of the JPM was Don Finto and Belmont Church in Nashville, Tennessee. In the early seventies, Finto was both a pastor at the then Belmont Church of Christ and a teacher at David Lipscomb University when he began to desire conversions like the large, southern California beach baptisms he saw in the pictures of *Look* and *Time* magazine. Soon after this, not only did Finto claim to have been baptized in the Holy Spirit, but the entire church also reportedly entered into an "awakening" of Pentecostal spirituality and witnessed a rapid acceleration in youth conversions.[246] Entering into charismatic praxis meant the church exited the Church of Christ denomination and left behind a tradition of non-instrumental worship to become an influential part of the CCM industry. These examples of Evangelical "coming outers" are presented as a sample of what was occurring on a large scale during the days of the JPM. And in addition to these, there are a number of American church leaders, like Bill Hybels, John MacArthur, Chuck Swindoll, and Ray Stedman who have admitted the influence the JPM had upon their church growth and personal ministry, but who never migrated into Pentecostalism.[247]

Links With the Full Gospel Business Men's Fellowship International

Armenian born dairy farmer, Demos Shakarian (1913–1993) founded the FGBMFI in 1951 as an organization to spread the Christian message of salvation, the fullness of the Spirit, and divine healing.[248] Through its growing network of local chapters around the country, the FGBMFI came into contact with many JP leaders and financially sponsored numerous JP initiatives. These included Tony and Susan Alamo, David Hoyt, Bob Weiner, Mario Murillo, Bill Lowery's CITA, the JP Milwaukee's trip to Scandinavia, and Scott Ross, to name only a few. Their engagement with the JPM did not include participation in street level, JP outreaches, but was instead limited to the offer of financial assistance in the initial stages of outreaches. The JP were not merely puppets on the hands of the FGBMFI. They were most often given financial help and a great deal of liberty to get on with their work.

246. "Belmont Church."

247. On Hybels, see Eskrdige, "God's," 367; on MacArthur, see Mohler, "Faithfully"; on Swindoll, see Old, *The Reading*, 530.

248. Zeigler, "Shakarian, Demos," 1058.

However, given the mission of the FGBMFI, there was an expectation that the sponsored outreaches continue in their belief and practice of Pentecostalism. This is not to suggest that JP did not embrace Pentecostal spirituality of their own volition, or that their motivations were disingenuous. However, some of the credit for the spread of the JPM and its Pentecostalism is owed to the financial contributions and goals of the FGBMFI. Without the help of the FGBMFI, many independent JP initiatives would have never existed.

Links to Other Movements

By way of a very brief mention, there were other movements that either arose from or crossed paths with the JPM and as such entered into a relationship of reciprocity with the JP. First was the ex-gay movement, as already mentioned, which was born out of JPM leaders' responses to the LGBT movements. Second, the "anti-cult movement" sprung up as a direct response to JPM groups like David Berg's COG, The Alamo's The Christian Foundation, and Victor Paul Wierville's The Way International. Third, the "mega-church movement" began to appear in America during the years 1960–1978, and according to Scott Guffin ("Examination") the JPM was one of the key causes. Fourth, as the JPM grew it also attracted the attention of the leaders of the Shepherding Movement (SM)—Bob Mumford, Ern Baxter, Derek Prince, Charles Simpson, and Don Basham—also known as the "Ft. Lauderdale Five." These men established relationships with numerous JP leaders by visiting them and participating in their events. Bob Mumford, for example, met with Chuck Smith when Calvary Chapel assembled in the big tent in order to see if he could partner with Smith's ministry. Even though Smith declined his offer, Mumford successfully recruited Lonnie Frisbee and four other JP to join the SM in Ft Lauderdale.[249]

Kent Philpott and GO were more accommodating than Smith, and both were almost completely subsumed under the SM for a season. Philpott wrote, "For many Jesus People these men were our mentors and teachers. They had a status and a recognition that virtually none of the Jesus People leaders had—they taught, we listened."[250] Scott Ross also participated with the SM, but through the coxing of Pat Robertson he eventually withdrew from them.[251] Derek Prince gathered over a thousand JP youth in Kansas City, Missouri for Charismatic seminars and Bob Mumford could be found

---

249. D. Moore, *Shepherding Movement,* 50–51.

250. Philpott, "Jesus People," 6.

251. D. Moore, *Shepherding Movement,* 89–90.

teaching at many JP gatherings like the Jesus '73 festival.[252] By the mid to late seventies, the same reach of the SM across charismatic Christianity had also spread across numerous segments of the JPM, enveloping them into their quasi-ecclesiological umbrella.

Not only did the CCR and the JPM begin in 1967, but the Six Day War in June of that year also sparked an interest among many people of Jewish origin to believe that Jesus was Israel's Messiah. After their conversion in the JPM, some founded Jewish focused, evangelistic organizations like Moishe Rosen's Jews for Jesus, and others began small Messianic fellowships or synagogues.[253] Although the Messianic movement is a phenomenon that has a long and slowly emerging identity, according to Daniel Juster, "The actual rise of the Messianic Jewish movement in the USA was particularly triggered by the Jesus movement of the late 1960s, with its accompanying charismatic component."[254] The JP's influence is reflected in the charismatic nature of many Messianic Fellowships, and Peter Hocken also underscored how the JPM's Pentecostalism played a major factor in the change of name from "Hebrew Christians" to "Messianic Christianity."[255] Some of these fellowships and synagogues were associated with denominations like the Baptists, the Presbyterians, and the AG, while others were started as independent charismatic fellowships.[256] Not all JP from Jewish background joined a Messianic fellowship as some chose instead to integrate into various types of Christian churches or JPM groups. In any case, Charismatic Messianic Fellowships began to appear in major cities like San Francisco, Chicago, Philadelphia, New York, and Miami. With approximately 300 congregations in America, Daniel Juster claims that the power center for the Messianic movement is in the United States and that most Messianic Fellowships associate with either the International Alliance of Messianic Congregations and Synagogues or the Union of Messianic Jewish Congregations.[257]

252. "'Jesus People' Seminar," 29; and Zidock Jr., "Jesus People Gather in Paradise," 12.

253. Plowman, "Turning on to Jeshua," 33–34.

254. Juster and Hocken, "Messianic," 15.

255. Hocken, *Challenges*," 100.

256. See "Jewish Ministry Flourishes," 15; "Assemblies of God Jewish Evangelism," 25; and Kalapathy, "Chicago Hebrew Mission," 20.

257. Juster and Hocken, "Messianic Jewish Movement," 10, 32.

Conclusions

Prominent Christian leaders, authors, newspaper editorials, and singers offered an abundance of interpretations of the JPM. In 1971, addressing his weekly general audience, Pope Paul VI acknowledged his awareness of the JPM and assumed that it was an unexplained paradox within the hippie movement.[258] Billy Graham (*Jesus Generation*), while pointing out some inherent weaknesses and its need to be more firmly grounded in Bible teaching, was rather optimistic and saw the JPM as a part of an end time revival before the second advent of Jesus Christ. Although his interest is not in Pentecostalism, Eskridge's thesis ("God's Forever Family") sees the JP as a youth movement and connects it to other youth movements in American history. While Elton John was cynical of the JP, country music star Johnny Cash, who, according to Michelmore "rededicated his life to Jesus" during the JPM, was more approving. He said, "I think the 'Jesus People' are doing a great thing."[259] Quite a few JP interviewed for this book believed the movement to be a revival distinctly different from but also part of the CM and Evangelicalism. Swedish Pentecostal leader Lewi Pethrus' offered a supportive evaluation, interpreting the JPM and the CM as different branches from the original Pentecostal movement.[260] Popular and scholarly evaluations during the early 1970s also considered the JPM to be a third charismatic movement, distinct from, but also part of the CR and the CCR; forming a triad of overlapping movements.[261]

Since the JPM was such an enormous movement of Pentecostalism that impacted many in its heyday and has continued to influence American Christianity into the present day, it is only to be expected that there would be Pentecostal and Charismatic analysis of the movement and that its location within the American historiography of Pentecostalism would be well established. Yet perplexingly, there is a paucity of reflection among scholars of America Pentecostalism and a complete absence of the JPM from the historical accounts. The few scholarly comments that can be found are restricted to very minor mentions and most often trivialize the size and influence of the JPM. This limited sampling of vignettes has been written in order to tell the account of the JP as a story of American Pentecostalism and to unveil some of its myriad links to classical Pentecostal, charismatic, and non-charismatic movements.

258. "'Jesus People' Puzzle the Pope," 3.
259. Michelmore, *Back to Jesus*, 89. Trott, "Johnny Cash," 18.
260. Davidsson, "Lewi Pethrus," 205–6, 209–10, 212.
261. Bustraan, "Jesus People," 31–33.

While it is possible and necessary to make distinctions between the movements, it is equally important to leave them entangled and to muse over the mutual benefit they derived from each other. A normal pattern of reciprocity can be observed any time a church or organization opened their doors to the hippies and the JP. Most often an initial and controversial decision to let the hippies into meetings was followed by a period of numerical growth and a transformation of the ministry's ethos to align with the new counterculture trends emerging from the sixties and seventies. Compared to the ICFG the AG showed more resistance to the hippies and as such was probably less transformed. While a number of AG churches participated in the JPM, there was no parallel to the cluster of ICFG's churches that arose under Ralph Moore or Roy Hicks Jr. And two of the large JPM church movements were formed by ex-ICFG ministers, Chuck Smith and Wayman Mitchell.

While the labels CR and CCR have served to identify and clarify differences, they have also created blinders that have inadvertently turned attention away from looking within mainline Protestant and Catholic Churches as a place where the JPM thrived. Charismatic youth activity in the Lutheran Church in Scandinavia and Europe offers clues of another place to investigate the spread and impact of the JPM internationally. If the differentiating lines between the movements are blurred too much, then it is possible to overstate anything youthful and charismatic within mainline churches as the JPM. It is also just as problematic to see the youth in these churches in isolation from the JPM, cut off the natural connection within the youth culture that also fed the currents in the CR, CCR, classical Pentecostal, and Evangelical churches. Classical Pentecostals, CR, and CCR churches all participated in the JPM, both shaping it and experiencing growth and transformation from their interplay with it.

While recognizing the overlap between these movements, it is just as important to delineate and see that there was a distinct stream of the JPM that did occur outside the established denominations. It is nearly impossible to picture characters like Linda Meissner, Jim Palosaari, Lonnie Frisbee, or Scott Ross functioning within denominational churches. Like the analogy of new wine in new wine skins, the street level outreaches, the communes, the birth of a new music industry, and the new churches movements needed a space outside existing churches structures for their phenomenon to flourish and spread. The label JPM is best applied to the vast and diverse collection of counterculture and Pentecostal hybridizations that lasted as a visible movement from 1967 through the end of the 1970s, whether it is the steams inside or those outside existing churches.

The aftermath has, however, remained an active and influential part of American, and in some respects, global Christianity to the present day.

While the movement had died out by the end of the 1970s, the influence of the new hybrid organizations, the migration of JP youth into various kinds of churches, and the youth who were already part of existing churches, all became the agents that assimilated the values of the JPM wherever they took root. It is possible to find former JP across a wide spectrum of American Christianity, having held leadership positions in churches and various Christian organizations, having worked in secular employment, or having stayed home to raise children. Many JP are now retired grandparents, singers in choirs, worship leaders, pastors, and missionaries.

Chapter 4

A Sociological Identity

Embattled and Thriving

READING THROUGH MAGAZINE AND newspaper articles from the sixties and seventies it is easy to be allured by the photos that capture the quintessential styles of that period in time. Particularly interesting is how the dark horn rimmed glasses fashionable in the sixties can be seen giving way to the large, round frames of the seventies. In much the same way, sociologists use analytical lenses that bring certain features into focus or out of focus. Consequently, two different social scientists can see a completely different image of the same group of people. Like the change in fashion, the lenses that sociologists used to analyze religious movements during the sixties and seventies have also changed and are now considered to be outmoded and in many cases, completely unacceptable. This chapter will place a different lens over the eye of the reader; one that sees the JP as a religious subculture that shared a sociocultural family resemblance with American Pentecostalism. This lens will clarify that the JP were neither Fundamentalists nor irrational, religious people as they were depicted in the sociological studies of the sixties and seventies. Instead they will be presented as those who rationally and intentionally constructed a unique subcultural identity that can be differentiated from Fundamentalism and located within the family of movements associated with American Pentecostalism.

To demonstrate the family resemblance, the chapter relies on the theoretical framework of Christian Smith's Subcultural Identity Theory (SIT) presented in *Evangelicalism: Embattled and Thriving* (1998). Smith presented three potential postures as a way to differentiate between Evangelicalism, Fundamentalism, and Liberalism. He concluded that Evangelicals have taken an embattled stance with modernity and thus have thrived as a subculture. He argues that this embattled stance is differentiated from

Fundamentalists, who separate and build a protective shield against secular modernity and survive in an enclave, and Liberals, who accommodate modernity. The JP can be seen as aligning with Smith's SIT. That is, they were not resisting and separating from the culture by creating an enclave in the margins of the society, as Fundamentalists do, and neither were they accommodating the culture, as Liberals do. Instead they intentionally and rationally created moral identities and they embattled with the culture in order to establish and globalize their own subcultural identity. They stand squarely in the camp of Smith's embattled and thriving subcultures and for that reason should be sociologically distinguished from Fundamentalism.[1]

Noting the testimony of common participants and not simply elites in the JPM, it can be seen that the JP were not always submissively obliging and thus uniformly aligning with their leaders' beliefs and their individual opinions were also not overridden by the groups' beliefs. Instead, they were individually and intentionally clustering under collective umbrellas for the purpose of erecting unique, subcultural, moral identities. The JP's moral identities were expressed in symbols that delineated boundaries lines and clarified who was is in their "ingroup" and who was in their "outgroups." They were not only aware of who they were but just as aware of who they were not. And like all subcultures, they believed their own moral identities to be ethically superior to those of their outgroups. Thus it is not enough to simply clarify the moral identity of the JP, as expressed in their symbolic boundaries. It is also necessary to understand that their moral comparisons were the method they used to differentiate themselves as a subculture that was better than their near outgroups. As Smith wrote, "People do not simply categorize, they also always evaluate categories through 'social comparison,' . . . Thus our Irish Roman Catholic man certainly believes that being employed, heterosexual, and church going are morally and functionally better than being jobless, gay, and unchurched."[2]

Moral comparisons are normal and the friction and tension they create is normal. Understanding this alleviates the study from the burden of choosing sides or defending and criticizing the moral comparisons made by the JP or those made against them by their outgroups. Moral comparisons are clues for interpreting where the JP located themselves as a subculture. Eight symbolic boundaries will be examined to illustrate the tension of their subculture as set against their outgroups. But before presenting the Jesus People as an embattled and thriving subculture, it is first necessary to point out the common and outdated lenses used in the 1960s and 1970s and to unfetter the JP from the way they were envisioned in earlier writings.

1. There were few exceptions to this. See Enroth et al., *Story*, 214–17.
2. Smith et al., *American Evangelicalism*, 94.

Jettisoning Pejorative Assumptions

The sixties was an era of an intense religious interest among the American public and it included ventures into eastern religions, newly invented religions, as well as the CM. This revival of religious activity attracted the examining eye of sociologists, who categorized the entire spectrum of religious interest under the label New Religious Movements (NRMs). Hence the JPM was included in a broad discussion of religious plurality alongside groups like the New Age Movement, Jim Jones' People's Temple, Scientology, the Moonies, and ISKCON; organizations with whom Pentecostals, Charismatics, and JP would rather not be associated. This undesirable association for American Pentecostals may be one of the main reasons that they have not included the JPM in their historical and theological considerations as a revival movement.

It is necessary to note that a large portion of the historical data available on the JPM was produced by sociologists who spent untold hours in interviews with JP and as participant observers in JP communes, outreaches, and marches. And while acknowledging and appreciating their endeavors it is just as critical to also point out how drastically the field of the sociology of religion has changed since the 1960s and 1970s. As such, many of the underlying assumptions that guided the studies on the JPM and NRMs are now considered to be passé and even improper.

The Modernization/Secularization Theory substantially influenced the interpretive lenses in the sociology of religion up to the early 1970s. This view pitted religion against modernity and promoted the notion that as society became more modernized, mechanized, and more reliant upon science, religion would inevitably become more privatized, less relevant, and less visible in the public square. Thus a secularized society was one in which religion was removed from its place of dominance within society and was pressed to the margins and privatized. Around the year 1957 church attendance began to decline among the mainline Protestant churches and for many this was evidence that validated the notion underlying theory. In fact, during the pinnacle years of the theory, the 1960s, the more ardent supporters envisioned Secularization's fast-approaching triumph and religions impending decline. For example, Gabriel Vahanian wrote of a "post Christian era" in *The Death of God* (1961), Peter Berger of Secularization's dismantling of religion in *The Sacred Canopy* (1967), Harvey Cox of the great values Secularization in *The Secular City* (1968), and even *Time* magazine (1966) ran a cover story entitled "Is God Dead?"

The 1960s also marked the decline of the Modernization/Secularization Theory from its place of dominance. The onslaught of religious movements in the sixties was evidence that religion in America was not dying, but was thriving and remained public in a modern world. Scholarly works like Dean Kelley's *Why Conservative Churches are Growing* (1972) and popular news reports in *Time* magazine, "Is God Coming Back to Life" (1969) and "Alternative Jesus" (1971) confirmed this general observation. Most supporters of the Modernization/Secularization Theory have since either significantly modified their original opinions or abandoned them altogether. Pentecostalism itself was responsible for two main proponents, Harvey Cox (*Fire from Heaven* [1995]) and David Martin (*Pentecostalism* [2002]), shifting away from their original positions on Secularization. Other theories, such as Market Models, or Rational Choice, and Globalization, have dominated discussions of how religion has thrived in a modern world; theories in which the posturing of modernity against religion is not necessary to the success or failure of their arguments.

Consequently up to the early 1970s it was a standard practice to pit religion against science and modernity and to reflect this in a writing style that pessimistically imagined religious people as those making the final, desperate grasps at magical beliefs before science would ineluctably prove their beliefs to be mythical. Pentecostalism, NRMs, and the JPM, being religious movements, fell victim to this pejorative stereotyping. It was assumed that NRMs were marginal or non-mainstream religions and that only certain types of non-mainstream, marginal, or irrational persons would seek to join them. This assumption often imputed vulnerability due to the presumed childhood socialization of the participant and a rather sinister and exploitative motivation on the part of the NRM. Thus, in order to validate the hunches of their own theories, the objective of many sociologists was to unearth the psychological and religious preconditioning of irrational and marginal religious people. Religious participants' "irrationality" was negatively stereotyped in deeply pejorative and value-laden concepts like maladaptive, anomie, deprivation, psychosis, and Fundamentalism. Abigail Halci identifies the irrational typology as one of the primary guiding assumptions of the "classical social movement theory," which she argues ran from the 1920s into the 1970s.[3]

Evidence of this can be seen in writings on Pentecostalism as early as 1927, when George Cutten concluded that people of low and underdeveloped mental capacities who evidenced hysteria and schizophrenia spoke in tongues.[4] In 1964, Nils Bloch Hoell's concluded that the "emotionalism" in Pentecostalism was in part caused by the high percentages of "woman and

---

3. Halcli, "Social Movements," 464–66.
4. Cutten, *Speaking with Tongues*. See discussion on pages 157–83.

Negroes" that made up their ranks.[5] In 1968, George J. Jennings wrote, "the success of glossolalia in contemporary Western culture is due to the increment of anxiety syndromes characterizing Western man."[6] And E. Mansell Pattison wrote that speaking in tongues was "a modification of the conscious connection between inner speech and outer speech, that may serve various psychodynamic functions."[7] In 1971, Marvin H. Mayers wrote, "Those who practice tongues have a potential for extremism in their life experiences."[8] And again in 1971, Robert Simmonds commented on the JP stating, "religious people in general tend to exhibit dependency on some external source of gratification."[9]

Some wrote of "deprived" types of religious people whose socioeconomic, psychosomatic or general social privations were fundamentally causal of their joining religious movements. Robert Mapes Anderson (*Vision of the Disinherited*) most famously applied this typology to classical Pentecostalism and Peterson and Mauss (*Cross and the Commune*) applied it to the JPM. However, Stephen Hunt, in a survey of various deprivation theories among both classical Pentecostals, neo-Pentecostals, and the JP, concluded that there are indeed many variations of deprivation typologies, but that they are filled with oversimplifications and "carry the acute danger of establishing stereotypes and are now largely outmoded."[10] Others applied the cult/sect/church typologies to NRMs, analyzing the cycle of new religious groups that begin as inventive initiatives outside established religious boundaries and often lead to the formation of new religious institutions or denominations. Initially influenced by Richard Niebuhr (*Social Sources*), cult/sect/church typologies have been greatly modified over time.[11] While they have been applied to the JPM in Jacobson and Pilarzyk ("Croissance") and Richardson ("From Cult to Sect"), Richardson ("Mergers, 'Marriages,' Coalitions, and Denominationalization") has suggested that Calvary Chapel's growth through "mergers and marriages" demonstrates a different pattern of growth than that which is assumed in the cult/sect/church models. There was also the strict religious typology that emerged mostly from the works of Dean Kelley (*Why Conservative Churches Are Growing*; *Why*

---

5. Bloch-Hoell, *Pentecostal Movement*, 173.

6. Jennings, "Ethnological Study," 5.

7. Pattison, M.D., "Behavioral Science Research," 73.

8. Mayers, "Behavior of Tongues," 89.

9. Simmonds, "Conversion or Addiction," 910.

10. S. Hunt, "Deprivation and Western Pentecostalism Revisited," 23.

11. See Stark and Bainbridge ("Of Churches, Sects, and Cults"; *Future of Religion*), Iannaccone ("Formal Model"), Zellner and Petrowsky ("Sects, Cults, and Spiritual Communities").

Conservative Churches Are Still Growing) and Rosabeth Kanter ("Commitment"). Kelley observed that there was a type of church, the "conservative" church, which through its "strict" requirements on members had continued to grow in numbers since the 1950s. Perrin and Mauss ("Strictly Speaking") however, challenged Kelley's premise of the relationship between "strictness" and "social strength" by suggesting that aspects of The Vineyard Christian Fellowship are evidence to the contrary.

Far more derogatory were the concepts of "anomie" and "alienation" as applied by Emile Pin ("En Guise") and "maladaptivity" by Simmonds et al. ("A Jesus Movement Group"). These overly essentialist typologies condescendingly misconstrued the JP as a homogeneous group of young people who seemed to be lost in a new world of religious plurality in which their childhood religion, Fundamentalism, had been challenged and shattered. For example, Mauss and Peterson ("Les 'Jesus Freaks'") presented the JP as "stigmatized" and in need of a religious phenomenon to act as a "waystation" assisting them to be reabsorbed back into the Fundamentalism in which they were originally socialized. Robert Adams and Robert Fox believed that due to their original socialization in Fundamentalism, the JP were crippled in an adolescent crisis that hindered them from progressing on into normal adulthood.[12] David Gordon stated, "It is my view that the Jesus Movement combines elements of the moral code into which these young people were originally socialized."[13] Besides being condescending, these typologies ignore the diversity of JP backgrounds which included those from non-religious, Catholic, liberal Protestant, and Jewish upbringing. Finally, Richardson et al., provide the quintessential specimen of irrational typologies when they wrote, "We have chosen to apply the findings of the thought reform [brainwashing] literature to the Jesus Movement because of the striking similarities between this contemporary phenomenon and the brainwashing that took place in China and Korea during the early 1950s."[14]

Though it is readily conceded that irrationality, maladaptivity, alienation, or deprivation may have played a role in some JP's participation in the movement, it is not the concepts per se that are at issue. Rather it was the way that the researchers' presuppositions caused them to dismiss the claimed experiences, beliefs, and practices of the JP as immaterial or insubstantial. Perhaps the first to lay challenge to the assumptions of deprivation, maladaptivity, alienation, and anomie in Pentecostalism were Gerlach and Hine ("Five Factors") and Hine ("Pentecostal Glossolalia"). In 1971, Rodney

12. Adams and Fox, "Mainlining Jesus," 50–56.
13. Gordon, "Jesus People," 159.
14. Richardson et al., "Thought Reform," 186.

Stark also criticized, "To put it plainly, many social scientists are inclined to regard conservative religious beliefs as abnormal. Because they reject the truth of such beliefs, they find it difficult to imagine that a truly normal person could believe them."[15] More recently, David Martin robustly charged that these kinds of irrational assumptions were the "emperor's eye" and the "ontologies" of "defunct intellectual empires" of the sixties, rescripted as if "what believers say is fantasy waiting for analytic solvents to transfer it to some more basic category."[16]

Jettisoning the assumptions of irrationality as an outdated sociological lens of the sixties and seventies, this chapter begins conversely with the assumption that the JP were rational individuals who understood their choices and were intentional in their actions. By doing so, it not only treats the meaning-content of JP's testimony as substantial and consequential, but also as clues for understanding the identity of the subculture they constructed and where they located themselves as a religious phenomenon.

Severing the Association With Fundamentalism

There remains one final assumption from which the JP need to be unfettered and that is their association with or location in Fundamentalism. The label Fundamentalists(ism) has been consistently applied to the JP and JPM in sociological and historical studies on the phenomenon since the first published works to the present day.[17] There are rare examples, like William McPherson (*Ideology & Change*), who argued that the JP were a form of "New Fundamentalism," based on what he believed to be several thematic resemblances. However, he failed to establish how his themes were unique to Fundamentalism or to take into consideration what self-identified Fundamentalists said about the JP. On occasion, cursory summaries of the tenets of classical Fundamentalism are listed. But these lists of Fundamentalists' beliefs serve as little more than very scant overviews of what Fundamentalism was in the 1920s.[18] Not one of these works attempts to demonstrate links between the Fundamentalists and the JP or to challenge whether or

15. Stark, "Psychopathology," 172.

16. D. Martin, "Undermining," 18, 20.

17. For example, see Enroth et al. (*Story of the Jesus People*), Lyra ("Rise and Development"), Simmonds ("People of the Jesus Movement"), Stones ("Jesus People"), Richardson and Davis ("Experiential Fundamentalism"), Isaacson ("Delicate Balances"), Jensen ("(Re)Discovering"), Di Sabatino (*Jesus People*), and Eskridge ("God's Forever Family").

18. For example see Lyra ("Rise and Development," 44), Richardson and Davis, ("Experiential Fundamentalism," 389, 398), and Di Sabatino (*Jesus People*, 11).

not it is right to locate the JPM in the camp of the Fundamentalists. And most critically, not one of these lists of Fundamentalists' beliefs were produced by the JP themselves, but instead have been forwarded by scholars as an anecdotal evaluation of the JP's beliefs. Streiker (*Jesus Trip*) admitted that there were a few differences between the JP and Fundamentalists and Ellwood (*One Way*) exercised a rare and welcome choice of labels for the JP as "Pentecostals" and "Evangelicals." But it was Hiley Ward who almost uniquely argued that the JP were not Fundamentalists.[19] Ward wrote, "But the Jesus People cannot relate to the Fundamentalist churches as such any more than they can relate to a formal Unitarian Universalist book discussion or an Episcopal women's afternoon card party."[20]

It is not uncommon for Pentecostals to be labeled as Fundamentalists and for scholars of Pentecostalism to bemoan this point. Russell Spittler rightly says that when applied to Pentecostals, "The term *Fundamentalist* is usually a put-own."[21] And beyond the intended derision, Spittler observed that "adjectives such as *Evangelical, Fundamentalist, charismatic* and *Pentecostal* could be exchanged at will for stylistic variety."[22] In this way, the application of the Fundamentalists label works on the oversimplified notion that all of American Christianity, and especially Protestantism, can be bifurcated into two streams: liberal and conservative. The phrase conservative Protestant is most often a synonym for Fundamentalist, Evangelical, or Pentecostal; in other words all that does not fit into liberalism. When applied in this manner, the "Fundamentalist" label demonstrates a profoundly unacceptable lack of rigorous investigative interest in differentiating an enormous and heterogeneous portion of American Christianity.

Based on the lack of links between the two movements, it is proposed that the JP were not Fundamentalists and that the JP should not be, and never were, located in the camp of Fundamentalism. To begin, the influence of Fundamentalists had already greatly diminished since the formation of the NAE in 1942. James Davidson Hunter wrote, "Although there are clear remnants of the '1920s Fundamentalism' still to be found within conservative Protestantism (the ACCC and ICCC, Bob Jones University, Hargis and his Christian Crusade), they no longer make up the formidable cultural force they once did."[23] In addition to their increasing marginality, Fundamentalists lacked diachronic links to the JPM. In fact, an examination of several prominent Fundamentalists, Bob

19. Ward, *Far-out Saints*, 154–67; Ward, "Are Jesus People Fundamentalists?," 4.

20. Ward, *Far-out Saints*, 155.

21. Spittler, "Are Pentecostals," 103.

22. Ibid.

23. J. Hunter, *American Evangelicalism*, 45.

Jones (*Is Jesus a Revolutionary?*), Bob Jones III (*Look Again*), and Robert Walter (*"Jesus Movement"*), reveals their vitriolic criticisms and intentional dissociation from JPM. They most often lashed out against the JP for the following reasons: The JP loved rock music. They did not support the government. They disdained the local church. They wore hippie attire and grew their hair long. They only used the gospels and not the whole Bible. And, they practiced the "wildfire counterfeit" of tongues, healing, and prophecy found in Pentecostalism.[24] This chastisement by Bob Jones III is perhaps the best summary of Fundamentalists' general sentiments, "Revival is not spawned in pot parties, love-ins, hippie pads, dens of iniquity, and rock orgies; but that is where the Jesus Movement was spawned."[25] The increasing marginality of Fundamentalists coupled with their intentional disaffiliation with the JPM, makes it rather unreasonable to suggest that the movement be located under the umbrella of Fundamentalism. Further evidence will be given throughout the chapter to show Fundamentalists' intentional disassociation with the JPM.

Sociologically speaking, there is a vaguely defined, but generally accepted interpretation of Fundamentalism that sees it as a broad descriptive typology of any group that resists social and cultural change and that practices strict behavioral restraints. For example, Jensen ("(Re)Discovering") depicted the Calvary Chapel movement as discontents that rediscovered Fundamentalism through resisting the culture in the margins of society. Or Enroth, very comically and simplistically claimed that all JP as Fundamentalists neatly fit into Niebuhr's "Christ against culture" model.[26] It may be true that Fundamentalists exercise strict behavioral constraints and resist cultural change and especially against pluralistic modernity. And this was the cause of their decreasing significance. However, the JP did not fit this sociological characterization of Fundamentalism. They opted for a different posture than Fundamentalists, one of embattlement with the culture. It was for that reason that, unlike Fundamentalism, the JPM thrived as a subculture and continued to influence American Christianity through the end of the century.

Eight Symbolic Boundaries

Names

Perhaps the best symbolic boundary to begin with is the sobriquet "Jesus People" or "Jesus People Movement" and those who self-identified as a JP.

---

24. Jones III., *Look Again*, 3.

25. Ibid., 14.

26. Enroth et al., *The Story*, 168.

As stated earlier the names JP and JPM did not originate endogenously, but were labels given by outsiders as a more endearing replacement for the original labels of Jesus Freaks, Hippie Christians, and Street Christians. Interviews and other sources reveal that quite a few of those involved in the movement were reticent to self-identify as a JP for several reasons. For example, some felt the name represented Evangelical Christianity's corruption or quelling of what was originally a real work of the Holy Spirit among the hippies, while others felt it would associate them with what they saw as marginal groups like the COG and The Alamo's Christian Foundation. Others saw the name as too closely associated with what they believed were gimmicks like bumper stickers, slogans like "getting high on Jesus," or Jesus marches. No one interviewed was unaware of the name JP or JPM and even those who were hesitant to identify with the movement were willing to do so once their reservations were expressed.

The primary symbol of the JP was Jesus himself, the symbolic revolutionary who was leading a revolution of young people that also took on his name, "Jesus People," or at times "Jesus Freaks." The harmony between Jesus and their hippie culture created an attraction for a large number of hippies and was reflected in the adoption of the sobriquet "Jesus Freaks," which wed together "Jesus" from the text of the Bible with "Freaks" another name for hippies. In appearance Jesus was "the world's first hippie" and in practice He was a revolutionary who, like them, stood on the side of the weak and against religious institutions.[27] The Jesus Freaks symbolically erected Jesus as someone who not only lived in their hearts, but also resided in their communes, attended their meetings, and carried banners at their marches. Jesus was portrayed as embattling alongside the JP against other religious subcultures, as one poster proclaimed:

> JESUS CHRIST ALIAS: THE MESSIAH, THE SON OF GOD, KING OF KINGS, LORD OF LORDS, PRINCE OF PEACE, ETC. Notorious leader of an underground liberation movement. Wanted for the following charges:—Practicing medicine, winemaking and food distribution without a license.—Interfering with businessmen in the temple. —Associating with known criminals, radicals, subversives, prostitutes and street people. —Claiming to have the authority to make people into God's children. APPEARANCE: Typical hippie type—long hair, beard, robe, sandals. Hangs around slum areas, few rich friends, often sneaks out into the desert. BEWARE: This man is extremely dangerous. His insidiously inflammatory message is particularly dangerous to young people who haven't been taught

27. For "world's first hippie," see B. Kelley, "Christ," 14.

to ignore him yet. He changes men and claims to set them free.
WARNING: HE IS STILL AT LARGE![28]

Many names were clustered under this one symbolic boundary of the "Jesus People" and have become famously and infamously associated with the name. To one degree or another, Chuck Smith and Calvary Chapel, David Berg and The COG, Linda Meissner and The JPA, Carl Parks and The VoE, Jim Durkin and GO, and Scott Ross and The Love Inn all joined with Jesus in his revolutionary engagement against established religious subcultures.

The name "Jesus People" and the phrase "Jesus People Movement" enabled the heterogeneous subculture to globalize with a presumed singular identity. And with newspapers featuring articles like, "'Jesus People' Are out to Convert the World," "'Jesus People' Are Locating in County," "'Jesus Movement' Attracts Following across Country, on Campuses," "Jesus People settle in U.K.," "Jesus People Move to Latin America," or in New Zealand, "10,000 March for Jesus," the media helped to emblemize the advance of a homogenous religious phenomenon that was vaguely Christian, youthful, and hippie. The name also gave sympathetic outgroups a chance to respond in support of the subculture as these article and book titles indicate: "'Jesus People' Really Doing Good Job," "'Jesus People' Call Nation Back to God," "'Jesus People' Winning over Street Youth in Southland," and *Jesus People Come Alive*.

The assumed homogeneity of the JP's subcultural identity placed it in tension with various outgroups and provided a single target to strike at with concerns and criticisms. Authors of books, magazines, and newspaper articles did not conceal their moral judgments as outsiders, but railed against the JP's subcultural identity as something inferior to their own. For example, Enroth's criticized, "We disapprove of their simplistic mentality, their excessive emphasis on experience and feeling, and their bias against intellectual pursuits, social involvement, and human culture in general."[29] Disapproving tones are also printed in article titles that state, "Church Leaders Note Dangers in Youthful Jesus Movement," "'Jesus People' Worry Rabbi," or "Calls Jesus People 'Faddists, Not 1st Century Christians.'"[30] One editorialist disdainfully mocked, "It [the JPM] may be better than drugs in the same way that diabetes is better than cancer."[31] The greatest resistance to the JP's identity of Jesus the revolutionary came from self-identified Fundamentalists, as this comment captures, "The man who says

28. "Alternative Jesus."

29. Enroth et al., *The Story*, 17.

30. Cornell, "Church Leaders Note," 15; "'Jesus People' Worry Rabbi," 94; Rodney, "Calls Jesus People," 10.

31. "Only Another 'Trip,'" 6.

Jesus was a revolutionary stands in grave danger, for to make this statement is to come very close to committing the unpardonable sin."[32] These
judgments clarify who the JP's outgroups were. They are the sounds made
by irritated outgroups as the name "Jesus People" engaged with them. The
many groups that clustered under the name "Jesus People" were disparate,
but the name itself remains one of its most recognizable and unifying
symbolic boundaries.

Conversion Experience

The extremely high value placed on conversion is highlighted in many sociological works and some have used conversion models to analyze the how,
the why, and predispositions of JP conversion.[33] But attention is turned here
to the value of the experience to the individual JP, how they symbolized it,
and how they globalized it. While some sociologists interpreted conversion
as the equivalent of recruitment (M. Harrison, "Sources") or swapping ad-
dictions (Simmonds, "Conversion or Addiction"), the JP spoke of conversion as something real, personal, spiritual, and not as a recruitment tool or
a rite for joining a JP group. For many, the group to which they belonged
seemed incidental compared to the value they placed upon their conversion
experience. For most, a personal conversion experience was the entry point
into the JPM and without it, someone did not belong to the movement.

A central motif common in individual testimonies was a conversion
experience, preceded by a season of sojourning into drugs and eastern religions. Their conversion caused a subsequent departure from hippiedom.
This motif was critical to constructing and globalizing the JPM's identity
as a movement of youthful conversion that had exited out of the American counterculture. While not all JP shared this experience, the more banal
conversion stories were brushed to the side to make space for the more dramatic, hardcore, ex-hippie and ex-counterculture conversion stories. For
example, the biographies selected for the book *Harvest*, are accounts of the
conversion experiences of several prominent Calvary Chapel leaders that
were anything but mundane. The testimonies are titled "A Heartbeat from
Hell," "Drug Dealer to Shepherd," "A Quest for Psychic Powers," "Meditating

---

32. Jones, *Is Jesus a Revolutionary?*, 13.

33. See Ward (*Far-Out Saints*), Jacobson and Pilarzyk ("Croissance"), Richardson
and Stewart ("Conversion Process Models"), Simmonds ("Conversion or Addiction")
and Tipton (*Getting Saved*). For conversion models see Richardson et al. (*Organized
Miracles*).

Undercover."[34] When Bob Dylan, Allan Cohen, Paul Stookey, and other counterculture celebrities claimed a similar conversion experience, they became trophies for the JP. This is not to doubt the sincerity or truthfulness of these testimonies, but to underscore the way that the more breathtaking stories were adorned with greater credibility since they promoted the archetypal conversion from the heart of the hippie movement.

In interviews, it was very common for an interviewee to frame the entire conversation around their conversion experience. Their childhood background, other religious or drug experiences, and the first days in a commune were all presented as events that led to their conversion. For some, their spouse and children, their career, and education were never mentioned, as their conversion experience was the centerpiece of their entire personal narrative. The conversion experience was often expressed in Pentecostal rhetoric like "born again," "accepting Christ," being "saved," or "being a new creation." It was described by adjectives like "beautiful," "wonderful," and "sweet" to emphasize how positive and meaningful the experience was to them. Most conversion accounts were as equally centered on the theme of salvation from a ruined life as they were on salvation from hell or salvation from sin. "Emptiness," "hungry," "depressed," "miserable," and "lost" were often used as a descriptive of their life before their conversion, while words like "fun," "exciting," "loved," "full," and "happy" of their life after conversion. A few interviewees were willing to overlook very unpleasant abuses in communes and churches, claiming the value of their conversion experience outweighed the difficulties.

The conversion experience was sung about as a very popular theme in Jesus Music. It was also popularly emblemized in a symbol that, according to Don Williams, was introduced by a young man named Lance as an adaptation of the Harvard University strike symbol.[35] From the fully clenched fist, he drew one finger pointing to heaven with a small cross above the fist and the phrase "One Way" printed below the fist. This symbol, often called the "One Way" symbol, quickly found its way onto signs, t-shirts, and was frequently displayed by JP at marches, festivals, and meetings from Singapore to New Zealand, from New York to California. It was also just as popular for JP to make the symbol with their hand and point their index finger in the air when at meetings or on marches. The symbol pointed to their conversion experience and the belief that Jesus was the one way to heaven.

To the JP, their conversion experience was something beautiful that they wanted to "share" with others and it was something they also claimed

---

34. Smith and Brooke, "Harvest," Table of Contents.

35. D. Williams, *Call*, 43–45.

was necessary for all. The necessity and "beauty" motivated them to global-ize the message to others, often in a haphazard way. Their baptisms, tracks, bumper stickers, outdoor festivals, street meetings, communes, and cafés all became vehicles for sharing what they believed to be God's love and salva-tion for others. The globalizing interests of the conversion experience were sung about in songs like Kurt Kaiser's *Pass It On* that expresses a primary sense of being overwhelmed by God's love. The result was an irresistible compulsion to share this experience with everyone else. Many JP communi-ties counted numbers of people who claimed to have had this conversion experience. Songs, bumper stickers, and posters had little intrinsic value apart from their instrumentality in globalizing the message. Thus, conver-sion became the ultimate filter through which the JP seemed to evaluate who was in and who was out of the JPM.

As a symbolic boundary it placed them in tension with other reli-gious subcultures like eastern religions and the Jewish community. This mostly because personal conversion also often included a conversion from these other religious subcultures and as such implicitly judged them as in-ferior. This also placed them in tension with other Christian communities as their conversion stories often included accounts of people who claimed they were previously a Lutheran, a Catholic, or a Baptist. By saying that they once were, but were no longer, they distinguished their subculture identity as better than these other Christian groups and other religions. A few JP admitted that some believed that those outside the JPM were not "real disciples" of Jesus.[36]

Many Evangelicals, Pentecostals, and some Fundamentalists cel-ebrated the JP's conversion experience as a common symbol of their sub-cultures. However, the tensions between classical Pentecostal Churches and the JP underscores the dissonance caused by the JP's non-compliance to the expected norms that should accompany a classical Pentecostal conversion; a greater disassociation with the hippie subculture. Most Fundamentalists did not acknowledge the JP's conversion experience as legitimate and assumed that a truly converted young person would at-tempt to escape out of the JPM. For example, Bob Jones wrote, "Some Jesus People have, indeed, been regenerated. Some of them, in spite of the Jesus Movement, have their sins under the blood of Christ and are there-fore on their way to heaven."[37] As such, the JP embattled their conversion experience as a symbolic boundary that they differentiated from that of other religious subcultures and other Christian subcultures.

---

36. Harry Hewat, interview with author, December 10, 2008.

37. Jones III, *Look Again*, 5.

Communes and Jesus People Churches

The JP communes are a rather puzzling anomaly; for while they were a part of the largest communal movement in American history, almost all had completely disappeared by the end of the seventies. Many JP churches on the other hand have endured to the present day as "new paradigms" (D. Miller, *Reinventing*) in post-sixties American Christianity. Communes as symbolic boundaries, for a relatively short period of time, defined real spatial areas through property, homes, and other tangible assets. Communes and JP churches as spatial arenas were utterly essential in the construction of the JP's moral identities as a subculture contrasted to, and outside of, the established churches and hippie communes. Within these boundaries, the symbols of JP fashion, hair, music, art, conversion experience, and Pentecostalism all found a place to flourish. In the communes, the daily regiment, leadership structure, doctrinal teachings, and group expectations shaped the behaviors of communards and were reciprocally shaped by the communards. The communards were not mere victims of indoctrination and brainwashing, but were participants in shaping the moral identities that emerged from the communes. This is, in part, because communes were more fluid than might often be assumed, with large numbers of people visiting or passing through for short periods of time, leaving only a relatively small committed core of communards.[38] According to T. Miller (*6os Communes*), no two communes were perfectly identical and most operated with a large degree of autonomy, including those that functioned as part of larger collectives.

Generally speaking, to the JP, their communes and churches were comparatively better than the hippie communes and established churches and this brought them into tension with both. Not only did they believe their practices were more biblical, but their communes and churches operated 24 hours a day, seven days a week compared to the few opening times of conventional churches. One JP lamented, "But you were too far in debt paying for cathedrals to help a man buy a shirt for his son . . . We advise you churches to sell your buildings, give the money to the broken little people of the earth . . . Did not Jesus say, 'Go, sell all that thou hast and give it to the poor and come and follow me?'"[39] Paradoxically, however, many communes were financially dependent upon the generous contributions of established Christian churches.[40] To them, communal life was warm and accepting, shared all things in

38. See Jackson (*Coming Together*), Richardson et al. (*Organized Miracles*), and T. Miller (*6os Communes*).

39. Moody, *Jesus Freaks*, 51.

40. Richardson, "Financing," 255–56. Quite a few communes were also

common, and witnessed God at work daily as contrasted with established churches that they often presumed to be dead. It was frequently admitted in interviews that increases in the numbers of conversions, healings, baptisms in the Holy Spirit, and even the simple provision of daily needs were interpreted as stamps of divine approval upon their better and more biblical form of communal Christianity.[41] And unlike the drugs, alcohol, and sexual promiscuity of the hippie communes, the JP communes were, to them, places of establishing a comparatively better ethical standard.

Opinions between established Christians were polarized and many tolerated the JP communes and churches as long as the JP remained outside of their church buildings. Fundamentalist Christians launched the sharpest rebukes of the JP communes and JP churches, as these citations exemplify. "If they [the JP] know the Scriptures, they will recognize that the failure of Christians in LOCAL CHURCHES [sic] does not invalidate the concept of the LOCAL CHURCH."[42] "It is my sincere hope that the JESUS MOVEMENT will learn this basic teaching of Scripture, and, as a result, will begin to affiliate with LOCAL CHURCHES."[43] Fundamentalist Dr. Joseph Stowell, the chief executive officer of the General Association of Regular Baptist Churches, said, "We decry the movement's apparent rejection of the spiritual teaching on the local New Testament church. Also we believe strongly in the divine institution of the family and regret to hear of some Jesus People living in communes. Any movement ignoring these two matters cannot survive as a Christian movement."[44] The communes and churches were the primary spatial areas through which the JP embattled their nascent subcultural identity and globalized the movement's symbols.

Pentecostal Spirituality in Tension with Non-charismatic Christianity

To say that the JP practiced Pentecostal spirituality would be true, but to say that many JP treasured and cherished Pentecostal spirituality as something deeply meaningful would more accurately reflect their testimony. The most emphasized experiences among the JP were the BHS, tongues, healings, words of prophecy, visions, and dreams. And while most JP interviewed were

---

self-supporting.

41. Jackson, *Coming Together*, and Jackson and Jackson, *Living Together*, sees communal living as a better form of church.

42. Walter, *"Jesus Movement*," 19.

43. Ibid., 19–20.

44. Ward, *Far-out Saints*, 160.

disinterested in the classical Pentecostal issues surrounding these experiences, they were not indifferent about the meaning of these experiences. All who claimed to have had Pentecostal experiences highly valued them and remembered them as pleasurable highlights in their Christian experience. As with their conversion, adjectives like "awesome," "amazing," "released," "free," and "overwhelming" accompanied their descriptions of the experience. In some interviews the individual spoke from the position of a passive recipient of spiritual gifts and in these cases more emphasis was laid upon the feelings that accompanied the experiences they claimed. Other interviewees spoke from a position of being "mobilized" or "equipped" to go somewhere and accomplish a task that they believed God had destined them for. In these cases there was a tendency to lay more emphasis upon the works that followed their experience than upon the feelings accompanying the experience.

In a similar way to the conversion experience, Pentecostal spirituality was promoted as part of their subcultural identity and something for all to participate in. The JP not only embraced Pentecostal spirituality as a moral identity, but they intentionally engaged American religious institutions with what they believed to be its axiological superiority. Although great variance could be found across the entire movement, most JP meetings intentionally created space for healing, for tongues, and for prophecy. The JP took advantage of testimonies in meetings as a means to communicate to others the meaning of Pentecostal spirituality and to invite others to receive and experience the spiritual experiences of Pentecostalism.

Resonating within the testimony of the JP were strong comparisons and judgments about the deprivations in Christianity, in established American religions, and in NRMs that had failed to give them the depth of spiritual experiences they claimed to have found. The JP considered their Pentecostal spirituality to be superior to and more fulfilling than other forms of Christianity that were non-charismatic. So while the JP shared a common conversion experience with Evangelicalism, their appreciation for Pentecostal spirituality gave them a closer affinity to the CR, CCR, SM, and classical Pentecostalism. This also helps explain their migration in and out of CM and classical Pentecostal meetings. The common experience of Pentecostal spirituality brought them together with these other movements in spite of the differences in counterculture values, hair, fashion, and music.

Yet all was not harmonious between classical Pentecostals and the JP and the indifference to classical Pentecostals' sensibilities about what should accompany the BHS resulted in rifts and fissures and the creation of new subculture called the JPM. And the JP's Pentecostal spirituality as a symbolic boundary formed deep fissures between them and American Fundamentalism. The following citation from Bob Jones III illustrates that

Pentecostal spirituality was one of the main reasons for Fundamentalists' condemnation of the JP's subculture. He wrote, "Thousands of young people looking for the way to heaven are being deceived by a popular, charismatic, undergrounded, wildfire counterfeit which talks about Jesus."[45]

Pentecostal Spirituality in Tension with the Political

The vast majority of JP saw themselves as a spiritual people and the JPM as a spiritual movement, not as a political movement. While there was never a shortage of opinions offered that supposedly described their political views, there was a shortage of thorough research that defined term "political" and sought answers to precise questions. The best attempt was made by Richardson et al., in a survey of SYRC participants in which they noted a massive shift in political attitudes from 27 percent being politically indifferent before joining to 71 percent being politically indifferent after joining the commune.[46] While the survey yields some helpful responses, the ambiguity of what was meant by political makes their conclusions rather dissatisfying and raises more questions than it answers. A more precise question would ask, "Were the JP engaged in the African American battle for civil liberties?" The answer, by-and-large would have most probably been, "No." Or "Were the JP ever known to have held anti-Vietnam protests or marches?" For the most part, the answer would most probably have been, "No." In this way Senator Mark Hatfield's chastisement for their failure "to grapple with issues such as war and racism," was probably justifiable.[47]

Jesus Marches may have been the closest that some came to political protest. However, these marches never seemed to have a focused political agenda and were seldom more than groups of young people carrying signs, raising their fingers to indicate the "One Way" symbol, and chanting "J-E-S-U-S." Richardson's survey reported that 82 percent of the JP in SYRC believed that "acceptance of Jesus as God would provide the solution for the major world problems."[48] If this is true of most participants in the JPM, then it shows that many JP believed that an important part of the answer to world peace lay in the spiritual answer of Jesus. For example, Sammy Tippit spoke to hostile crowds immediately after the Kent State shooting with the message of "Only Jesus can bring peace."[49] After his preaching, he claimed that peace and

45. Jones III, *Look Again*, 7.

46. Richardson, et al., *Organized*, 218.

47. Plowman, "Explo '72", 32.

48. Richardson et al., *Organized*, 221.

49. Sammy Tippit, interview with author, February 1, 2011.

order "fell on the campus."[50] He stated, "Peace in the world begins with peace in the heart. It is only when we experience that deep level of spiritual peace that we can truly be reconciled with our enemies."

The question of social action however brings a more diverse response. For example, Jürgen Moltmann lamented their lack of social action by labeling them as ascetic John the Baptist types.[51] One Harvard staff psychiatrist, however, concluded that the JP on Harvard's Campus were commendable because their "intensive social interests have by no means diminished."[52] And Walter Hollenweger envisioned the JP as a force for social change.[53] Following Hollenweger's thought, if their communes were taken into consideration, then the JP could potentially be credited with having launched one of the largest social action programs in American history. That is, Timothy Miller concluded that the JP communes, in terms of sheer numbers, might have been the largest identifiable communal type during the 1960s era.[54] And the JP communes arose at a time when the numbers of youth runaways in America reached the highest levels for the twentieth century. They served the basic function of providing food, housing, clothing, as well as the gospel and miracles, for enormous numbers of transient American youth. For example, SYRC provided food, housing, and the gospel for an estimated 100,000 young people between the years 1969 and 1979. And although their commune building habits were borrowed from the Hippies, the JP saw this as a biblical form of Christianity taught in the book of Acts 2:42–47. The research for this book did not investigate their political action and the question of their social action is simply forwarded for further investigation.

Preston Shires's investigation *Hippies* shows that some JP in the 1980s became involved in the politically conservative movement called the religious right. Beyond this, little research has been invested in answering political questions on the JPM. So until further examinations are carried out, it is assumed that with Pentecostal spirituality at the moral center of the JPM, political systems were rendered impotent for accomplishing the more necessary, spiritual outcomes they desired. In addition, the nearness of Christ's return probably bolstered the feeling that there was little time to deal with political matters and the political institutions themselves would be toppled and destroyed. If there was a general tendency for the JP to be indifferent to

50. Ibid.

51. Ward, *Far-out Saints*, 74–75.

52. Jorstad, *That New Time Religion*, 81.

53. Hollenweger, *Pentecost Between*, 10.

54. T. Miller, *60s Communes*, xxiv.

engagement in the political process, then Pentecostal spirituality was most likely partially responsible for this. In this way the JP located themselves as a subculture with its identity in Pentecostal spirituality and therefore in tension with concurrent political movements.

Sexuality and Gender Identity

The sexual revolution of the sixties and seventies turned upside down the American traditional values on sexuality and gender identity. The traditional, taboo frontiers of sexual relationships outside of marriage were openly trespassed by many in the counterculture movement and in American society at large. For this brief discussion, the sexual revolution is here taken as a broad umbrella of liberation movements that could be broken down into three primary arenas: sexual liberation generally, Women's Liberation—as in feminism and womanism—and LGBT Liberation.[55] Each of these movements saw themselves as forces for liberating and empowering minority groupings of individuals they believed to have been wrongfully oppressed for their alternative sexuality and/or alternative gender identity. Under the banner of liberation there has also ensued a moral struggle for the redefinition of religious, civil, and human rights since the late sixties to the present day. The moral battle has grappled with redefining maleness and femaleness, submission and headship, fathering and mothering, careers, earnings, divorce and remarriage, homosexual civil partnerships, and adoption to name a few. Since the types of possible relationships had been expanded, the identity in each new role needed redefinition.

Engendered in the midst of this revolution, the JP erected symbolic boundaries to differentiate themselves from their sexual revolution outgroups and to engage their sexual and gender identity with their outgroups. The JP's sexual identity could be defined as strongly heterosexual and forbidding of sexual relations outside of marriage. In marriage, their gender identities reinforced the conventional American roles of male headship and a wife's submission. Their religious structures reinforced the position of male leadership. The JP's sexual identities were enforced through the separation of men from women into separate communal living quarters, a requirement placed upon visitors and members alike. The JP communicated their gender identity directly through the content of their teaching and indirectly through the lack of

---

55. The suggestion of these three movements coming under the banner of Liberation movements comes from Stephen Hunt, "Saints and Sinners," who proposes that "Queer theology" can be located as a branch of liberation theology because of its methodological similarities.

leadership positions made available to women, by expectations of dress codes, and the assignment of daily chores in communes.

It is most often assumed, as in Isaacson ("Delicate Balances"), that the JP's sexual and gender identity was rooted in American Fundamentalism, since, after all, the assumption was that the JP were Fundamentalists.[56] However, it is suggested that their gender and sexual identity were rooted in a combination of the Bible, in conventional American values, and in hippiedom. Although it may seem strange to suggest hippiedom as contributing to their gender identity, since the hippies participated in the sexual revolution, more recent scholarship has suggested that the hippies were not as sexually liberated as they are often stereotyped. According to Timothy Miller the rumored stories of group sex and frequent rotating of partners in communes were quite rare.[57] As for their gender identity, Alice Echols argues that the hippies were sexist, very heterosexual, and a subculture guilty of "reconstructing" the "inequalities" of the traditional American family.[58] She writes, "Although many hippie guys managed to avoid nine-to-five jobs, few hippie girls avoided housework. Baking, cooking, sewing were a 'woman's thing.'"[59]

Generally speaking, the JP's sexual and gender identities were not misogynous. The high portion of males and the prominence of male leadership in the JPM's structures undoubtedly served to enhance the JP's male and female gender identities.[60] As for female identity, Mary Harder noted that high percentages of JP women in SYRC had considered careers, had attended university, and were open to sexual relationships outside marriage before joining the commune.[61] She stressed the "supra-human legitimization" of the male leadership roles over females; that is to say that God was presented as being supportive of their gender roles.[62] However, she also concluded that the simplicity and informality of the communal structures significantly reduced tensions and conflicts over roles between males and females.[63]

With the exception of the few years of Linda Meissner's leadership in the JPA, Melody Green's in LDM, or the obscure individuals like Bobbi Morris, no other prominent woman leader emerged from the movement. The wives of famous JP leaders are rarely mentioned in historical accounts

---

56. For example see, Richardson et al., *Organized Miracles*, 182.

57. T. Miller, "Sixties-Era Communes," 346.

58. Echols, Shaky Ground, 34.

59. Ibid.

60. Richardson and Reidy, "Form," 189; and Richardson, "Jesus Movement," 4852.

61. Harder, "Sex Roles," 352.

62. Ibid.

63. Ibid.

or are most often portrayed as the behind the scenes Mom or the supportive wife.[64] Not one of the women interviewed admitted to holding an alternative gender identity, but neither did any of them hint at feeling repressed or coerced against their will into a stereotypical, mainstream gender role. There were two women interviewees from two separate communities who felt that the females were treated as subordinates and servants to the men. To them, the assignment of certain quotidian duties to women and the organizational structures themselves reinforced the stay at home women who cooked and cleaned for the men, whose job it was to lead, teach, and go out to work in ministry. Most women, however, expressed a willing compliance with their gender identity, stating that they were content with raising children, with being a wife, or with being single a woman communard in the communal environment. This indicates that these women rationally and intentionally participated in the sexual and gender identity of the JPM.

While the JP drew on the Bible, traditional American values, and hippiedom for the formation of their sexual and gender subcultural identity, they were not simply reconstructing the sheltered enclave of Fundamentalism's sexual and gender identity.[65] The JP's embattled posture on sexual and gender identity made outgroups of feminism/womanism and LGBTism and enabled them locate their subculture as distinctly different from these movements. One means of battling their identity was through the expectation that conversion include repentance from alternative gender and sexual identities. The creation of an "ex-gay" category made any association with sexual liberation movements permissible if it remained part of the preconversion experience. This stance also gave rise to the formation of the "ex-gay movement" from the heart of the JPM in San Francisco and to many small, informal ministries within local churches that sought to help those who were exiting the sexual revolution. The policing of this boundary not only enabled JP to identify individual cases of heterosexual and homosexual "moral" failings, but also enabled them to identify the COG's "flirty fishing" methods of recruitment and the MCC's inclusion as taboo sexuality.[66] Consequently, these groups' were exclued from the mainstream JPM.

While it would be overstated to claim that the JP were aggressively anti-LGBT or anti-feminist/womanist, they did see themselves as embattled against LGBT values. JP attitudes, especially towards LGBTism, would align with the observation of Kirstin Aune that Evangelicals "sympathise with

---

64. Durkin, *Living the Word*, 65–70.

65. For "sheltered enclave," see Smith et al., *American Evangelicalism*, 67–69.

66. "Flirty Fishing" was the term used by the COG to describe the practice that encouraged single and married women to entice and gain male recruits through sex acts.

those who are trying to resist same-sex sexual relationships, not with those who are unrepentant."[67] The JP's "ex-gay" category also aligned with mainstream American and Christian values that believed the LGBT lifestyle was morally wrong.

Interviewees have testified to the presence of people from LGBT backgrounds that accepted the sexual and gender identity of the JP. Some individuals sought to align with the JP's moral identity and made a "successful" exodus from LGBTism while others "failed." Marsha Stevens and Lonnie Frisbee were among the better known JP whose sexuality and gender identity varied from the JP's moral identity, and their lives highlight the tension this presented to JP churches. One interview revealed a dilemma that arose among the leadership of a commune over whether to place a transsexual communard in the men's or women's accommodation. The way the leaders handled the individual by treating her with respect and according to her new gender identity, indicated a high level of care and sensitivity. Whether or not their posture is interpreted as morally right or wrong, the very fact that they had to make such decisions and "deal with" such circumstances are the consequences of engagement with LGBTism. They never would have faced such issues had they remained separated from LGBTism and in a protected enclave. Although they embattled their identity, the interviewees did not speak in an aggressive tone toward those who remained in the sexual revolution.

According to Isaacson ("Delicate Balances"), Chrasta ("Jesus People") and Goldman and Isaacson ("Enduring Affiliation") there were subtle shifts in the JP's gender identity to align with the larger societal trends, however these shifts were negligible and limited to gender roles. Concurrent with the JPM were individual churches like Glide Memorial Church in San Francisco and new church movements like Metropolitan Community Church (MCC) that took an inclusive position with the LGBT people. Today LGBT groups have risen under nearly all the established denominations in American Christianity and a few LGBT organizations have emerged on the periphery of Pentecostalism: namely the Global Alliance of Affirming Apostolic Pentecostals and the Affirming Pentecostal Church. Scholarly analysis of Pentecostalism's interaction with LGBT people is almost non-existent and this brief examination does not pretend to even begin to scratch the surface. But, from the beginning into the present day, the JP located their subculture as something distinct from the sexual revolution and outside the sexual liberation movements.

---

67. Aune, "Between Subordination," 49.

Counterculture Identity

The hair, clothing, music, art, newspapers, and jargon of the JP were distinct, visible symbols of their intentional identification with hippiedom and the counterculture. There was great meaning in these counterculture practices, as through them the JP were able to be part of Christianity and also maintain the symbols of and identification with the counterculture. For example, Jesus newspapers of various types were valued for their utilitarian use of communicating the JP's conversion message and also for their function as a networking tool. It seemed to be one of the unwritten rules of the subculture that once the movement localized it began to produce its own newspaper. The most enduring of these symbolic boundaries, however, was the JP's music, and it is difficult to limit this conversation to only a brief mention where others (Romanowski, "Rock'n'religion") and (Baker, *Why Should the Devil*) have written extensively. The JP borrowed and reinvented the hippies' music both for its intrinsic and artistic value, but also for its utilitarian function as a means of globalizing their subcultural identity. Young people stood in wonder at Bands like Love Song whose appearance and musical style and quality was similar to other hippie bands, yet their lyrical content centered on Jesus. The music and appearance of the Jesus Music bands were highly influential in recruiting youth to join the subculture. Clothing, hair, and music were two of the most common symbols and they served as easily observable boundaries of who was "in" and who was "out," establishing a visual homogeneity.

Forty years on, it may seem difficult to imagine that hair, fashion, and music were so controversial as to bring them into tension with both the counterculture and established Christianity. Hair and clothing communicated sameness with the hippies and this allowed them access into hippiedom. But the lyrical content of the music was intentionally differentiated from hippiedom to create a separate subculture from the hippies. Since secular music labels rejected it and Gospel music labels considered it taboo, a new market emerged for their own music. Classical Pentecostals, Evangelicals, and Fundamentalists in particular saw the JP's hair, clothing, and music as an accommodation of the evils of hippiedom and according to them, the conversion experience was to include a conversion from the counterculture and its symbols. A young man standing in front of a microphone with a beard and long hair, singing hippie styled music on a guitar was an iconic and powerful symbol that embattled against symbols of the piano, organ, choir, and a music director leading hymns from behind a podium. In its day these symbols of the JP's subculture clashed with the symbols of established classical Pentecostal, Evangelical, and Fundamentalist churches and served to locate the JPM as a subculture with a very different identity.

The hair, fashion, Jesus newspapers, and art all faded along with the counterculture, but the Jesus Music and the outdoor Christian music festivals remain as one of the most enduring contributions to American Christianity. Although the music did locate the JPM as a unique religious subculture in its heyday, the tensions have lessened over time as churches have assimilated the JP symbols into their own identities. It could be said that it is more the exception than the norm to find a church or denomination that has not adopted the JP music symbols into their worship services.

Race and Age

Race and age can be combined to form a distinctly recognizable boundary marker, for which a few simple observations are necessary. First, race erects visible boundary markers that have inherited and inalienable qualities over which individuals have no choices. That is, most JP were born as white Americans and as such were reared in white American cultural norms. Consequently, much of the antagonistic drama that played out between the JP and classical Pentecostals and Fundamentalists was acted out within the theatre of White American Christianity. Race is a main reason why the JP's concerns were alien to African American, Latin American, and Asian American Christians and probably why the JP were not engaged in their political causes. The success of Pentecostal enculturation within the JPM lay behind its ability to engender a subcultural identity with Pentecostal spirituality and to spread within the white American culture. It is also a factor in why the JPM did not spread among these other communities and why there were few non-whites among the JP's ranks.

This observation is not intended to imply that the JP were racist against non-whites nor that they embattled against non-white cultures with a form of white Pentecostalism that was superior to Black Pentecostalism, as Iain MacRobert claims existed among early classical Pentecostals.[68] In fact, small numbers of people of other races counted themselves as part of the JPM. One African-American JP communard said, "It never occurred to me, my color . . . Jesus appeared to all. He died for me as he did for white people."[69] It is simply to draw attention to the self-limiting nature of the JPM and that the affects were primarily within white American Pentecostalism and white American Christianity.

Second, the age of the JP must always be kept in mind when discussing their subcultural identity. The JP were self-conscious of their age, they

68. MacRobert, *Black Roots*, 95.
69. Ward, *Far-out Saints*, 84.

valued their generation and its new identity, and they exploited concepts like the "generation gap" through expressions like "trust no one over thirty." The fashion, hair, music, art, and also Pentecostalism were unique qualities in the identity of the younger generation that found their meaning, in part, from being set in tension against the older generation. The empowering nature and imaginative space within Pentecostalism appealed to the restlessness of the 1960s and 1970s counterculture generation and they embraced it as their own. Evidence shows that the churches famously tagged as "JP churches" were most often comprised of all ages and that those over 30 worshiped harmoniously alongside the young JP. However, in the "JP churches," it was the JP subcultural identity that shaped the ethos and it was the older generation that had to choose to either get on board with the JP or to move elsewhere and identify with the older generation.

The JPM was not a collective of church sponsored youth meetings for bored second and third generation Pentecostal youth led by denominationally trained Pentecostal youth leaders. During the movement's early years and heyday it was the young people themselves who globalized their subcultural identity. They embattled it through the urban centers and the countryside, not seeking permission from anyone to use guitars and drums, speak in tongues, preach on the streets, baptize in the ocean, or to nomadically wander from commune to café to church. As one minister said, "It's the greatest awakening in the history of the church, . . . and it's kids. Kids are leading it."[70] Consequently the JP subcultural identity found common appeal to the under thirties irrespective of their denominational affiliation or the differences in the Pentecostal belief and praxis. The JP located themselves as a youth movement of Pentecostalism and arguably perhaps one of the largest that America has ever seen. It is now forty years since the heyday of the movement and JP, aged between fifty-five and seventy-five years old, can still be found serving behind the scenes or as leaders in ministries and missionary organizations around the world. The young age of the JP has given the aftermath longevity and contributed to the continuity of some of the JP's subcultural identity into the beginning of the twentieth century.

Conclusion

It is necessary to draw this discussion to a close with a few concluding comments regarding the JP's subculture and its sociological location. First, the JPM should be located as a subculture that is part of but unique within the family of movements that constitute American Pentecostalism. By

---

70. Vachon, "Jesus Movement." 21.

jettisoning the assumptions that undergirded many sociological works of the seventies, it can be seen that the JP were architects of a unique subculture who with rational intentionality, constructed and differentiated their subcultural identity as one which was comparatively better than their near outgroups. While sharing family resemblances with American Pentecostalism they also differentiated themselves from it sociologically by the moral identities they borrowed from hippiedom. And all this embattlement occurred both within and outside of established churches.

Second, by unfettering the JPM from its previously assumed association with and location in American Fundamentalism, it can be differentiated from that of American Fundamentalism in two ways. First, the notion that the JP were Fundamentalists is impossible to support when the evidence of testimonies shows that the JP never claimed to be Fundamentalists and that self-identified Fundamentalists intentionally disassociated themselves from the JPM. And although it may be true that Fundamentalists shared certain moral identities with the JP, like sexual and gender identity, it must also be noted that these moral identities did not originate within American Fundamentalism and neither are they unique to American Fundamentalism. Thus it is rather far stretched to maintain that certain JP moral identities that aligned with the majority American cultural values were derived from the Fundamentalists of the 1920s. The most pronounced area of tension between the Fundamentalists and JP moral identity centered on the JP's view of church, their Pentecostalism, and their identity of Jesus as a revolutionary. These areas of tension are an important key that clarifies how the JP distinguished themselves from Fundamentalism as a separate religious phenomenon. The JP's symbolic boundaries allow their nearer outgroups of Pentecostalism, and hippiedom to come to the fore and Fundamentalism to be seen as a more remote and distant outgroup.

In addition, the JP's posture of embattlement against pluralistic modernity sets them apart from American Fundamentalists, who, according to Christian Smith choose a posture of withdraw into an enclave. And the posture of embattlement helps explain why the JPM flourished as a subculture and why Fundamentalists continued to decline. While it is not the entire pursuit of this chapter to understand the JPM's relationship with Fundamentalism, untangling the two subcultures leads to the chapter's central question of locating the JPM. In a sociological analysis, it can be concluded that the JP were not Fundamentalists, but were a flourishing collection of hybrid communities most broadly associated with their nearer outgroups of hippiedom and Pentecostalism.

Third, the construction, maintenance, and globalization of the JP subcultural identity relied upon the ongoing maintenance of tension with their outgroups. This means the JP were dependent upon their nearest outgroups as hosts from which they borrowed values and reinvented them as their own, ingroup, moral identities. Yet paradoxically, while they embattled against their outgroups, they also needed their outgroups to survive, as their own subcultural identity derived its significance as something contrasted against and in tension with their outgroups. Without this tension their subcultural identity diminished in meaning and either needed to be redefined or simply could not exist.

It is for this reason that the JPM as a large, visible religious movement disappeared together with hippiedom at the end of the seventies. The ending of hippiedom and the counterculture meant the end of one the JP's primary outgroups and, consequently, the loss of an identity that was set in contrast to hippiedom. With hippiedom dying, the JP's contrasting identity also diminished. As the years passed, the lessening tension meant the JP's subcultural identity became less unique and alternative and facilitated their assimilation into American Christianity. It is also due to the lack of tension that the JPM struggled to thrive outside the United States. That is, as the JP attempted to globalize their subculture transnationally they sought to embed in societies where the outgroups were very dissimilar to those from which they had originally derived their identity in America. With the exception of Canada and some exceptions in Scandinavia, the United Kingdom, Australia, and New Zealand, the subcultural identity of the JP had limited purchase abroad and perhaps appeared to be little more than a novel American anomaly.

As the JP settled into their denominational churches or migrated into American Pentecostalism and Evangelicalism, with their unique identity in hippiedom reduced to a less meaningful state, they were able to transition with less tension into these other religious subcultures in America. While their similarities with Pentecostalism and Evangelicalism had in part legitimized the mainstream JPM by the end of the seventies, the loss of the hippie identity that had differentiated the JP from Pentecostalism also enabled them a smoother transition into Pentecostalism. The unique ethos of the JPM remained strongest in the new church movements and in the music.

However, legitimization among established Evangelicals, Pentecostals, or Charismatics is not the only consideration at hand. Since the JP subcultural identity was infused into these other branches of American Christianity, it could be said that the JPM assisted them in making a transition into a post-1960s America. The fact that the tension had reduced and the uniqueness of their subcultural identity had lessoned is also an indication of the degree to which many churches and denominations had adopted the JP's subcultural identity. The JP in this way assisted many other churches in American Christianity to make a successful transition through the counterculture and into a post-1960s America.

Chapter 5

A Theological Identity

The Need for a Theological Assessment

NOT A FEW PEOPLE have scoffed at the notion of the JP having a coherent theology. While it is true that they did not articulate their beliefs in writing, it is rather simplistic to equate their lack of spoken or written theological precision with poor theology. In fact, Walter Hollenweger noted a common pattern within Pentecostalism that is also observable in the JPM. He said that Pentecostals are "strong on experience of the Spirit, on pneumapraxis, but they are weak on the interpretation of their experiences."[1] The catchphrases of Jim Durkin, "Practice the Word," and John Wimber, "Do the stuff," are indicative of this characteristic of Pentecostalism noted by Hollenweger. It is an act now and reflect later orientation that makes praxis take chronological and axiological precedence over theological reflection and articulation. This Pentecostal tendency of praxis over articulation means that while the theologies and theopraxes of individual JP and of JP churches have morphed and crystallized over time, they have by and large remained unarticulated. For example, instead of releasing a detailed doctrinal statement, Potter's House Christian Fellowship directs people to the main ICFG theological text, *Foundations of Pentecostal Theology* (1983), as a thorough explanation of their beliefs. The praxis orientation means the JP's beliefs are best understood by deducing conclusions from the words of their testimony, the actions of their practice, and the statements of church beliefs.

Before venturing into their theology, however, it is critical to point out how little reflection has been offered on their beliefs. Beyond the many small works that offered passing, anecdotal comments, there has yet to emerge a substantive treatise that discusses the JP's theology. Neither has there arisen

---

1. Hollenweger, *Pentecostalism*, 218.

a notable JP theologian or even a JP who has written extensively about the theology of their movement; this perhaps further evidence of their rather blasé attitude toward theological articulation. An early attempt was made by Frederick Wagner, whose DMin sought a "A Theological and Historical Assessment." Yet on closer examination, the thesis was primarily an early historical account with little theological content. John Rodman Williams founded and taught at the Melodyland School of Theology from 1972–1982 and admitted there was a large influx of JP into the school during these years.[2] But disappointingly, he never discussed their theology and did not incorporate them into his *Renewal Theology*. Williams' disinterest in their theology mirrors the general Pentecostal and Charismatic disinterest in the JP's history. Stephen Hunt described the JP's theology as "paltry," comparing it to the same content of pre-routinized classical Pentecostalism, and Enroth claimed it was "simple and doctrinally unsophisticated."[3] These opinions typify that of many who rendered the JP's theology as nugatory, thus worthy of little regard.

James Richardson and his colleagues produced several works that touched on theological concepts couched in sociological language. While these lend themselves to this discussion, this chapter makes a departure from sociological argot like routinization, cult/sect/church, and conversion models in order to indulge more in theological conversation. Thus, without a major theological work to use as a dialogue partner, this chapter is attempting a very focused twofold aim of description and location of the JP's commonly shared charismatic expression. The description is of the mainstream theology and theopraxis of the JPM, not only in its heyday, but also as it has continued into the present day, especially through the agency of new church structures. Second, the descriptive assessment of the JP's belief and praxis is intended to confirm that, based on theological resemblance, the JPM should be located within American Pentecostalism.

As in the historical and sociological chapters, the heterogeneity and the sheer breadth of the phenomenon weaken the generalizations that are made. At times, some may wish the conversation to plunge further in where is it only wading knee deep, while others may want more thought given to the interplay of the JP's theology with concurrent emergent theologies on the environment, gender, and transcendental meditation. In addition the descriptive nature of this chapter lacks the critical engagement or corrective suggestions that others may desire. This should not be mistaken as support for the beliefs and practices of the JP, but rather as an effort to stay on task

2. J. Williams, "Preface—A Theological Pilgrimage."
3. S. Hunt, "Were the Jesus People," 2; Enroth et al., *Story*, 163.

with the aim of locating their theology in American Pentecostalism. So this assessment does not pretend to be exhaustive and incontrovertible, yet it will hopefully propose a way forward with which others may wish to engage.

Admittedly however, a banal description and location of the JP's theology would seem insufficient without also addressing the implications of their theology and theopraxis on American Pentecostalism. So, it is proposed and argued in this chapter that the JP's beliefs and practices negotiated greater flexibility within American Pentecostalism's theology and theopraxis and that this flexibility has been primarily, but not exclusively, preserved through the ecclesiological structures that emerged from the movement's heyday. To demonstrate this, five premises are forwarded that lead the discussion from broad classifications to more narrowly focused descriptions of the JP's theology that ends with comments on eight ecclesiological organizations. This is a historically informed theological analysis and as such relies on evidence from statements in interviews, as well as other source material like books, and denominational, doctrinal statements to argue its theory. It is intended to capture and, in a fair and balanced way, represent the beliefs and experiences of the elites as well as those of the common JP and their communities.

Premise One—The Hallmarks of Evangelicalism

Premise One: The JP did have a theological system and its major tenets were borrowed from, guided by, and built upon the essential hallmarks of American Evangelicalism. David Bebbington condenses the hallmarks of Evangelicalism throughout the English-speaking world into four tenants: crucicentrism, conversion, biblicism, and activism.[4] He elaborates further stating that these are, "the typical emphasis of the atoning work of Christ on the cross, the need for personal faith through conversion, the supreme value of the Bible, and the binding obligation of mission."[5] This first premise is intended to provide a simple classification of the majority portion of the JPM. In fact, putting together the childhood religion of the JP and the types of churches that the JPM permeated, it is necessary to recognize the overlap between Evangelicalism and other branches of American Christianity. For example, there were strong currents of the JPM flowing within Catholic and mainstream Protestant churches and there were JP communities like the COG and the MCC, all of which shared major tenants of Evangelicalism, but also subscribed to beliefs and practices that fall outside the boundaries of mainstream American Evangelicalism.

4. Bebbington, *Dominance of Evangelicalism,* 19–48.
5. Ibid., 21.

In addition, there were considerable numbers of JP from non-Evangelical family backgrounds who were assumedly relying upon, to some degree, the theologies from their childhood upbringing. For example, in Mauss and Peterson's study, they reported that 61 percent were from Protestant homes and 19 percent were from Catholic homes. The remainder fell into Jewish and non-religious.[6] This led them to compare the JP to the prodigal son of Luke 15 who had not converted, but had returned home to his childhood religion. Among the SYRC participants Richardson, et al., recorded: 46.7 percent were from Protestant, 26 percent from Catholic, 1 percent from Jewish, and 17 percent from non-religious families.[7] Of those interviewed for this research, 50 percent were from Protestant, 17 percent from classical Pentecostal, 8 percent from Catholic, 4 percent from Jewish, and 21 percent from non-religious homes. These statistics demonstrate that Gerlach and Hine's observation that "most converts to Pentecostalism are drawn from the ranks of nominal Christians" also holds true with the JPM.[8]

This also concurs with quite a few testimonies, as one JP from a Catholic background stated, "One day I was hitchhiking and a guy picked me up and said he'd like to share the gospel with me. He was talking about stuff I had heard all my life but this time it really blew my mind."[9] Hence, growing up as a Catholic he was familiar with the message presented to him, and at this point in time he seemed to have a personal epiphany over his childhood beliefs. Therefore, stating that the mainstream JPM can be located within the boundaries of American Evangelicalism is not suggesting that all the JP could be exclusively and neatly fit into the American Evangelical paradigm. The boundary lines on several fronts were too indistinct to make such a notion plausible. While Catholicism, Protestantism, and independent churches of all sorts can be differentiated, there are elements of Evangelicalism to be found among all that also permitted JP a level of transience.

Before differentiating between Evangelicalism and Pentecostalism, it is also important to point that the essential hallmarks of Evangelicalism create a strong bond of unity between American Pentecostalism and American Evangelicalism. Like Catholic and Protestant churches, there were JP to be found among the ranks of classical Pentecostal and Conservative Evangelical churches. As such, locating the mainstream theology of the JP under this main Evangelical rubric accommodates both its charismatic and non-charismatic strands. The JP's beliefs were significantly informed by

6. Mauss and Peterson, "Les 'Jesus Freaks,'" 298.

7. Richardson et al., *Organized*, 182.

8. Gerlach and Hine, "Five Factors," 34.

9. Vachon, *Time to Be Born*, 20.

their older leaders, many of whom were not only theologically trained in Evangelicalism and Pentecostalism, but also spent untold hours in face to face contact with the young people they mentored. This means that many JP were not only explicitly taught beliefs but they observed and mimicked the practices of their leaders. This imitative nature of ministry praxis can be seen in Lonnie Frisbee, for example, who not only admired Kathryn Kuhlman, but also appeared on her *I Believe in Miracles* program and borrowed elements of her praxis. Many JP and JP leaders openly admitted their admiration of Pentecostal and Evangelical leaders as John Wimber did of George Ladd, Mario Murillo of Aimee Semple McPherson, and Scott Ross of Pat Robertson. With major Evangelical leaders like Billy Graham (*Jesus Generation*) warming to JP and affirming their beliefs, it adds to the case that their beliefs could be located in this camp.

Indeed, many JP were not from Evangelical or Pentecostal homes, many were not well versed in denominational doctrinal statements, and, given their young age, even those from Pentecostal and Evangelical families still had much to work out in their own personal theologies. However, their broad doctrinal synthesis of American Christianity and especially Evangelicalism took hold quickly throughout the entire movement and could be seen operating in several ways. First, it can be seen guiding the JP to identify groups like The Way International as Evangelically heterodox and enabled them to filter these groups out of the mainstream. In 1967, for example, Lonnie Frisbee, Ted Wise, and Kent Philpott all debated with Way International leader Victor Wierwille and rejected his non-Trinitarian views. Second, it informed their belief in the necessity of individual metanoia, or repentance from, other religions and the sexual lifestyles of the hippies and consequently pushed groups like MCC and the COG to the margins of the JPM. Third, as for theological discussion, it precludes regression into the triunity of God or the hypostatic union as these types of confessions were never explicit in their testimony and are assumed to be latently underpinning their Evangelical, theological framework.

Finally, it also facilitates a conversation on certain theological themes that nestle comfortably within both Pentecostalism and Evangelicalism. To illustrate only one such possible discussion, an abundance of statements in source materials confirm a Christological belief in the immanent Christ who incarnated himself among and identified himself with the hippies and the JP. This immanent Christological motif could be acutely contrasted with the former view of many JP, which saw the transcendent god or gods of their hippie journey as those that the devotees were ever approaching and never finding. They were always contemplating, but never fully knowing these gods and their amorphous visage was seen only while on psychedelic trips, but not in the real world when sober. Contrasted to this, many JP claimed that Jesus Christ had appeared to them personally, touched them, and healed them. The JP never questioned the divinity of Jesus Christ. But they did emphasize his nearness and his humanity as someone who could be known and who understood them. Jesus' poverty and identification with the down trodden was also stressed, as one JP stated, "Jesus never became rich in this world's goods . . . THE SON OF GOD put on humanity that sons of men might put on divinity."[10]

In addition, the JP's One Way sign underscored an unmistakably christocentric belief in solus-Christos as the via salutis, all of which could be elaborated upon in conventional Evangelical, theological language. Since, the christocentric core in the JPM was also a non-negotiable and central motif in both Evangelicalism and Pentecostalism, it facilitated high levels of cooperation between the two camps and permitted many JP to be found among the ranks of both. Christology was so central in the JPM that Richardson and Ellwood felt the movement had a lopsided Jesus-centric belief system.[11] While their fear is unwarranted, the JP's Christology serves to underscores how Bebbington's theory on Evangelicalism could be applied to the JPM. Other categories of JP belief and praxis could be discussed, in a similar way, under Bebbington's core Evangelical beliefs of the cross of Christ, the Bible, conversion, and missions to reaffirm their location under this broad doctrinal umbrella. The primary implication of the premise is that the JP's theology was neither trivial, nor an attempt to challenge and redefine the core of Evangelicalism, but it was instead hosted upon and operational within this theological core.

Premise Two—The Hallmarks of Pentecostalism

Premise Two: The JP's beliefs and practices can be differentiated from conservative Evangelicalism and Fundamentalism and located within Pentecostalism. Scholars often debate what constitutes a Pentecostal or a charismatic theology. For example, Veli-Matti Kärkkäinen rightly raises the question "is it really the case that the Spirit is the 'first theology' for Pentecostals?"[12] Certainly, Pentecostalism cannot be reduced to the BHS and glossolalia, yet these are often the first identifiable qualities of Pentecostal spirituality and offer a starting point for discussion. As Allan Anderson has said, it is not merely the belief in the BHS and the gifts of the Spirit that makes a church,

10. "Shepherds Inn Canton Ohio Jesus People."

11. Richardson, "New Religious," 398; and Ellwood, *One Way*, 80.

12. Kärkkäinen, "Pneumatologies," 223–24.

a movement, or a person Pentecostal or charismatic. It is the emphasis upon these qualities that does so.[13] This section categorizes and discusses five hallmarks of the JP's Pentecostal spirituality. It is not suggested that all JP shared a homogenous perspective of the gifts of the Holy Spirit or that this is an exhaustive list of the only qualities of Pentecostal spirituality present in the JPM. Rather, these hallmark beliefs and practices best facilitate a discussion into what makes the JP's theology Pentecostal. While operating broadly within the arena of Evangelicalism and Pentecostalism it is these doctrines, explicit in the JP's testimony and praxis, that make it possible to differentiate them theologically from conservative Evangelicalism and Fundamentalism and to locate them in Pentecostalism.

The Baptism of The Holy Spirit and Tongues

As previously stated, high percentages of JP not only claimed to have experienced the BHS and tongues, but they were also highly cherished as valued blessings. Not all within Evangelicalism shared the JP's appreciation for the BHS and tongues, however, and as their ranks spread among established denominations it was inevitable that the tension over charismatic praxis would intensify and for boundary lines to be erected. By far, Fundamentalists offered the most acrimonious resistance to the JP's Pentecostalism.[14]

With the JP permeating and affecting the SBC's structures (Reid, "Impact"), it was inevitable that their Pentecostalism would create controversy. Albert Schenkel observed that while the CR presented a "threat" to the SBC, they maintained an "irenic tone" up to the mid-seventies, after which point they adopted a more aggressive mood in their publications.[15] In 1974, for example, the Dallas Association of Southern Baptists called for member churches to either "desist" from charismatic practices or "voluntarily withdraw" from the association.[16] At the center of this controversy was Beverly Hills Baptist Church; a church that not only promoted the practice of Pentecostalism, but that had participated in the JPM and experienced transformation and growth from the JPM. The call to desist or voluntarily withdraw, was indicative of what would become the SBC's firm strategy of non-accommodation that forbade the public praxis of tongues when the church was gathered. It addressed the theopraxis of Pentecostalism within

13. A. Anderson, *Introduction*, 11.

14. See Bob Jones (*Is Jesus a Revolutionary?*); Bob Jones III (*Look Again*); Walter ("*Jesus Movement*").

15. Schenkel, "New Wine," 158–60.

16. "Baptist Ask Charismatics to 'Desist or Withdraw,'" 24.

the context of ecclesiology as something disruptive to SBC koinonia, and as such, sufficient to warrant its prohibition. Sammy Tippit and Kent Philpott both acknowledged this SBC posture towards the charismatic practices in the JPM. While Schenkel states that the SBC remained "flexible enough to retain large numbers of charismatic believers," they also managed to drive others away with the firm establishment of boundaries.[17] Although the SBC participated in the JPM and benefited from it, they distanced themselves from the charismatic practices in it. In the end, Beverly Hills Baptist Church did withdraw from the Dallas Association of the SBC.

Missionary organizations like IVCF, Operation Mobilization (OM), and CCC were affected by the JPM; mostly through missionary recruits who were drawn from a broad cross section of Evangelicalism and Pentecostalism. Of these three, CCC had the greatest interplay with the movement and is also the most self confessed non-charismatic. The use of glossolalia became enough of an issue for CCC that they responded with specific barricading measures to impede the practice of Pentecostal spirituality in their outreaches. The following *CT* article illustrates the barricading measures of CCC and the tension they experienced over Pentecostalism during Explo '72, an event that they organized. It states, "Pentecostals . . . took leadership roles with the understanding that they would not promote speaking in tongues, but some groups at Tent City held charismatic meetings, and Army General Ralph Haines spoke warmly of the 'baptism of the Spirit' in testimonies at the Cotton Bowl and in a military seminar.[18]"

During the 1970s as recruits entered CCC from the JPM, internal organization policies were also adjusted to specifically address public glossolalic practice. The changes were not expressed in vociferous language or argued on theological grounds. There was not, for the most part, this kind of strong animosity. In fact there was great cooperation. They permitted charismatic JP to join the organization, but simply forbade the public practice of Pentecostalism.[19] In a CCC Staff Personnel Handbook, a section titled "Charismatic and Other Controversial Doctrines" states, "Any staff member who feels that he has the gift of tongues is to refrain from any public use of the gift of tongues, from the emphasis of and promotion of the public and private use of that gift, and is to restrict any practice of tongues to private

17. Schenkel, "New Wine," 163.

18. Plowman, "Explo '72," 32.

19. According to CCC leadership, the policy changes related to the recruits coming from the JPM.

use in his individual and personal devotional life. Staff members are entrusted with this expectation, and any who violate this trust are to resign."[20]

These barricading and policing measures indicate that Pentecostal spirituality, especially the gift of tongues, was "controversial" enough to create a differentiation between charismatic and non-charismatic practice at the core of CCC's structure. Comparatively, YWAM also experienced growth from an influx of JP, but being a charismatic missionary organization, it accommodated the Pentecostalism of the JP without altering any internal policies. These two examples of the SBC and the CCC are meant to highlight the fact that not all in American Evangelicalism agree with Pentecostalism's core beliefs. Some JP may have readily conformed to these restrictions, but others did not. While these examples have only considered the practice of glossolalia, there were also the other core beliefs of Pentecostalism that differentiated the JP even further from Evangelicalism that will now also be examined.

Christophanies, Visions, and Prophecy

Not a few JP claimed to have had Christophanies and visions of Jesus, and these most often occurred while they were still hippies and under the influence of drugs. The experiences usually led to their subsequent conversion and new vocation as an evangelist or community leader. For example, Lonnie Frisbee, said that while he was naked and stoned on LSD in Tahquitz Canyon, the atmosphere in the canyon "tingled" and "lit up" and that "there was a light on me, that he was placing on my life. And it was Jesus Christ and that I was going to go bear the word of the Lord."[21] Oden Fong claimed that after an overdose of LSD, while he was slipping off into death, out of a frightful darkness Jesus appeared in front of him with a bright light emanating from his body.[22] According to Fong, His voice "sounded like many waters" and He said, "I am the Alpha and Omega the Beginning and the End."[23] An early JP group called The Fellowship of Freaks got its start after "Blake Steel and his sister Marge were smoking dope and meditating when they saw a vision of Jesus Christ."[24] And the Modesto Church in the Park reportedly began after "a young doper met Jesus Christ in a vision, not unlike St. Paul's,

20. "Campus Crusade for Christ International: US Staff Personnel Handbook," 42.

21. Di Sabatino, "Frisbee."

22. "Oden Fong interview," One-Way.org.

23. Ibid.

24. P. King, *Jesus People*, 6.

and became converted."[25] It seemed that these alleged occurrences were more frequent in the early years than in the later years of the movement. Newspaper articles and books are replete with such stories and many JP believed that LSD did open them up to a spiritual dimension that was just as dark and demonic as it was full of color and light. So frequent were these stories that David Wilkerson accused the JP intentionally and regularly taking drugs to enhance their Bible studies.[26] Evidence shows that such charges were baseless.

More frequent, and less dramatic, were the claims made by Carl Parks, Linda Meissner, Jim Durkin, Kent Philpott, and Chuck Smith that they heard the voice of God, but without an accompanying visual and sensory experience. In some cases the voice of God was indirectly mediated through a prophet or prophetess in a church meeting. Most of these occurred to ministers who were already Evangelical or Pentecostal and immediately preceded their involvement in the JPM. They interpreted these to be prophetic calls, in which God spoke to them directly about their personal destiny and commissioned them for the work they carried out in the JPM. In most cases the prophecy led them to a providential interpretation of the their involvement in the JPM; as fulfillment of the prophecy given by God himself.

While the examples of Christophanies, visions, and prophecy mentioned here most often constituted a decisive change of the direction of the person's life, there is also ample evidence of the JP relying on prophecy to direct a myriad of quotidian affairs. The directives included prophecies regarding who people should marry, where they should marry, where they should give birth, which property to purchase, where they should evangelize, and the names that should be given to ministries. It was not that the JP and their leaders merely discussed the theoretical plausibility of such experiences, they emphasized them as valid Christian experiences. They believed that these were viable means for God to directly reveal Himself, a practice that is commonly shared and emphasized in American Pentecostalism.

Demonic Exorcism

Demonic activity and exorcisms were reported to have been commonplace, however, it is a little difficult to actually find testimonies from individuals who describe what it is like to be delivered from demonic possession. Bil Gallatin's story offers a rare exception.[27] This is not to say that the JP did

25. Ibid., 7.

26. D. Wilkerson, *Purple*, 23, 42.

27. Smith and Brooke, "Harvest," 71–73.

not talk about the devil and demons or claim to have practiced witchcraft. In fact, Hiley Ward encountered so much rhetoric about the devil that he dedicated a chapter to "Links With the Occult," concluding that the "Jesus movement does have some strange similarities to the occult."[28] Mel Hatampa, for example, said that Satan stood next to him asking him to kill himself until the Holy Spirit filled the room with His presence and chased away Satan.[29] David Hoyt wrote about his conversion saying, "I was set free from an evil spirit that had kept me from the truth."[30] Kent Philpott stated that beginning from his work at the Anchor Mission in 1968, "without exaggeration, I would estimate that I have seen thousands of demons cast out of people, and the result was very good for the person involved."[31] There were numerous questionable testimonies like that of Mike Warnke's in which he claimed to have formerly been a high priest of Satan. An investigation by John Trott and Mike Hertenstein cast doubt on the truthfulness of his claims.[32] Whether real or rhetorical, the emphasis on satanic activity and deliverance from demonic spirits, is another characteristic of the JP that they share in common with American Pentecostalism.

Hermeneutics

Do Pentecostal and Charismatic Christians have a unique way of interpreting the text of the scripture? Amos Yong (*Spirit-Word-Community*) and Kenneth Archer (*Pentecostal Hermeneutic*) make a convincing case that they do. Assuming their claims present a distinguishable Pentecostal hermeneutic, then what about the JP, did their hermeneutical methodology resemble that outlined in Yong and Archer's work? It seems that it did. Before addressing the Pentecostal nature of the JP's hermeneutics, it is, first of all, important to clarify a presupposition about the text of scripture that seemed common among the JP and also among other branches of Christianity. This presupposition was that the JP embraced a high view of the Bible, considering it to be the inspired, the infallible, and perhaps the inerrant, written word of God. While it is difficult to prove this assertion from comments made in JP testimonies, they can be found explicitly written into the doctrinal statements of the many Protestant, Evangelical, and Pentecostal churches and para-church organizations that participated in the JPM. For this reason, it

28. Ward, *Far Out Saints*, 103.

29. P. King, *Jesus People*, 130–31.

30. Plowman, *Jesus Movement*, 50.

31. Philpott, "Jesus People Movement," 7.

32. Trott and Hertenstein, "Selling of Satan."

is not implausible to assume that these concepts also latently underpinned the JP's understanding of the Bible, albeit, for many, on a rhetorical level. For example, Balmer and Todd wrote, "The doctrine of inerrancy does not appear explicitly in Calvary's [Calvary Chapel's] brief statement of faith, but Rick Dedrick, one of Smith's associates, acknowledged that if one of the staff members denied biblical inerrancy, he would be called to account for his views."[33] A very simple and very limited survey conducted by Hiley Ward, indicated that the JP did not give a high priority to either biblical inerrancy or to the Bible as "propositional revelation from God."[34]

Some, like Harriet Harris, have demonstrated that the early twentieth-century, Fundamentalist movement championed the high view of scripture and that this belief can be traced into today's modern Evangelicalism.[35] Those inclined to a simple essentialism may argue from here that all those who have a high view of scripture, including the JP, are Fundamentalists. However, early twentieth-century Fundamentalists never had a seminal or exclusive claim to a high view of scripture as Kärkkäinen has pointed out; there is strong agreement between Roman Catholics and Pentecostals over inspiration and infallibility.[36] While inerrancy may be a unique feature of Fundamentalism, it is difficult to prove that the JP strongly embraced this concept. And, it would be unrealistic to reduce Catholicism, Fundamentalism, and Pentecostalism into a single movement due to their similar views of Scripture. Highlighting the JP's high view of scripture merely establishes a connection with other branches of Christianity based upon a similar view of scripture and does not indicate anything unique or Fundamentalist.

It was also frequently said that the JP interpreted the Bible literally. But rarely is there an attempt to explain what is meant by a literal interpretation of the Bible. This phrase is very ambiguous and was probably little more than borrowed rhetoric. The JP were avid Bible readers, many preferring the King James Version above others, and they seemed to frequently indulge in trifling and squabbles over the meanings of passages. However, it is not reasonable to identify their hermeneutical methodology as a literal interpretation without a lengthy discussion on this topic. Thus, as a starting point, it is assumed that the JP embraced a high view of the scripture and that this most likely included inspiration and infallibility. While these value-laden terms do not frequently appear in their own testimonies, it is also assumed

33. Balmer and Todd, "Calvary Chapel," 682.

34. Ward, *Far-out Saints*, 128.

35. Harris, *Fundamentalism*, 319.

36. Kärkkäinen, "Toward a Pneumatological," 25.

that they underpinned their understanding as they occasionally surfaced on a rhetorical level.

To understand what made their use of the text of scripture Pentecostal, it is time to turn to Yong and Archer and see what their models present. While they are not identical, and this is not the place for a discussion on the differences in their views, they both observe a similar method in Pentecostalism for interpreting the Bible; a non-hierarchical, non-sequential dialogical interplay between the Holy Spirit, the Word, and the Community in which the individual has embedded him/herself. Yong explains his theory this way, "My thesis in this volume is that method in theology begins with the Spirit which is always informed in some respect by Word and Community, and moves through, not necessarily in sequential order, the moment of the Word which is also never entirely bereft of either Spirit or Community, and the moment of Community which is also never entirely disconnected from Spirit and Word."[37] Archer summarizes his theory this way, "The hermeneutical strategy will be a narrative approach to interpretation that embraces a triadactic negotiation for meaning between the biblical text, Pentecostal community, and the Holy Spirit. Meaning is arrived at through the dialectical process based upon an interdependent dialogical relationship between Scripture, Spirit and community."[38]

While the Bible was significant among the JP, so was their community's interpretation, and the claimed experiences of the Holy Spirit. Claimed experiences with the Holy Spirit are integral to the narrative of Charismatic and Pentecostal Christians and they must be incorporated when considering their use of the Bible. However, incorporating the claimed experiences of the JP is not an attempt to prove or disprove their claims, but simply to make space for them alongside the community and the Bible in the emergent, hermeneutical narrative. And while spiritual experiences mattered to the individual JP, using the three-fold paradigm of Yong or Archer helps to avoid the temptation of positing the locus of epistemology too exclusively in human experience, by balancing it with the observable elements of the Word and the community. For although their individual experiences were epistemologically significant, testimony also reveals an oscillation between their personal experiences and what they believed to be unchanged truths as revealed in the text of scripture. So, on one hand the JP can be found laying claim to the exclusive nature of Salvation in Jesus Christ as a truth epistemologically rooted in the Bible, while on the other, they lay strong claim on their personal experience as the judge of what is truthful. For

37. Yong, *Spirit-Word-Community*, 220.

38. Archer, *Pentecostal Hermeneutic*, 5.

example, one JP stated, "All the other religions won't get you to Heaven. Salvation through Jesus Christ is the only way to Heaven."[39] This statement was accompanied by the recitation of John 14:6, demonstrating his belief in the Bible as epistemologically authoritative; "Jesus Christ said, 'No one comes to the Father except by me. I am the Way, the Truth and the Life.'"[40]

At the same time, the uniqueness of Jesus is equally appealed to on the grounds of his ability to prove his existence through individual experience. This surfaces in the typical JP expressions like "get high on Jesus" that present Jesus as someone who can provide a superior experience to drugs or other religions. Or as one JP stated, "So at that time at that night I asked Christ into my life. And I'll tell you it's been a joy ever since. He's given me everything I've always wanted. He's given me peace and joy and life and just everything. He's given me a way I could express myself. And he has shown me that he is the only Son of God."[41] From the basis of personal experience, an invitation was often made to others that was grounded in the understanding that the ultimate way for the listener to test the truthfulness of these claims was to try them for him/herself. For example one JP said, "We're not asking you to believe us. We're not asking you to believe God's Word . . . You give God an honest chance to bust into your heart, and I guarantee you, you will not be disappointed."[42] This normal oscillation demonstrates an epistemological reliance upon the Bible and individual experience in their hermeneutical methodology.

Alleged prophetic words abounded in the days of the JPM they were a normal part of community life. It is important to create a necessary space for considering the community's claims for prophecy as something inspired by the Holy Spirit and as a separate but connected element of the interpretive process. For example, the following testimony from Mike Messer's captures the role of the community in his prophecy. "The first time I gave a [prophetic] message I went to Carl with my heart pounding and some words inside me. He encouraged me to give it and let the rest judge as to whether it came from the Holy Spirit. Everyone bore witness and I continued to give what I had received."[43]

Kent Philpott's Church of the Open Door in San Rafael and GO regularly sought words of prophecy for direction in people's lives. Harry, for example, remembers a visiting speaker whose prophecy implied that he and

39. Ortega, *Jesus People*, 37.

40. Ibid., 36.

41. Cording and Hardenbrook, "Son Worshippers."

42. Ibid.

43. Mike Messer, email correspondence with author, August 24, 2011.

his wife would leave the community and serve as missionaries. The prophecy also aligned with Durkin's regular teaching from the Bible that world mission was central and mandatory for the whole church. Thus, the community confirmed that the prophecy was valid since it agreed with the text of scripture. Thus the prophecy was not active in isolation but was operational together with the Word and the community. Dreams and visions, like prophecies, were incorporated into the normative praxis of Harvest House in San Francisco, the afterglows at Calvary Chapel, the power evangelism of John Wimber, and the prophetic emphasis of the fivefold ministry that arose across much of the JPM by the mid seventies.[44] The Holy Spirit was thought to be the source of prophecies and also the one who inspired songs and, according to Ward, entire song books.[45]

With so much emphasis placed upon extra-biblical or para-biblical revelations, the notion of sola scriptura in their hermeneutics was undermined— or enhanced, dependent upon the perspective taken. The Bible's relationship was at times primary, at times supplementary, and at times subordinate to these types of experiences and revelations. In his lengthy tome, *Renewal Theology*, J. Rodman Williams categorized the revelation gifts of prophecies, dreams, visions, and tongues as "subordinate revelation," arguing that these types of revelation were "subordinate or secondary to the special revelation attested to in the scriptures."[46] Perhaps if questioned many JP would have theoretically agreed with Rodman's statement, but in praxis his notion of "subordinate revelation" would not hold true for many JP groups. A deeper probe in the subsequent sections into the use of revelation gifts in the JPM proves that even operating within Rodman's boundaries of subordinate revelation did not preclude serious and menacing ecclesiological tensions. The agreement on the high view of scripture or the rhetoric of literal Bible interpretation is where the similarity between the JP and conservative Evangelicals or the JP and Fundamentalists ends. The JP's high value for the Bible coupled with extra-biblical revelations differentiates their hermeneutical process from Fundamentalists and Evangelicals. Holding in tension the three elements of the community, the Spirit, and the Bible gives a more complete understanding of their use of the Bible and their overall interpretive method.

The JP also had a method of imitating and mimicking the text of the Bible that is perhaps best summarized in the words of Ted Wise, "a few of us agreed on one thing: that we ought to live out the Book of Acts like a

44. Enroth et al., *Story*, 218. Ward, *Far-out Saints*, 126; Balmer and Todd, "Calvary Chapel," 682; J. Wimber, *Power Evangelism*, 44.

45. Ward, *Far-out Saints*, 125.

46. J. Williams, *Renewal Theology*, 1:43–44.

script."[47] The early Christians in Acts 2:44–47 shared all things in common, broke bread in their homes, and went house to house to share the faith and the JP felt they should do the same. In Acts, the Holy Spirit was poured out, the people saw miracles, and they spoke in tongues; and the JP felt should see the same. The religious leaders rejected the early Christians and the JP believed they should expect the same treatment from leaders of established Christianity. In this way, the JP intentionally collapsed the historical and cultural distance between themselves and the text of scripture—a distance that is often sought and respected in other hermeneutical methods—and believed themselves to be imitatively living out the New Testament.

The JP also used the Bible as a prophetic text through which they expected God to speak to them and to direct them. For example, they believed God used specific scriptures to guide their choices of the names of their communities; as in the case of SYRC that came from the name Shiloh in Genesis 49:10, or the name Potter's House Christian Fellowship that came from Jeremiah 18:10.[48] In addition, the JP read the Bible with a filter through which Jesus was eisogetically imported into nearly every Bible story. Jesus could be found in a story from the life of Abraham in the book of Genesis, or in Proverbs, or in Jeremiah.[49] And there is plenty of evidence to suggest that it was a common practice for JP to couple the rhetoric of literal biblical interpretation with an allegorical view of the Bible. For example, Chuck Smith interprets the Churches of Revelation chapter 2 and 3 as figuratively representative of seven periods of church history. Or Dick Eastman, who believed Joel 3:13 was a prophecy about a harvest of salvation in the JPM, when the context may be more suggestive of a harvest as God's judgment.[50] Gordon Fee's comments could be readily applicable to the JP, "In place of scientific hermeneutics there developed a kind of pragmatic hermeneutics—obey what should be taken literally, spiritualize, allegorize, or devotionalize the rest."[51]

This brief examination has not been an attempt to argue for a unique JP hermeneutic within Pentecostalism. Rather, it has described a hermeneutical methodology that was not only centered in an understanding of the text, but that also oscillated between the community and what they claimed to be the Holy Spirit. It is suggested that this process aligns with Yong's and Archer's view of a Pentecostal Hermeneutic and thus shows a similar thematic resemblance

47. Cronn, "Jason Questions a Jesus Freak."

48. Maseko, "Potter's House," 126.

49. Ibid.

50. Chuck Smith, "Revelation 2, 3." Eastman, *Up with Jesus*, 40.

51. As cited in Hollenweger, *Pentecostalism*, 313.

between the JP's interpretive method and that found in Pentecostalism. Other segments of American Christianity may employ some of these same elements. But intentionally mixing extra-biblical or para-biblical revelation in the interpretive process does set the JP apart from non-charismatic groups that would consider this an affront to the authority of the Bible, the closing of the canon, and the principle of sola scriptura.

Eschatology, Missiology, and Pneumatology as a Triadic

Examining eschatology, pneumatology, and missiology as something uniquely Pentecostal is slightly problematic, mostly because these areas of theology did not emerge as unique expressions of Pentecostalism. For example, in the area of eschatology, while not all JP held the same eschatological views, most accounts concur that the predominant position of the JP was dispensational premillennialism; with pre-tribulational, mid-tribulational, and post-tribulational rapture varieties all being present.[52] Some JP communities were difficult to locate due to an unarticulated position while others, like GO, carried overtones of impending doom and may have leaned toward post-tribulationalism. Also, by the early eighties historical premillennialism began to arise as a popular eschatological variant mostly through the influence of the Vineyard Fellowships and John Wimber's appreciation for George Ladd. While presumably the vast majority of JP were premillennial and also dispensational, this does not indicate anything uniquely charismatic in their eschatology, as these perspectives were also shared by both charismatics and non-charismatics alike. The same could be said of the pneumatology, or missiology.

However, Allan Anderson has noted a unique and common triadic within Pentecostalism that brings together the BHS with missiology and eschatology.[53] Veli-Matti Kärkkäinen also observed this common feature stating, "Pentecostal-Charismatic Christians, however, have intuitively grasped something about the essence of mission, which, even if it is not articulated in theological terms, is theologically speaking extremely revealing about the integral relation between mission, Spirit, and eschatology."[54] Within Pentecostalism there is the strong feeling that the end is near and Jesus is coming soon. For this reason, the Holy Spirit has been poured out in the end times, just before Jesus' return, so that the church may be empowered with gifts to fulfill its mission of world evangelization. So, following Anderson's and

52. Enroth et al., *Story*, 179–90.
53. A. Anderson, *Introduction*, 217–18.
54. Kärkkäinen, *Toward a Pneumatological Theology*, 219.

Kärkkäinen's observations, these three areas of theology—missiology, pneu-matology, and eschatology —are not going to be examined in isolation as though there may be something that makes each one distinctly Pentecostal. Instead, the following paragraphs will demonstrate that this triadic of the imminence of Christ, missions, and Spirit empowerment were commonly wed together in the JPM and this common feature makes their theology Pentecostal and Charismatic.

To begin, the triadic can be heard in numerous testimonies of JP leaders and participants alike.[55] For example, Duane Pederson stated, "For the Jesus People Movement—this is just the beginning. I believe it is going to grow and spread, enveloping the entire world in the most tremendous outpouring of the Holy Spirit the world has ever known. It has already be-gun . . . and it will continue till He comes! Praise the Lord! Jesus is coming soon!"[56] One reporter summarized, "Many people in the movement . . . feel the world is in the middle of the last great revival and that Jesus will come soon to Earth to judge."[57] The Bible texts of Joel 2:28 and Acts 2:16,17 were commonly cited or alluded to as being fulfilled in the JPM. Chuck Smith said, "It is prophesied in the Bible that the Lord will pour the Spirit down upon all men, and I believe that is happening. And I believe that it won't be long until we see the Second Coming of the Lord."[58] For example, Ray Rempt saw the JPM as evidence of the imminence of the Second Coming of Jesus, saying, "There is no doubt about it. Take this Jesus Movement as one of your proofs."[59] He then cited Acts 2:17.

Not only did many explicitly make this connection between the JPM and the outpouring of the Spirit in Joel 2, Acts 2, but numerous JP leaders recognized their dependency upon the young people to fulfill the task of world missions and especially to reach other hippies with the gospel. Most JP leaders were acutely aware of the generation gap between themselves and the hippies and that they were personally unable to cross that divide. To ac-complish the goal of evangelism and mission, leaders often impressed upon the youth the value of the empowerment of the Holy Spirit as an experience of greater worth than theological training or higher education. This belief lay behind Wayman Mitchell's dislike for Bible colleges and preference of the local church for the place of leadership training and qualification. One JP

55. See Ward, *Far-out Saints*, 125; Ortega, *Jesus People*, 125, Enroth et al., *Story*, 179–83.

56. Owen, *Jesus Is Alive and Well*, 118–19.

57. Bisceglia, "'Jesus Movement' Attracts Following," 9.

58. Enroth et al., *Story*, 179–80.

59. Vachon, *Time to Be Born*, 135.

stated, "When I think of higher education, there is only one high education in my books, that is the Holy Word of God."[60] Or another believed, "All you need to know is the Bible. Why learn about anything else but the Bible?"[61]

Leaders often emphasized the Spirit's ability to empower the common, ordinary individual and the outcast. They also connected this teaching to the way many hippie youth saw themselves; that they were rejected outcasts of society. For example, Chuck Smith stated,

> [I]n raising up pastors to shepherd Calvary Chapel churches with thousands of members, God did not necessarily look for Phi Beta Kappas from Yale or Harvard. He did not look for magna cum laude graduates with impressive resumes. Instead, God chose people like a Mexican street fighter who had dropped out of high school, a hippie who had gone insane on drugs, a drug dealer who was into sorcery, and a motorcycle gang member to build His churches in the Calvary Chapel movement. God has used many such unlikely leaders to turn worn traditions upside down.[62]

His young protégés were, according to Smith, "men with varied, wild, and even Satanic backgrounds, with one thing in common. They were touched by the grace of God and now are being used to touch thousands of other lives."[63] To him they were "representative of the transforming work of the Spirit of God."[64] In the same way, Linda Meissner saw the Jesus People Army as a fulfillment of the prophecy of an army of kids that would be raised up to accomplish an evangelistic goal that she could not do by herself. As testified by Jim Palosaari, "Meissner's emphasis in the height of her ministry was on the empowerment of the Holy Spirit for young people and drug addicts."[65]

Irrespective of variations in eschatological perspectives, the single unifying feature in the eschatology of the JP was the imminence of the second advent of Jesus Christ. Nearly every person interviewed for this research admitted that they had felt an expectancy that Jesus could appear at any moment and consequently they felt an urgency to evangelize everyone. Most JP did not expect that they would grow old and die, but would instead be "raptured" away, as John Mehler commented, "Jesus was supposed to

60. Ortega, *Jesus People Speak Out*, 94.

61. Ibid., 93.

62. Smith and Brooke, "Harvest," foreword.

63. Ibid.

64. Ibid.

65. Jim Palosaari, interview with author, March 24, 2009.

come years ago. Jesus is still coming."[66] In 1972, Ruben Ortega recorded the following responses to his question, "Do you think Jesus is coming again soon?"[67] Neil from Detroit said, "Very soon, probably, I see the year 1971 just about right."[68] Ken from Spokane said, "Within thirty years."[69] Gary from San Francisco said, "I feel He'll be here within 2 to 20 years. He could come tomorrow but it might be 20 years."[70] The lyrics of Larry Normans' song "I Wish We'd All Been Ready," became an anthem among the JP and conveyed the meaning that those who were not converted would, in a very short time, be tragically left behind on earth when Jesus returned.

The formation of Israel as a nation in 1948 heightened the belief in the imminent return of Christ. This event was interpreted by some as the sign of the fig tree recorded in Matthew 24 and that within a "generation," or forty years, Jesus would set his feet on Mount Zion. Consequently, the rhetoric of "this generation" caught on and could be heard in many accounts and testimonies. Duane Pederson cited Matthew 24:33–34, the sign of the fig tree, as being fulfilled in his generation, as did Hal Lindsey's *LGPE*.[71] It was reported about Hal Lindsey, "His talk was apocalyptic, and the kids went wild when he thundered, 'Christ is coming in this generation.'"[72] One JP said, "I believe Christ will return in this generation."[73] Based on the notion of "this generation," Chuck Smith came very close to setting a date for Jesus' return writing,

> We're the generation that saw the fig tree bud forth as Israel be-
> came a nation again in 1948. As a rule, a generation in the Bible
> lasts 40 years. The children of Israel journeyed in the wilderness
> for 40 years until that generation died. Forty years after 1948
> would bring us to 1988 . . . From my understanding of biblical
> prophecies, I'm convinced that the Lord is coming for His Church
> before the end of 1981. I could be wrong, but it's a deep conviction
> in my heart, and all my plans are predicated upon that belief.[74]

The date was determined from simple mathematical calculation: 1948 (the year Israel became a nation) + 40 (a generation) = 1988–7 (the Tribulation) =

66. John Mehler, email correspondence with author, December 6, 2008.

67. Ortega, *Jesus People Speak Out*, 124.

68. Ibid., 125.

69. Ibid.

70. Ibid.,126.

71. Owen, *Jesus Is Alive and Well*, 120. Lindsey, *Late Great Planet Earth*, 42–58.

72. Bastien, "Hollywood Boulevard," 40.

73. Ortega, *Jesus People Speak Out*, 126.

74. Chuck Smith, *End Times Report*, 17, 20.

1981. Now that so many years have passed, Smith's personal belief that Jesus would return in 1981 may seem extreme. But it reveals how the profoundly convinced the participants in the JPM were in the imminent return of Christ.

The belief in Jesus' imminent return was also accompanied by the overtones of impending doom common in dispensational premillennialism and resulted in the JP's view of the future being labeled pessimistic and negative. The ominous sense of foreboding hung so heavily over some communities that their antics and hateful messages appear, in retrospect, rather humorous. Enroth told how the COG once invaded and disrupted an unsuspecting church meeting and frightened those in attendance by shouting judgments against the established church and by thumping people on the heads with their Bibles.[75] One doomsday, "prophet," legendary in the forests of Northern California, was David Leon. Of him, Peter Michelmore wrote, "David Leon, who went about scaring people out of their wits with booming biblical language and horrendous prophecies. Christians have been known to flee from Leon, even the Children of God find him overpowering, and what torments he had put into the spongy hippie minds can only be imagined."[76]

The belief that the end was at hand affected their view of the world around them. Thus, established educational, religious, and political institutions carried little functional or intrinsic value; a disposition not only informed by Pentecostal Spirituality, but also by dispensationalism and hippiedom. However, to say that their eschatological views only produced pessimism is to understand only half of their disposition. The doomsday message sounded optimistic to the JP who preached it. To them, it meant the future eschaton was at hand; and this was far more desirable, peaceful, and beautiful than the present, trouble filled world. Also like hippiedom, the JP's harsh pessimism and dissent were directed toward the people and structures of this present world but their interpretation of their own movement was very optimistic. Allan Anderson made an astute observation about the paradox of pessimism and optimism in Pentecostalism when he said, "But this premillennialism was not entirely pessimistic, for there was a certain tension between the negative view of the world and the very positive view of their place in it."[77] To the JP, their movement was the place of blessing in which God had poured out his Spirit on dry ground, a harvest just before the end; and to them, this was very positive.

The pessimistic/optimistic paradox can also be heard in Jim Durkin's prophecy in which he claimed God said, "Very shortly there is coming to

75. Enroth et al., *Story*, 34.

76. Michelmore, *Back to Jesus*, 71.

77. A. Anderson, *Spreading Fires*, 220.

the earth a major worldwide economic collapse, and a world-engulfing war. In its scope and severity this coming crisis will be greater than anything in modern world history."[78] He admitted that there was horror in the prophetic words, but believed the consequence to be positive, stating, "those who have prepared themselves, this will be the greatest day for the gospel of Jesus Christ."[79] His instructions for preparation included advice on living debt free, investing cautiously, and having a personal food storage program— that is, how to store enough wheat, honey, and water for each member of a family for one year. His preparations also included a strong appeal for Christians to maintain links with other Christians and to bring the gospel to all nations.

Some, upon hearing the news that their phenomenon was spreading globally, seemed to feel confirmed that their religious movement played a positive role, that it was divinely inspired, and beneficial to the world. As one newspaper article stated, "An army of long-haired 'freaks' is on the march to conquer the world—with Bibles."[80] Or as Pat King wrote, "If the Jesus People aren't in your city they'll be along shortly. (You could invite them if you want to speed things up.) . . . Their impact will be felt and lives will be changed. Pushers will lose business and Bible sales will rise."[81]

There were two primary vehicles responsible for conveying premillennialism to the JP: churches—mostly classical Pentecostal churches and the new JP churches—and Hal Lindsey's book *LGPE*. First, many of the classical Pentecostal churches, especially the AG and the ICFG, had their fingerprints all over the movement from its earliest days and their high level of involvement in the JPM also meant that they informed the JP's eschatology. Both the AG and ICFG explicitly state in their denominational doctrinal statements that their eschatological positions are premillennial and both align with dispensationalism. However, the AG reject dispensational's cessationist teachings on spiritual gifts and so do the ICFG, and the other JP churches.[82] Both Hope Chapel and PHCF align with ICFG doctrines and Calvary Chapel has also maintained a strong commitment to a premillennial, pre-tribulational rapture; Smith's eschatological views spread via his widely distributed teachings on cassette tapes. Admittedly, the JP churches would have been of lesser influence in the earlier days than the AG and ICFG, but as the years pro-

78. Durkin, *Coming World Crisis*, 4.

79. Ibid., 7.

80. Gessell, "Bible-Carrying 'Freaks,'" 16.

81. P. King, *Jesus People*, 139.

82. Poloma, "Charisma and Structure," 13; "Assemblies of God, "Core Doctrines"; and Foursquare Church, "Declaration of Faith."

gressed they served as vehicles to maintain and enhance the eschatological views already infused from classical Pentecostal churches.

Second, through his book *LGPE*, Hal Lindsey took up the mantle of C.I. Scofield and the *Scofield Reference Bible* by becoming a primary vehicle for informing dispensational premillennialism in the 1970s. The same way that the *Scofield Reference Bible* influenced classical Pentecostals earlier in the twentieth century, the *LGPE* solidified dispensational premillennialism among the JP in the 1970s.[83] In the *LGPE* Lindsey re-envisioned an apocalyptic form of dispensationalism from the books of Ezekiel, Daniel, and Revelation that animated the current events of Israel's nationhood, the Six Day War, and the other "signs of the times" with prophetic meaning. It would not be wise to assume that all JP adhered to everything in *LGPE*, but given that it was one of the most widely read book among the JP, and one of the best selling non-fiction books of the 1970s, few have doubted its influence. In fact, the book is probably responsible for influencing similarly themed films and books beginning with "A Thief in the Night" (1972) and running through Tim Lahaye and Jerry Jenkins' *Left Behind* book series published from 1995–2007. Yet amazingly, while Lindsey animated the dispensational imagination of the JP, he shunned their Pentecostalism and did not share their motivation for mission in his commune called The Light and Power House; as Enroth records, "The Light and Power House further distinguishes itself from the more fanatical segments of the Jesus Movement by denying that the presumed nearness of the second coming is a call for Christians, all of them, to fling themselves into fulltime personal evangelism."[84]

Further, Lindsey's position can be contrasted to that of the AG, ICFG, PHCF, and Calvary Chapel, all of which explicitly connect eschatology to the BHS and missions.[85] So, while not all JP beliefs were so easily categorized as premillennial dispensational, these were arguably the dominant eschatological views. And while some non-charismatics shared the dispensational belief embraced by many JP, these premillennial and dispensational views were not held in isolation. Rather, the JP wed together their eschatology, pneumatology, and missiology in a way distinctly different to others who may share points of commonality with their eschatology or missiology. There was in the JPM an inseparable, triadic belief that the Spirit had been poured out upon them in the end times to accomplish the role of bringing a worldwide harvest for the gospel. And this is a common distinctive within Pentecostalism.

---

83. G. King, "Disfellowshiped," 131–35, 140–42.

84. Enroth et al., *Story*, 138.

85. Chuck Smith, *Calvary Chapel Distinctives*, 17, 33.

Other areas of theology could also be examined to argue the point that the JP's theology was Pentecostal and Charismatic But these five—the BHS and tongues; christophanies, visions, and prophecy; demonic exorcism; hermeneutics; and the eschatological, missiological, and pneumatological triadic have been forwarded as evidence to support the premise that the JP's theology could be differentiated from non-charismatic families of theology and located in Pentecostalism.

Premise Three—Variations in Subsequence and Consequence

Premise Three: The JPM negotiated greater flexibility in classical Pentecostals' core beliefs of subsequence and consequence of BHS and sign gifts. This section seeks to demonstrate that in the 1960s and 1970s, the JP had a variance in the belief and praxis of the BHS and gifts of the Spirit and a tolerance for variance unlike classical Pentecostals. It is now quite well established that in the opening years of the twentieth century, when the Pentecostal movement in America began to flourish, there was much debate over the BHS, its timing, the number of baptisms, how it was to be received, and what outcome was to be expected. As the years progressed, classical Pentecostal denominations constructed theological statements for the purpose of maintaining distinctives that created rigid, singular demands regarding the timing and expectations of the BHS.

In classical Pentecostalism these teachings are often summarized as subsequence and consequence. Subsequence is the belief that the BHS must be a separate experience that occurs after the conversion experience. Consequence is the belief that the person who receives the BHS will definitely speak in tongues as a sign that they have had the experience; often called the initial evidence. William Kay writes of an ongoing struggle between historians and traditionalists within classical Pentecostalism over denominational dogmatism on subsequence and consequence. He wrote, "On one side traditionalists in a Pentecostal denomination three or four generations old are building up doctrinal defenses so as to prevent the erosion of a distinctly Pentecostal form of Christianity. On the other side, historians and theologians are questioning the dogmatism of this position in light of the original intention of the ministers who first founded these denominations."[86]

While this struggle occurs within classical Pentecostal denominations, Vinson Synan points out that there were dramatic variations from classical Pentecostal distinctives on subsequence and consequence in the CM in

---

86. Kay, *Pentecostalism*, 229.

the 1960s and 1970s.[87] The JP's perspective toward subsequence and consequence aligned with these broader developments in the CM. The following paragraphs survey the doctrinal statements of churches, practices within churches, and the personal experiences of the JP to show that the there was a great variety of claimed experiences in the Holy Spirit and that the JP tolerated this diversity.

Variations in Church Statements of Faith

The statements of faith for the AG, ICFG, PHCF, Calvary Chapel, and Hope Chapel all emphasize the BHS. All but Hope Chapel and Calvary Chapel, insist on the BHS as a subsequent event; while only the AG, ICFG, and PHCF insist on evidential tongues as a consequence. Calvary Chapel writes, "We believe in the Baptism with the Holy Spirit as a distinct and separate experience to that of regeneration, occurring, either subsequent to or simultaneous with salvation."[88] This leaves space for an all-in-one experience or for a two-stage experience of the BHS, depending upon each individual's own personal experience. Calvary Chapel and Hope Chapel emphasize empowerment of the Spirit for mission and Calvary Chapel also stresses fruit of the Spirit as a consequence. Jack Hayford believes that tongues should be seen as provision and privilege open to all Christians instead of a proof of the Spirit. This slight deviation from the ICFG statement potentially alleviates the obligation on members to speak in tongues as a consequence of the BHS.[89]

Vineyard Churches also emphasize Spirit empowerment, this at the point of conversion, but drop the use of the phrase BHS. Nathan and Wilson explain that the Spirit is received at conversion, but that it is as an "event with many dimensions."[90] No mention is made of "separate and subsequent" and neither do they single out tongues as a sign gift for initial evidence.[91] These deviations from classical Pentecostal subsequence and consequence are probably best explained as a reflection of each leader's personal journey. For example, Chuck Smith and Ralph Moore had shifted away from the classical Pentecostal denomination, the ICFG, and John Wimber never was part of a classical Pentecostal denomination.

---

87. Synan, "Role," 75–81.

88. Calvary Chapel, "Statement of Faith."

89. Synan, "Role," 80.

90. Nathan and Wilson, *Empowered Evangelicals*, 156. See broader discussion on 151–68.

91. Vineyard USA. "Statement of Faith."

Variations in Church Praxis

As helpful as they are, the statements of faith do not perfectly represent or explain the practice during the heyday of the JPM or in the aftermath. When comparing the churches' statements of faith to the praxis in meetings a more complicated picture emerges. For example, while Calvary Chapel is at times more explicit in statements about the BHS than Vineyard Churches, Vineyard Churches are more expressive in the public practice of spiritual gifts than Calvary Chapels.[92] Or, while Calvary Chapel's emphasis on "orderly practice" of the gifts of the Spirit finds its basis in not distracting people from Christ during worship, Jim Durkin's GO and Breck Stevens' Bethel Tabernacle permitted the open display of gifts, which they also interpreted as "orderly practice," to attract the curious to Christ.[93]

Variations in Personal Experiences

When comparing the statements of faith and praxis in churches to the testimonies of the JP an even more diverse picture emerges. Some of the JP's experience aligned with a typical classical Pentecostal method of a separate and subsequent experience with tongues that followed. However, King (*Jesus People*) wrote about numerous people in the Seattle area whose testimony collapsed their conversion and BHS into a single experience. For example, one JP said, "The words sputtered out, 'Jesus come into my life . . . forgive me for what I've done . . . baptize me in the Holy Spirit.'"[94] Similar testimonies could be found in other locations like this JP from Southern California, "Then one day, I just realized how wretched I was. And I found Jesus . . . No. Jesus found me. And he filled me with the Holy Spirit. And now I know there is eternal life."[95] Or as another JP said, "Dear Jesus, come into my heart, Take away all my sins, Wash me in Your blood, Write my name in the Book of Life, Give me the Holy Spirit, in Jesus name, Amen."[96]

In addition to personal testimonies, Frank Reynolds, an AG minister and leader of TC from 1963 to 1987, claimed to have witnessed many hippies "get saved and baptized in the Holy Spirit all in one sitting."[97] According to

92. Chuck Smith, *Calvary Chapel Distinctives*, 29–32.

93. Ibid., 29–32. For Gospel Outreach, see Harry Hewat, interview with author, December 10, 2008.

94. P. King, *Jesus People*, 86–87.

95. Vachon, *Time to Be Born*, 44.

96. Rodney, "Calls Jesus People," 10.

97. Frank Reynolds, interview with author, September 16, 2010.

Reynolds, their BHS was simultaneous with their salvation and for others it was only ten or fifteen minutes subsequent to their salvation; an experience he found to be very different to the way he had been brought up to tarry for days, weeks, or months.[98] J. Rodman Williams made the same observation writing, "Many of these young people [JP] had a total experience of turning to Christ and at the same time of receiving the Holy Spirit."[99] According to him, their experiences in Pentecostalism came "not usually by virtue of a later charismatic experience, but because they became such in the initial breakthrough of Christian faith."[100]

While Reynolds and Williams seemed pleased, Linda Meissner observed the same, but was less conciliatory with the variance from classical Pentecostal orthopraxis. Her teaching on the obligatory nature of tongues as a sign gift created tensions with the JP whose experiences did not align with hers. Some claimed to have had an all-in-one experience and others never spoke in tongues after their BHS. Carl Parks, Meissner's Seattle based neighbor, did not teach the necessity of a subsequent experience and the initial evidence of tongues as a consequence. In interviews, some JP expressed an appreciation for Park's tolerance of differing experiences.

Other testimonies reveal that some of those who spoke in tongues did not explicitly link it to an experience of the BHS. For example, Kent Philpott's first experience of speaking in tongues while asleep behind a pulpit occurred at a time when he was "strongly opposed to all things Pentecostal."[101] He was reticent to label this glossolalic experience as his BHS, but he did interpret the subsequent, rapid expansion in his ministry as a consequence. In a similar way, Mike Messer recounted an experience of being "overpowered by the Holy Spirit" during a prayer meeting in a car. While all the band members in the car shared the experience of empowerment, some never spoke in tongues and Messer did not connect his glossolalic gift to the experience of empowerment in the car. He believed the consequence to be a subsequent and miraculous rise in numbers of conversions at Wilson McKinley concerts.

The same disconnection between the BHS and tongues is found in the testimony of Harry Hewat, who claimed he was riding his bicycle the first time he began to speak in tongues, and John Wimber, who randomly spoke in tongues while walking alongside an irrigation ditch.[102] These few

98. Ibid.

99. J. Williams, *Renewal Theology*, 22.

100. Ibid.

101. Kent Philpott, email correspondence with author, July 9, 2010.

102. Harry Hewat, interview with author, November 1, 2010; and C. Wimber, *John Wimber*, 74–75.

examples are intended to demonstrate that the JP claimed a variety of experiences that did not align with the classical Pentecostal denominational teaching on subsequence and consequence. Most the JP were themselves tolerant of a variety of experiences.

Suggested Reasons for Variations

It is suggested that there were four main reasons why the JP tolerated a variety in spiritual experiences, unlike the classical Pentecostal denominations. First, the JP placed a high priority on conversion and healing; especially healing from drug addiction and most often at the point of their initial conversion. The themes of conversion and healing from drug addiction emerge much more prominently than the BHS and speaking in tongues. While observers took notice of the high percentages of the JP who spoke in tongues, the JP's testimonies speak abundantly more about the instantaneous power of the Holy Spirit to convert and heal from drug addiction. With the emphasis on conversion and healing, the timing of tongues in relation to conversion or BHS simply was not an issue for most JP. Neither was the place nor agency of healing an issue. It was claimed that healing took place in church aisles, on the streets, and in communes. The prayers of people mediated some healings, while some alleged that Jesus Christ himself had healed them. Large-scale, healing meetings were not the norm, and there was no evidence to suggest that debates arose over the timing or agency of healing.

The primary agency for solidifying a connection between the BHS and healing was *TCTS*. While the book mentions the typical classical Pentecostal connection between the BHS and tongues, as in Wilkerson's conversation with Jesuit Priest, Father Gary, the BHS and tongues theme is overshadowed by Wilkerson's fascination with connection between the BHS and healing.[103] For example, the book records the following conversation with Nicky Cruz, who connected the BHS to his freedom from drug addiction. "I spoke to Nicky, who had been taking goof balls and smoking marijuana. I asked him when it was that he felt he had victory over his old way of life. Something tremendous had happened to him, he said, at the time of his conversion on the street corner. He had been introduced at that time to the love of God. But it wasn't until later that he knew he had complete victory. 'And when was that, Nicky?' 'At the time of my baptism in the Holy Spirit.'"[104]

Based on Cruz's experience, Wilkerson wrote about the heuristic, evolutionary development of a methodology that connected the BHS to healing

---

103. D. Wilkerson, *Cross*, 157–61.

104. Ibid., 156–57.

from drug addiction. He began by practicing on soft drug users. He said, "At first we experimented, rather cautiously, on a marijuana user. Luis was one of our boys who had been smoking this weed, which addicts the mind but not the body. He received the baptism of the Holy Spirit, and his mind addiction left him completely."[105] Then he progressed to hard drug users. He stated, "Time and again we got the same results. Harvey had been referred to us by the courts; he had been deeply addicted to heroin for three years, but after the baptism [in the Holy Spirit] he said the temptation itself went away."[106]

The same BHS and healing methodological connection was invariably dominant in the TC programs and in Meissner's Teen Harvest Headquarters' ministry to drug addicts in Seattle in 1965. The connection between healing from drug addiction, initial conversion, and the BHS was also an inseparable strategy at Bethel Tabernacle, which claimed a "30-second cure from heroin addiction, with no withdrawal pains."[107] Breck Stevens' conversion and healing at TCC in Huntington Beach probably influenced his method of healing from drug addiction in Bethel Temple. In fact, interviews with Lyle Steenis, the pastor at Bethel, record him synonymously interchanging the concepts of conversion, healing, and the BHS.[108] Whether it was Carl Parks in Spokane, Kent Philpott in San Francisco, Scott Ross in New York, or John and Anne Gimenez in Virginia Beach, the connection between healing, and at times conversion, and the BHS reverberated loud and clear throughout the JPM and formed a different paradigm to that of the BHS and tongues. Whether or not these ministries were imitative of Wilkerson or independently inventive, they served to reinforce a parallel theme of healing associated with conversion and the BHS. This theme seemed to cause a shift away from the classical Pentecostal view on subsequence and evidential tongues in the JPM.

Second, it is suggested that the hippie ideology of epistemological individualism, also adopted by the JP, mitigated against arguments for a singular, or universal pattern of experiences. That is to say, the hippies strongly emphasised the need for each person to have his or her own unique, religious or entheogenic drug experience. Everyone had his or her own trip or individual path. Religious and drug experiences were deemed right or wrong by the pragmatic benefit each individual received from them; whatever worked for each person was right for that person. This attitude was carried over into the JPM and pragmatically assessed conversion and healing

---

105. Ibid., 164.

106. Ibid.

107. Vachon, "Jesus Movement," 15.

108. Vachon, *Time to Be Born,* 46.

from drug addiction through the BHS as an experience of value that benefitted the individual. This outweighed any concern about the right timing of the experience in relation to conversion.

Third, the hippies talked and sang about love and, when they did not mean sex, it often conveyed a warm acceptance of others. Hippie love made its way into the JPM and found common ground with the Christian love of 1 Corinthians 13. So the Beatles sang "All You Need is Love," and the JP answered back with, "They Will Know We are Christians by our Love."[109] Love was frequently mentioned as one of the reasons for conversion, as this JP commented, "what really drew me was their love, their sincerity. And they were trying to help others—mainly hippies in the Los Angeles area, the orphans of the system."[110] Another concurred, "Faith and love are the keys to our movement . . . they go hand in hand."[111] The prominence of love over tongues as a gift of the Spirit was inscribed in the statement of faith of Calvary Chapel, which reads, "We believe that the only true basis of Christian fellowship is His (Agape) love, which is greater than any differences we possess and without which we have no right to claim ourselves Christians."[112] The JP's emphasis on love as a manifestation of the Spirit seemed to make them indifferent to arguments on subsequence and consequence.

Fourth, consideration must be given to the reciprocal interchange that also occurred between the JPM and the CR, CCR, and Evangelicalism. The influence of these other movements meant that classical Pentecostals were not the only ones informing the JP's Pentecostal spirituality. Not only did the CCR and CR perspectives on subsequence and consequence deviate from those in classical Pentecostalism, but the barricading measures erected by Evangelicals no doubt mollified the public praxis of Pentecostal spirituality in many JP gatherings. The JP often expressed an interest in cooperating with each other and this may have superseded an interest in supporting the conventional views of classical Pentecostals. All four of these reasons contributed to the lack of interest in pursuing a single, standardized theopraxis.

By arguing that the JP were tolerant of a variety of experiences in the Spirit is not to suggest that they were not without divisive tendencies, frivolous caviling, and quibbles, as Enroth pointed out.[113] But, where classical Pentecostal history is filled with written and sermonic quarrels about subsequence and consequence, and their denominational theologies reflect

109. McCartney and Lennon, *All You Need.* Scholtes and Arends, *They'll Know We Are Christians.*

110. "'Jesus People' Winning," 14.

111. Bisceglia, "'Jesus Movement' Attracts Following," 9.

112. "Calvary Chapel."

113. Enroth et al., *Story*, 175.

an insistence upon a prescribed, biblical pattern, this simply was not a concern for the JP. While they cherished Pentecostalism's core belief of the BHS and spiritual gifts, they were accepting of a broad range of experiences in the Spirit. As such, where classical Pentecostal denominational theologies sought to reinforce a singular and universal tradition, the JP negotiated greater flexibility in American Pentecostalism's core belief in the BHS during the 1960s and 1970s.

Premise Four—New Jesus People Churches Emerge in the Cultic Milieu

Premise Four: New Jesus People ecclesiological structures were birthed as Pentecostal hybrids in an adverse, cultic milieu that challenged their legitimacy. The final two premises of this chapter narrow the theological examination to ecclesiology. This section discusses the context of the sixties and seventies in which the JP ecclesiological bodies emerged, while the subsequent premise focuses on locating eight JPM church movements. This environment is often discussed as one that was "outside" the established churches and in a way that differentiates it from JPM strands that flourished "within" the established ecclesiological bodies of classical Pentecostalism, CR, and CCR. It was in this "outside" environment that the JPM's new church ecclesiological bodies were engendered.

The "Cultic Milieu" of the 1960s and the 1970s "Outside" Established Churches

The environment outside the established church of the sixties and seventies was supercharged with small and large ecclesiological collectives that thrived without the legitimization of American Christianity. As previously mentioned, this milieu included non-Christian or quasi-Christian NRMs; organizations like ISKCON, Scientology, Jim Jones' People's Temple, and the COG. Because the JP churches were birthed in this context, they were often lumped together and associated with these religious organizations. Consequently, the "cult" label that was attached to groups like the Unification Church was often placed upon the JP churches.

Colin Campbell ("Cult, Cultic Milieu") originally coined the phrase "cultic milieu," but the word cult and phrase cultic milieu are rather confusing and very disliked terms among sociologists and theologians these days.[114] Theologically speaking, to dub a religious body with the cult label was an attempt to locate the body in the non-Christian or quasi-Christian camp, by insinuating that they possessed dubious and dangerous teachings and practices. The word cult was strongly pejorative and mostly used as a rhetorical tool, which when left ambiguous, could be more effectively exploited than when it was clearly defined. Interestingly, the accusation of cult against JP churches was rarely centered on belief, but almost always on praxis. Over the ensuing years an enormous national controversy would erupt over cults and since the JP churches were at times associated with the cults, it placed them under enormous pressure in their battle for legitimacy. The choice to use the word cult in this discussion is meant to reinvigorate the history of the cultic milieu and to highlight the pressure JP churches faced, and is not meant to support the accusation that the JP churches were cults.

The Central Polity Motif of a Strong, Single, Prophetic Leader

As mentioned before, the JPM was very heterogeneous and would be best defined as a collection of locally led movements, most often with a strong, single, prophetic leader. Although infighting and schism had played a part in the formation of some JP churches, for the most part their beginnings were generally dissimilar to the fissiparous nature described by Gerlach and Hine ("Five Factors"). Most churches arose around a leader who claimed to have received a prophetic word or vision foretelling their future position as a leader of a community of people. This prophetic word accentuated their self-interpreted significance as an individual that God had selected to lead. To them, the ordination and appointment of an established ecclesiological body was trivialized, and at times contemptible, compared to the direct qualification and appointment of God himself that came through a prophetic word. As their community began to grow in number, they interpreted this as an affirmation and fulfillment that the prophetic words were indeed spoken by God.

The emphasis on this type of a single, prophetic leader over a community was bolstered by a concurrent revival in Pentecostalism generally; one that subscribed to the notion that God was in the process of restoring the fivefold ministry of apostles, prophets, evangelists, pastors, and teachers as found in Ephesians 4:11. The Shepherding Movement (SM), the front-runners in the restoration of the fivefold ministry, emphasized the laxity in morals and the leadership void in the CM and the JPM, and contrasted

114. See Campbell ("Clarifying the Cult"; "Secret Religion"), Richardson ("Definitions of Cult"), and Kaplan and Lööw, eds. (*Cultic Milieu*).

themselves and their model of leadership as something more biblical, healthy, and necessary.[115] Many JP leaders, already self-aware of their maligned and marginal location outside established Christian churches, found common ground in the restoration themes and this served to further enhance many JP leaders' sense of self-significance as a prophet leader over their ecclesiological body.

The locus of power residing in a strong, single, prophetic leader became a prominent motif in the JP ecclesiological bodies and it was from this leadership model that their belief and praxis would develop and gradually materialize into community traditions. The prophetic leader confessed a rhetoric of literal biblical interpretation and, most often combined this rhetoric with the use of alleged prophecy or revelations from God to solidify their position as a leader. Right belief, and especially right praxis, were articulated by the prophetic leader and combined with Bible verses and prophecies to establish their authority and validity. Beliefs articulated in written statements of faith were resisted or just slow in forthcoming. Instead, the prophet leader communicated beliefs and practices orally. In some cases titles were adopted, as in Jim Durkin, who was called a "prophet" or Wayman Mitchell, who calls himself an Apostle. Ian Wilson states, "an Apostle of Christ has been among us."[116] Church members were often urged to not ask questions but to, "obey those who have the rule over you, as they watch for your souls."[117] At times, the JP leaders' words were functionally more authoritative than the Bible, as Tipton says about Bobbi Morris and the Living Word Fellowship. "Pastor Bobbi is God's prophet and the Bible's authoritative interpreter. She is 'the shepherd who rules God's people, and leads them in His will. The voice of the shepherd is the voice of Christ,' and the faithful are to obey it without question."[118]

The Allegations of Abuse

It was not long before complaints began to emerge that centered on claims of emotional, spiritual, familial, and financial damage from unaccountable, abusive, and controlling leadership whose nebulous doctrines were never written down. Members and ex-members claimed that their finances, at times down to the level of daily purchases, their family decisions, their

115. D. Moore, *Shepherding Movement*, 45–49, 62–67.

116. Funnell, "Some Memories of Jim Durkin"; I. Wilson, *In Pursuit of Destiny*, 84, 92.

117. Linda Baker, email correspondence with author, June 23, 2009.

118. Tipton, *Getting Saved*, 35.

dress, and their whereabouts were subject to the regular scrutiny of lead-ers.[119] Members claimed that they were manipulated and coerced to sur-render finances and to attend all meetings; those who did not attend all meetings were considered as backsliders and leaving the religious body was tantamount to going to hell. There were extreme examples, like David Berg who led the COG's into teaching on "flirty fishing." In this case, Pentecostal rhetoric was combined with Berg's prophetic directives for single and mar-ried women to use their sexuality and sex acts to entice male members into joining the COG.[120] If the testimonies of ex-members are true, they include shocking descriptions of sexual acts that ranged from wife swapping to pe-dophilia. Less extreme cases from ex-members of other JP communities, like those reported by Enroth (*Churches That Abuse*), centred on the com-mon theme of unaccountable, abusive, and controlling leadership. These complaints and abuse claims almost exclusively focused on practice within ecclesiological bodies rather than identifying heterodoxy.

Response and Correctives

Reports from ex-members over claims of abuse raised concerns within Catholic, Protestant, and classical Pentecostal churches, but they could do little to address these concerns. For although their own ecclesiological bodies had structures and measures for policing, punishing, and purging internal abuses, these new ecclesiological bodies arose outside the juris-diction of these church structures. The same concerns for the JPM were also expressed over other new ecclesiological bodies arising from within the CM more broadly. J. Rodman Williams' "subordinate revelation" may have, in fact, been written as a reaction to address these concerns and as an attempt to clarify a different Charismatic belief in extra-biblical prophetic revelations.[121] But the concept of subordinate revelation was violated with regularity in the JPM and there was no structure present in this cultic milieu to address perceived violations. David Moore recounted at length the way that Charismatic leaders met together on various occasions to discuss and to confront SM leaders with their concerns over abusive teachings and prac-tices in the SM.[122] In this way they functioned as an ad hoc, polycephalous, ecclesiological leadership body over the CM. And to some degree the JPM

119. Linda Baker, email correspondence with author, June 15, 2009.

120. For claims from ex-COG members, see Thomson, "Children of God;" and Lat-tin, *Jesus Freaks*.

121. J. Williams, *Renewal Theology: Systematic*, 43.

122. D. Moore, *Shepherding Movement*, 99–178.

benefited from this process, given the many JP groups that were influenced by the SM. However, JP leaders never sought to come together in similar, large meetings in order to police or purge what they believed to be abuses from ecclesiological cults in the JPM.

One movement, however, that did arise as a corrective against perceived ecclesiological cults of the JPM was the anti-cult movement. The anti-cult movement was a term to describe a lose collective of different organizations whose self-appointed leaders imagined themselves to be people who rescued individuals from the clutches of religious bodies they deemed to be cults. It is readily accepted that the anti-cult movement began in 1972, as a reaction to the COG—a JP community—the first formal body to organize being the Free the Children of God (FREECOG). Ted Patrick and Margaret Singer, names famously synonymous with the anti-cult movement, armed themselves with self-created, deprogramming techniques that were intended to rescue people from cults and to free them from what they believed to be the effects of brainwashing.

The movement quickly snowballed to become a collection of various organizations that all shared a common mission of policing, purging, and making the American public aware of ecclesiological cults. Other names associated with the anti-cult movement were the Spiritual Counterfeits Project (1975), which formed at the demise of the JP group CWLF, the Institute for the Study of American Religion, and the Centre for the Study of New Religious Movements at Graduate Theological Union in Berkeley.[123] Worries also spilled over into a plethora of books, newspaper, and magazine articles. For example, after his work on the JPM, Enroth became interested in little else, cataloguing the activities and testimonies of "cultic" religious bodies over the course of twenty years.[124] An anti-cult, diachronic link and thematic resemblance is found in American Evangelicalism to the present day in groups like the Christian Research Institute, Rick Ross, and Lighthouse Trails; groups that have a large policing presence on the Internet.

With their influence growing, in 1974 the anti-cult movements pressured the New York State Attorney General and the State of California to launch enquiries into the activities of the COG. Also, from 1976 to 1977 similar failed attempts by anti-cult groups were made in Vermont and Texas, where they backed bills aimed at vaguely defined, cultic techniques. The FBI also got involved through its investigations of various organizations. The US Federal Government also found itself dragged into the cult battle by holding hearings from 1979 to 1981 to determine whether legal powers should be

123. Richardson, "New Religious Movements," 98–106.
124. See Enroth (1977, 1983, 1992, 1994).

granted to anti-cult groups to forcibly remove cult members from religious bodies.[125] This firestorm of controversy also sparked an anti-anti-cult reaction by groups like the National Council of Churches and the ACLU and individuals like Gordon Melton, who saw themselves, not as allies with the cultic milieu, but as guardians of religious liberty, a counterbalance to the anti-cult movements, and a challenge to the lack of objectivity of the claims of ex-members.[126]

The Effect on Jesus People Ecclesiological Bodies

In conclusion, without arguing for or against the anti-cult movements, its people and organizations filled a void and served a policing function in the arena outside the established church. While they have attempted to legitimize and delegitimize organizations based on their own evaluative criteria, many have testified to its benefit. However, they have also, rather successfully, portrayed this arena outside established churches as villainous, as dangerously unsafe, as a devil's playground, as a mystically religious, dark forest, where only the religiously vulnerable and gullible would dare venture; and from which they would most likely never return. Although not originally formed as critiques of mainstream JP churches, their scrutiny has perhaps touched every JP ecclesiological body. Much of their critique has centered on the JP church polity motif of a strong, individual, prophetic leader. A minor theme in the critique of the anti-cult movement has come from the Fundamentalists and non-charismatics who have targeted the Pentecostalism of the new JP ecclesiological bodies, not as aberrant forms of Pentecostalism, but simply because they are Pentecostal/charismatic. In any case, the scrutiny of the anti-cult movement has not died down and, with the growth of the Internet, it has arguably heightened. Internet searches like "Christian Research Institute Vineyard," "Calvary Chapel cult," "Wayman Mitchell," and "Maranatha Campus Ministries" produce an array of results listing pages of individuals and organizations whose self-appointed role is to watch and track the people and whereabouts of these churches; not always but not infrequently with disinformation.

The JP ecclesiological bodies arguably needed to appear legitimate to mainstream Pentecostalism and Evangelicalism if they were to emerge from the cultic milieu as acceptable ecclesiological bodies within American Pentecostalism. Some JP churches have used various means to legitimize themselves, like producing greater doctrinal clarity as their churches have grown,

125. See Richardson, "Regulating Religion," 2–5.
126. Melton, "Modern Anti-Cult," and Richardson, "New Religious Movements."

or making explicitly declared alliances as in Wimber's with Fuller Theological Seminary, Chuck Smith's with several well established Evangelical organizations, or Hope Chapel's and PHCF's alignment with the doctrines of the ICFG. Also, Wayman Mitchell on his website "waymanmitchell.com," has produced a page entitled "critics" that openly lists many complaints of anti-cult groups against PCHF along with his rebuttals. However, it can be generally concluded that the JP churches have not been preoccupied with an interest in appearing legitimate to American Christianity or the anti-cult movement. Neither have they offered much direct response to their cult accusers. For the most part, in spite of the firestorm of controversy, these new ecclesiological bodies have emerged from the cultic milieu undistracted from their mission. And they have managed to achieve remarkable growth since the days of the JPM in an arena outside established Catholic, Protestant, and classical Pentecostal denominations. They have focused on growing their particular hybrids of Pentecostal theopraxis through the multiplication of their own ecclesiological bodies and this, based on their size and influence, has been rather successfully achieved.

Premise Five—Jesus People Ecclesiological Hybridization in Pentecostalism

Premise Five: The new JP ecclesiological structures maintained the uniqueness of the JP theological hybridization in American Pentecostalism. From this cultic milieu of the sixties and seventies many ecclesiological structures have arisen and endured as unique expressions of JPM Pentecostalism. To bring this discussion to a close, a sampling of eight JPM churches, or church movements, has been selected and a brief overview of their unique theological locus is described in order to indicate the enduring ecclesiological developments of the JPM. But first several broad descriptive statements will be forwarded that are true of all eight of the samples selected. To begin, all of the churches presented below explicitly trace their historical roots to the JPM. Second, according to their statements of faith and praxis, they can be theologically located within Pentecostalism. Third, all of these ecclesiological bodies' beliefs and practices represent variations on the theme of BHS and spiritual gifts, some of which might more closely align with classical Pentecostalism's subsequence and consequence, while others do not. Fourth, these variations were not only common in the sixties and seventies among the JP, but these variations have been persevered through the ecclesiological bodies from the JPM to the present day. Fifth, each one of these churches nurtures the vast majority of its future leaders from within and emphasizes church planting as the primary means for multiplying and preserving their unique, ecclesiological hybridization of Pentecostalism and church polity models.

Finally, with the exceptions of GO and Maranatha Campus Ministries (MCM), these bodies continue to grow at a rather fast rate. Tracking individual membership in each body is elusive as many do not produce membership records and some do not even have church membership. This leaves counting the growth of these movements to the head counts of week by week attendances or as most seem to prefer, counting how many churches affiliate with their movement. But even this does not fully capture the size or potential influence of these ecclesiological bodies as each one has spawned thriving breakaway groups. For example, Morning Star International and Every Nations Churches formed out of Maranatha Ministries. Or there is Mike Neville's Praise Chapel, a church movement formed in 1976 after Neville broke ranks with Wayman Mitchell in Arizona. Praise Chapel claims to have 200 churches across America and hundreds in other nations.[127] In addition, each of these church movements have produced hundreds of independent ministries that in many cases maintain an affiliation and share the particulars of belief and praxis of the churches from which they have branched out. Finally, where a book with detailed analysis on each ecclesiological body is needed for each of the eight church models presented, a very brief and simple paradigm will have to suffice. The small summaries of the eight churches presented below are grossly simplified so as to capture the main paradigm of each church movement. As such, there is much that is omitted. The intention of this section is to show the theological trajectories from the JPM that these ecclesiological bodies represent and to demonstrate how they can be located within American Pentecostalism.

The Locus of Eight, Jesus People Ecclesiological Bodies

The first of these church bodies is Calvary Chapel, whose paradigm lies in a combined emphasis of chapter by chapter Bible teaching and love as the greatest of all charismatic gifts. Bible teaching, love, and evangelism take precedence over the public exercise of spiritual gifts and as a result large ministries like Greg Laurie's Harvest Crusades have arisen that cross-pollinate the praxis of Pentecostalism and Evangelicalism.[128] A number of Calvary Chapels have been in and out of the top twenty largest churches in America since the 1980s.

127. "Praise Chapel International." Also see Simpkins, *Open Door*, 137–40.

128. An attendance of 204,800 plus 558,923 online viewers were reported for 2010. "Harvest Crusade."

The second church, The Association of Vineyard Churches, finds their paradigm in power, as in Wimber's *Power Evangelism* or Nathan and Wilson's *Empowered Evangelicals*, and in intimacy of worship. Not only is Vineyard the most articulate in its written statements of belief, but the Vineyard church movement and Vineyard Music have undoubtedly influenced large portions of Christianity and, like Calvary Chapels, express a cross-pollinated version of Pentecostalism and Evangelicalism. Most notably has been Vineyard's influence on British Pentecostalism. Stephen Hunt believes it has been the most influential movement on British Pentecostalism in end of the twentieth century.[129] This has come about primarily through John Wimber himself, The Association of Vineyard Churches, and the "Toronto Blessing"—which has, in turn, influenced the expansion of the Alpha Course.[130]

Third, Gospel Outreach (GO) in its day and into the late 1970s existed as the most iconic combination of back to the land, hippie communalism and Pentecostalism. Their locus was in "practicing the Word" and shared community living which resulted in a pragmatic emphasis on preaching the gospel, practicing all the gifts of the Spirit, and a desire to establish self-supporting communities. GO aligned itself with the movement to restore the fivefold ministry, and has at times associated with other churches like Abbott Loop Community Church, Alaska that operated in the same vein.[131] A small remnant of the movement remains and is based out of Eureka, California as GO Reformational Church. Several missionaries still work outside the USA and its most successful offshoot is Verbo Ministries in Guatemala.[132]

Fourth, the Jesus People USA (JPUSA) remains as one of the most well known continuums of the JPM with its locus in an urban communal model of a self-supporting community. JPUSA has maintained two particular features since the JPM, its *Cornerstone* magazine and Cornerstone festival. The community has been through many changes and now aligns more closely with Evangelicalism by merging with the Evangelical Covenant Church. Fifth, the locus of MCM is very difficult to pinpoint because, by incorporating elements of the SM, Word of Faith, and restorationist themes into its praxis, it manifests a perplexing hybridization and a loss of some counterculture features. While it seems to be mostly defunct, it maintains an office in Gainesville, Florida, several overseas campus ministries, but has mostly been superseded by Morning Star International and Every Nation. Having

129. S. Hunt, "Anglican Wimberites," 105.

130. S. Hunt, "Alpha Course," 4–5.

131. See "Abbott Loop Community Church."

132. See "Verbo Christian Ministries."

said this, the locus of the ministry would be best placed as a university, campus outreach/church with restorationist leanings. Sixth, Dove Christian Fellowship International, headquartered in Lititz, Pennsylvania, would best be understood as a restorationist ministry that de-emphasizes large church by building cell groups. It is a growing international movement that operates under an "Apostolic Council," with Larry Kreider as its International Director. The influence of the JPM is maintained in its music and casual countercultural approach to church.[133]

Seventh, Potter's House Christian Fellowship has its locus in an edgy, urban version of classical Pentecostalism with restorationist leanings, and a primary focus on evangelism and discipleship. With Mitchell believing that he carries an apostolic mantle, PHCF has maintained a strong, centralized, ecclesiological polity and emphasizes leadership being raised up at the local church level in contrast to Bible colleges. Eighth, it is a little difficult to place the locus of Hope Chapel as something perfectly distinct from the ICFG under which it functions. It seems in some ways to have strong parallels to Roy Hicks Jr.'s churches that were launched out of the Eugene Faith Centre during the days of the JPM, but operates as a subcategory of the ICFG ecclesiological structure. In this sense, Hope Chapel's locus may be best placed as an ICFG cluster of churches strongly influenced by the counterculture of the 1960s and 1970s. It has lessened the ICFG emphasis on subsequence and consequence while stressing fellowship, small groups, and Bible teaching.

Due to the limitation of space, there are numerous other independent churches and church movements that have not been mentioned; churches that were rooted in the JPM and would find a locus in similar themes as mentioned above. For example the Church of the Open Door San Rafael emerged as a cluster of five churches from the JP communal homes in San Francisco and aligned with the SM and restorationist themes during the seventies. Other church movements like Larry Lea's Church on the Rock, or John Gimenez's The Rock Church, and independent churches like Trinity Gospel Temple and Belmont Church were rooted in and shaped by the JPM to varying degrees.

Summary

This brief survey of eight, JP ecclesiological bodies unearths several strands of churches not accounted for within American Pentecostalism, but which have made a significant contribution to the latter half of the century in Pentecostal and Charismatic ecclesiology. They were birthed in a cultic milieu

---

133. Larry Kreider, email correspondence with author, May 25, 2011.

very different to the Fundamentalist/modernist controversy of classical Pentecostalism's beginnings and different to the CM that occurred "within" the established Protestant and Catholic ecclesiological framework of the CR and CCR. These JP ecclesiological structures are more akin to the sixties and seventies counterculture ideologies and the Pentecostal belief and praxis of the JPM. They are part of the story of Pentecostalism by nature of their belief and praxis and they have served a critical function as agencies for maintaining hybridizations of Pentecostalism that came out of the JPM; especially hybridizations in the classical Pentecostal distinctives of subsequence and consequence. Yet they have also maintained a Pentecostal resemblance to their classical Pentecostal cousins and the CM.

Conclusions on the Jesus People Theology

This brief, descriptive exploration of the JP's theology is hopefully only the beginning of further investigations, but it should serve to support several claims. First, the JP should be untethered from their theological and theopraxis association with Fundamentalism. Second, while the JP shared theological resemblances to Evangelicalism and classical Pentecostalism, they can also be differentiated from both in their theological expression. Tongues were prominent in praxis, but accounts of healing were predominant in testimonies and very often the BHS and healing were simultaneous with the conversion experience. Third, the JPM demonstrates that Pentecostalism, in its theology, is fluid and flexible enough to contextualize in new environments and to form new hybrid expressions. Fourth, with many JP disinterested in debating classical Pentecostal distinctives of subsequence and consequence, large portions of JP found a home within the JP ecclesiological structures that would accommodate their variations. Testimonies from other JP, indicates that they were quite content to migrate into classical Pentecostal denominations, while others were more transient and moved through a wide variety of charismatic/Pentecostal churches. Fifth, a significant number of the new churches often associated with the "neo-Charismatic" or "neo-Pentecostal" movements that emerged from the late sixties to the eighties arose directly out of the JPM or were influenced by the JPM. Sixth, there remains a significant need for research to be carried out on the beliefs and practices of each of these hybrid church movements and especially their expression of Pentecostal ecclesiology. Finally, although the JP's theology can be differentiated from classical Pentecostalism on the particular issues of subsequence and consequence, there is a strong theological resemblance between the JPM and American Pentecostalism generally.

Based on this theological resemblance, the JPM should be located within the camp of American Pentecostalism.

Chapter 6

Conclusions on the Jesus People Movement

General Conclusions about the Jesus People Movement

This chapter draws the analysis to a close by giving concluding comments about the JPM, by comparing the JPM to other movements in American Pentecostalism, and discussing of the location of the movement in American Pentecostal historiography. By way of reminder, the goal of this book has been a rather simple one; to locate the JPM within the story of American Pentecostalism. The methodology guiding this aim has been Allan Anderson's family resemblance analogy, of which he wrote, "In the multidisciplinary study of global Pentecostalism, a broad taxonomy must use the family resemblance analogy to include its historical links and its theological and sociological foci."[1] It has hopefully been demonstrated that based on the historical links and the sociological and theological foci, the major portion of the JPM can rightly be identified as a Pentecostal/ Charismatic movement. Consequently, the JPM as a single label for a diverse collection or family of movements should be considered a part of the story of American Pentecostalism.

Since it was diachronically and synchronically linked to classical Pentecostalism, those coming out of classical Pentecostalism, the CR, and the CCR, there were a variety of different Pentecostal streams influencing the JPM's sociological and theological expression. Unlike these other movements, however, its expressions of Pentecostalism were also strongly shaped by the counterculture of the sixties and the seventies. By engaging with the counterculture, the JP forged a distinct subcultural identity that resulted in a multitude of localized, hybrid, Pentecostal communities. The JPM also cross-pollinated with American Evangelicalism, but had little, if any, historical, sociological,

---

1. A. Anderson, "Varieties," 27.

or theological connection to American Fundamentalism; perhaps with the exception of a commonly shared high view of scripture.

From the earliest days the JP intentionally sought to globalize their subcultural phenomenon. But due to its American countercultural identity, they faced limitations when moving cross-culturally to establish overseas outposts. JP communities found their most fertile ground overseas in Scandinavia, Germany, Netherlands, England, and Australia and in three primary locations: youth movements in established Protestant churches, missionary organizations, and in newly initiated ministries. When the counterculture died off in the seventies, so did the visibility and distinctness of the JPM. In the period of the aftermath, the JP's subcultural identity and theological beliefs and practices were assimilated into mainstream American Christianity primarily by its new musical expression, by the migration and settling of JP into established Christian churches, and also by the establishment of new churches, and para-church organizations.

Jesus People Movement—an Emic Interpretation

Being an emic study, it is necessary to consider how the JP interpreted the JPM; especially answering the questions of what caused the JPM and why so many young people were attracted to the religious phenomenon. Drawing on the testimony from the interviews, an overwhelmingly, unanimous evaluation emerged that cannot be overstated. The JP believed the JPM was a work of the Holy Spirit. Words like "revival" and phrases like "a work of the Holy Spirit" were commonly used when the JP explained why so many young people joined the JPM. Whether they had fond memories or appraised the JPM with harsh criticism, they all spoke adamantly that the heyday of the JPM was a revival brought on by the Holy Spirit. Almost all were convinced, and some would even argue the point, that there has not been a religious phenomenon like it in America since the 1960s and 1970s. Several said the heydays of the JPM were incomparably different to anything else they had ever experienced at any point in their lifetime. As such, in spite of the frustrations, disappointments, and bad experiences that some JP went through, their belief that the Holy Spirit was accomplishing something through the phenomenon gave most a positive interpretation of what took place. Again, this perspective was so common in testimonies that it cannot be overstated.

Second, most JP interpreted the human causes of the phenomenon to lie in the desperate condition of the youth and in the disillusionment with the hippie dream; this was especially true in the early days of the JPM and into the year 1971. During this time thousands of young people had migrated miles away from home and found themselves without food, money or housing, and in many cases addicted to drugs. Many who had not run away from home still found that experimentation with drugs had produced horrific and unsatisfying results. Forty years later, it is all too easy to gloss over the hopelessness and desperation expressed by the JP. Out of this desperate human need the young people responded positively to the food, housing, and message offered to them. Coupled with this was the self-understand that many had of their own generation being one of seekers that placed a high value in experimentation. To summarize, for many the message of salvation in Jesus and of the Spirit's power delivered a far superior and far more satisfying experience than hippiedom and often at a very low point of their life when to them the hippie dream proved to be an illusion. In interviews, almost all admitted that the JPM had become commercialized, fragmented, and diversified as the years progressed. Some interpreted this positively as the outworking of the Holy Spirit, while others saw this as human corruption of the Holy Spirit's work.

Metamorphosis from Healing into Various Themes

During the initial years and into the early 1970s, the JPM was primarily as a healing movement, and more specifically, a healing movement from drug addiction among the youth of North America. In this way it might align more closely with the proto-Pentecostal, healing revivals of the late nineteenth century and with those of the 1940s and 1950s; only the JPM was not noted for conducting large healing meetings. From 1960 through 1967 the message of instantaneous and miraculous healing from drug addiction through the BHS, developed primarily through David Wilkerson's newly emerging TCC and his book *TCTS*, can be seen to be seamlessly merging into Linda Meissner's early work in Seattle and other TCC outposts. By 1967 many churches and independent ministries around the country, unaware of each other, began tapping into this motif. They found an extraordinary receptivity with many young hippies who claimed to have had bad experiences from psychedelic trips. While glossolalia was practiced in abundance, the testimonies from these initial years arose from a bleak, street level, psychedelic youth claiming they had experienced an instantaneous and miraculous deliverance from drug addiction.

Watching the movement unfold over the years, a dramatic metamorphosis and fragmentation in its initial character can be observed as it shifted from this central motif of healing from drug addiction into a myriad other themes common in American Pentecostalism and Evangelicalism by the late 1970s. As the years passed, the JPM, like hippiedom, popularized and inveigled many disenchanted youth who never were addicted to drugs or embedded in the hippie culture. They did, however, relate to the generation gap and the youthful themes of the counterculture. The addition of many church going, disaffected youth added to the stability of the movement, but it also decreased the healing theme and saw the movement shift into an emphasis on discipleship and training. From its earliest days the JPM comingled with the CM and Evangelicalism. By the early seventies, large sections of the JPM had also joined in the SM so that by the end of the seventies the diversity in the JPM left the phenomenon difficult to even describe. The testimonies of healings continued, but were far less prominent, having been replaced by a growing interest in ecclesiology.

By the 1980s and 1990s the hippie generation had become outdated and the countercultural themes that were once revolutionary had become domesticated as normal and fashionable elements of mainstream society. The JP and JP churches had learned to engage with the sixties and post-sixties culture and to adapt cultural changes into their Christian praxis. The musical transformation, the variations in the experiences of Pentecostalism, the training of many young, counterculture Christians, and the new churches are among its most enduring legacies. In addition, the JPM has contributed to the growth and renewal of many non-denominational American Missionary organizations like CCC, YWAM, and IVCF. It has reached into other countries via the transnational growth of its new church movements and music.

Diversity as Essentialist and Normative

Many broad, descriptive statements have been made throughout this research that have sought something essentialist and normative among the diversity of the JPM. As André Droogers points out, "Essentialist and normative elements cannot be avoided in the study of Pentecostalism" as "essentialism can help to discover core characteristics."[2] This method of seeking essentialist qualities has been necessarily pursued in the research for this book in order to make generalized comments on the mainstream JPM. However, the JPM, as a heterogeneous collection or family of movements, produced a multitude of diverse Pentecostal hybridizations. Consequently, for every essentialist quality there are numerous exceptions, and no individual or community stands as the JP's sole representative voice or its single historical, sociological or theological locus. This means

2. Droogers, "Essentialist," 47.

that diversity itself should be identified as one of the JPM's core, normative, or essentialist characteristics.

Diversity between Statements of Faith, Leaders, and Common Participants

First, there was diversity in belief and praxis between the denominational
doctrines, the community leaders, and the participants of the community. This means that there was not a doltish agreement with and slavish
submission to all that the community leader or denomination taught. As
such it is not possible to establish a purely hierarchical or top down flow
of unquestioned belief between the community leader and the community
members. This raises questions about the degree to which any leader's belief
or any church statement of faith is representative of the entire community
they lead. The dissonance between the leader and the community members
was at times negligible and at others severe enough to cause schisms. For
example Frisbee, Gulliksen, and Wimber all represented variations from
Smith's Pentecostalism over which they were willing to divide. For others,
the dissonance resulted in a less schismatic response, where they simply
withdrew and distanced themselves from a JP church and attended elsewhere. For example, in interviews, some interpreted the Toronto Blessing to
be too "weird," others found Calvary Chapel as a disappointing retreat into
Evangelicalism, and other's found PHCF to be too controlling. On the other
hand, many more expressed a negligible interest doctrinal dissonance. For
example, Rick Hicks attended Calvary Chapel Costa Mesa from 1970 and
watched the church grow from 200 members to many thousands. While
regularly attending Calvary Chapel, he also migrated from church to church
where other JP attended, because he shared a feeling of solidarity and community with the JP. Ultimately, he considered his loyalty to lie in a church in
Whittier, California. So while he attended Calvary Chapel and enjoyed the
JP identity that the church engendered, he was rather indifferent to all the
doctrinal peculiarities of Calvary Chapel and Chuck Smith.[3] Hicks' disposition was very representative of the JP interviewed. More research along the
lines of Mark Cartledge (*Testimony in the Spirit*) should be conducted to
reconcile the variation between personal belief and church doctrines.

3. Rick Hicks, interview with author, September 24, 2010.

Fluidity in Jesus People Leaders' Beliefs and Praxes

Second, most JP leaders changed their beliefs and praxis over the course of their life and their Pentecostalism can only be fully appreciated by examining their entire life as a trajectory. Although many did operate from a fixed theme, the outworking of that theme resulted in changes in emphasis or at times a complete shift in belief and praxis. Beliefs and practices were at times more like heuristic tools through which trial and error experimentation was permissible and by which the limits of their own assumptions and theories were tested. This means that to better understand most leaders in the JPM, their beliefs and praxes have to be appraised in the context of certain stages or junctures in their own ministries; stages and junctures that they most often articulated.

For example, Wimber's desire for a more expressive Pentecostalism that was constrained within the Friends Church and within Calvary Chapel exceeded its limits in the Toronto Airport Vineyard Church. He withdrew his endorsement of Toronto in 1995 saying, "Toronto was changing our definition of renewal in Vineyard."[4] Or Kent Philpott, for example, was at first opposed to Pentecostalism and then was drawn into Pentecostal praxis through experiences in the JPM. During the mid to late 1970s he participated in SM and in signs and wonders at Church of the Open Door and finally retreated from these practices in the early eighties. He now believes that his experiences in the JPM were legitimate, but that the signs and wonders practiced in the seventies were not from God. He sees them as imitative, human attempts at maintaining what was a true work of the Holy Spirit's that occurred during the early days of the JPM. He now regrets some of what he practiced in the late 1970s, interpreting it as having been "toxic and dangerous" for the people that were under his ministry.[5] The examples of Wimber and Philpott show that a single description of a leader's belief may be true at one stage of their life, but not at another. Their theology and theopraxis need to be understood in the context of each stage of their lives.

Paradoxes in Individuals' Beliefs and Praxes

A third variation observed in testimonies was the content and dynamic of individual belief. Each JP's beliefs and praxis appeared to be multilayered, paradoxical, not fully worked out, not necessarily theological consistent or neatly articulated before they were implemented. And like their leaders, the

4. Stafford and Beverley, "Conversations."
5. Kent Philpott, interview with author, September 26, 2009.

JP's individual positions on the BHS and spiritual gifts, eschatology, and ecclesiology, to name a few, usually vacillated over time as they aged, married, and came in contact with different Christian teachings. Bundling each person into an orderly and static package does not do justice to this complexity and leaves conclusions rather anecdotal and bland. Although this creates a nightmare for historical, sociological, and theological assessment, it did not seem to hinder the JP from engaging with their culture. Quite the contrary, they were animated with liberty and courage to speak to others on the streets, preach in front of crowds, pray for healing, write songs, and lead singing from the very initial stages of their faith and with much of their belief still very fluid and unresolved.

The fluctuation of individual belief and praxis that has occurred over forty years can be seen in a variety of ways. By their own admission, some JP that could have been located in Pentecostalism in the seventies have changed their beliefs and therefore no longer fit under this rubric. Others did not participate in Pentecostalism in the JPM and yet are now more aligned with Pentecostal and Charismatic Christianity. Others have come full circle from a pre-Pentecostal to a post-Pentecostal paradigm. On the question of communal living, there are some who loved the community life during the heydays of the movement but would never return to it. Some who loved it still long for it, while others enjoyed it in the seventies, but detest it now and are still rather embittered by it. Each individual JP's belief and praxis has changed and their narrative communicates a journey of experimental and experiential Christian faith.

This is not an argument for pure relativism, but simply to note that the changing picture of the JP's faith does demonstrate how flexible and fluid their Pentecostalism was. Any attempt to capture this constant state of flux in still photos frustratingly and misleadingly results in flat, static, 2D characterizations. Recording their journey of faith is like watching a forty-year docudrama in full HD 3D. It reveals a seamless cast of regionalized and nationalized protagonists, antagonists, supporting actors, extras, and stage hands intertwined in a narrative of networks, alliances, disaffiliations, plots, and subplots. For the purpose of research, it has been necessary to press the pause button and examine isolated frames at a moment in time. But play must again be resumed and the beauty of the full depth and color of the entire drama of the JPM valued. It has also been necessary to draw lines around JP communities and ideologies in order to examination them. But hard and fast lines do not leave space in the analysis for the crosspollination or for variations in belief. So, although it has been necessary to define essentialist and normative traits, this has hopefully not robbed the beauty of the multifaceted and morphing nature of the individual Pentecostalism that occurred at a micro-phenomenological and intragroup level.

The JPM and the Amalgamation
of Pentecostalism and Evangelicalism

The JPM was quite arguably the primary location for the amalgamation of Evangelicalism and Pentecostalism in the latter half of the twentieth century. Ever since the onset of American Pentecostalism, the historical and theological relationship between the two movements has always been one of both cooperation and antagonism. Both movements represent flourishing branches of twentieth-century American religion and, as the century came to a close, the overlap or middle ground between the two has been shared by an increasingly larger portion of Christians. Consequently, at times the two words are interchanged synonymously in discussions on American religion.

Describing this twentieth-century relationship, Russell Spittler wrote, "Between World War II and the Vietnam War, say between the 1940s and the 1970s, there occurred the Evangelicalization of Pentecostalism. In the following quarter century the reverse process can be discerned: the Pentecostalization of Evangelicalism."[6] Problematically, Spittler's dates are arbitrarily assigned, his evaluation reflects a classical Pentecostal bias, and he does not offer support for the theory. However, he does point to a recognizable, reciprocal relationship between the two movements. The following comments are offered as a corrective to Spittler.

As Pentecostalism spread into various branches of Christianity in the 1940s, it not only influenced these other forms of Christianity that it came in contact with, but it also negotiated away certain classical Pentecostal traits through a process of reciprocal interchange. So it is possible to speak of the Pentecostalization of Protestantism and the Protestantization of Pentecostalism, since the 1940s. It is possible to speak both of the Pentecostalization of Roman Catholicism and of the Roman Catholicisation of Pentecostalism since 1967. So the phrases Pentecostlization of Evangelicalism and the Evangelicalization of Pentecostalism do not describe anything unique in the relationship between the two religious movements, but merely elucidate the normal bartering process as Pentecostalism globalizes and hybridizes.[7]

While the relationship between Evangelicalism and Pentecostalism is detectable from the beginning of the twentieth century, it is implausible to suggest, as Spittler does, that it is more unidirectional in its flow at certain

6. Spittler, "Are Pentecostals," 112.
7. See Poloma, *Assemblies of God*, 3.

junctures in the twentieth century. However, by moving Spittler's arbitrary date of the mid-seventies back to 1967, it is suggested that the JPM was the primary location for the reciprocal interchange between Evangelicalism and Pentecostalism in the latter half of the twentieth century. The evidence for this lies in several areas. First, numerous Evangelical organizations and churches that participated in the JPM would not class themselves in the camp of Pentecostalism. In interviews, many JP commented on the cooperation among many groups irrespective of labels like Evangelical or Pentecostal. There were a number of individuals like Sammy Tippit, Arthur Blessitt, and Leo Humphrey who associated loosely with the SBC, but whose experiences and praxis at times paralleled that found in Pentecostalism. For example, both Humphrey and Blessitt claimed to have had Christophanies and Blessitt wrote that prayer for healing from drug addiction was a normal practice in his Christian nightclub.[8] As already mentioned, the largest single JP gathering, Explo '72, was organized by CCC, a conservative Evangelical organization and included barricading measures on glossolalia for the purpose of "unity."

These and other conservative Evangelical groups have been excluded from this book because of the aims of this research, which were to trace out the Pentecostalism in the JPM. But they can be found, as already noted, in Alvin Reid's ("Impact") dissertation on the impact of the JPM on the SBC and in the recent academic works of Kevin Smith ("Origins") and Larry Eskridge ("God's Forever Family"), which have examined the Evangelicalism of the JPM. While bemoaning the lack of Evangelical scholarly attention, Eskridge concludes that the JPM was one of the greatest religious movements of the post WWII era and that it "continued to exert an influence upon American Evangelicalism decades after it faded away."[9] Both works also agree that the blended form of Evangelicalism and Pentecostalism was one of the byproducts and as such the JPM can be located under both umbrellas.

Second, JP of charismatic persuasion, many of whom believed the Holy Spirit had inspired their songs, were the initiators of the Jesus Music. But rarely do any of the songs make an explicit appeal to or promotion of Pentecostalism. Since the heydays of the JPM, the Jesus Music and its worship and CCM trajectories have not only been shaped by but have also shaped Evangelicalism and Pentecostalism. In this way, the JP's music has served as a place of unity and common expression of faith between the two camps since the late 1960s.

8. Blessitt, "*Turned On*," 94. For Leo Humphrey, see Michelmore, *Back to Jesus*, 18.
9. Eskridge, "God's Forever Family," 383.

Third, the JP churches have played a significant role in formalizing the blend of Evangelicalism and Pentecostalism of the JPM. It is amusing to note the perplexity among scholars over where to locate the JP churches. Peter Hocken wrote, "Calvary Chapel is not a charismatic grouping."[10] Whereas Balmer and Todd described the church as "soft Pentecostalism" that "defies easy characterization."[11] Stephen Hunt (*History of the Charismatic Movement*) classed Vineyard as a charismatic church while Nathan and Wilson (*Empowered Evangelicals*) gave it the label of empowered Evangelicals. Donald Miller thinks that words like Fundamentalist, Evangelical, Charismatic, or Pentecostal are deficient labels.[12] The JP churches have served as gathering places for Christians who find it difficult to fully appreciate the belief and praxis in the classical Pentecostal churches or in conservative Evangelical Churches, as well as for those who are also label averse.

So, while this study has focused on the majority expression of Pentecostalism in the JPM, it also possible to envision the JPM as the primary location for bartering and reciprocal interchange between the two movements from the late 1960s. While the movement died down by the late 1970s, its aftermath continued to influence the blending of the two religious movements through the end of the century. This not only allows much of the JPM's history and theology to be located in both camps, but makes simple dividing lines between them even more difficult to draw.

The JPM's Contribution to American Pentecostalism and Christianity

It is suggested that one of the JPM's foremost contributions was its function as a "Bridge Over Troubled Waters" that helped other movements in American Christianity and American Pentecostalism, to adapt to the post-sixties American culture. As stated in chapter 2, the 1960s was the most significant decade of change in twentieth-century America.[13] The changes wrought in the sixties and seventies were so transformational to conventional American society that historical and sociological conversations about the twentieth century could rightly be framed in a pre-sixties and post-sixties paradigm.[14]

10. Hocken, *Challenges*, 35n26.

11. Balmer and Todd Jr., "Calvary Chapel," 665.

12. D. Miller, *Reinventing*, 2.

13. See McLeod (*Religious Crisis*, 1), Fitzgerald (*Cities on a Hill*, 390), and Ellwood (*Sixties*, 19).

14. The phrase post-sixties is meant to be an abbreviated way to express the entire set of changes that were brought into American culture primarily during the 1960s and 1970s.

The JPM, infused with Pentecostalism and hippiedom, was itself birthed and matured synchronically with a plethora of counterculture groups that were considered marginal and that made their entry into the mainstream of American culture. As such, it shared the character and struggle for legitimacy of the counterculture and as such was more adept in this milieu than other branches of Christianity.

In the end the JPM managed to carve out a distinct subcultural identity connected both to the counterculture and the mainstream of society and to Pentecostalism and Christendom broadly; including Catholicism, Protestantism, and Evangelicalism. From the beginning of the JPM and into the end of the century the movement crossed over with other movements in Christianity and as such embedded much of its own ethos in American Christianity. Consequently, through the permanent structures emerging from the heydays of the JPM and by nature of their assimilation and comingling with other areas of American Christianity, the JP functioned as a bridge that assisted many in mainstream Christianity to also make a transition into the post-sixties American culture. As the JP's subcultural identity assimilated with mainstream Christianity many other individuals were either inveigled into the JP's structures due to their affinity with their counterculture or were inspired to imitate the JP's subcultural identity. In contradistinction, most Fundamentalists were polarized by the JPM and its aftermath and remained separated from the cultural changes of the sixties. But for many others, the JP's familiarity with post-sixties America has either inspired minor alterations or, in some cases, revitalized their institutional structures altogether.

While many agree with the notion that the sixties was the decade of great change in the century, some have argued too strongly for a bifurcated society experiencing a unidirectional shift from one location into another. These perspectives too often dichotomize American culture, which is very diverse and complex, into two, very tidy categories. This tendency can be found, for example, in James Davidson Hunter's *Culture Wars*, in which he places all people into two "polarized" camps: those who have "orthodox" tendencies and those who have "progressive" tendencies.[15] The JP's multilayered, multifarious, and transitional beliefs break down the notion that they can be neatly fit into one of two categories; either progressive or orthodox.

The same assumption that society is bifurcated and is experiencing a shift from one location to another also resonates in many of the modern/postmodern dialogues. For example Ellwood wrote, "In America the Sixties were fundamentally a time of transition from modern to postmodern

---

15. J. Hunter, *Culture Wars*, 43–54.

ways of thinking and being."[16] Or as Stanley Grenz wrote, "our society is in the throes of a monumental transition, moving from modernity to postmodernity."[17] The modern/postmodern dialogue has also been avoided in this book for two reasons. First, on definitional grounds it is a slippery slope. Namely, there are too many authors with too many definitions and the modernism/postmodernism concepts become elusive, meaningless, or too restricted to one author's set of meanings. Second, if for example Grenz's definitions were used, it could be strongly argued that both modern and postmodern tendencies were operational in the JPM and in American society both before and after the 1960s. Thus the notion of a bifurcated society in the "throes" of a unidirectional shift away from modernism and toward postmodernism seems too overly simplified and implausible. Finally, such a discussion for the purposes of this paper would unnecessarily result in a modernism/ postmodernism dialogue instead of identifying and locating the JPM story in American Pentecostalism.

Also this premise does not imagine an iconoclastic obliteration of pre-sixties America in place of a post-sixties America. By arguing a pre-sixties and post-sixties America it is meant that during the sixties the alternative religious, political, and social ideologies previously assigned an abnormal status on the margins of society, moved into the mainstream of conventional society. As they did, a multitude of new religious and political off-shoots also emerged and assumed a position of ever increasing acceptability and normality as viable competitors for defining American cultural values by the seventies, eighties, and nineties. This does not mean that pre-sixties mainstream American values were on their way out, as they too have remained as viable competitors for defining American values until the end of the twentieth century. Instead, the outcome in the post-sixties society was an amalgam of mainstream with alternative values on the main street of American culture. The assimilation of the alternative values of marginal movements into the mainstream of American society has resulted in a more pluralistic society than before the 1960s.

It is suggested here that the JPM be viewed as a phenomenon whose participants forged a way forward by producing many variations of a flourishing form of counterculture 1960s Pentecostalism. Due to its context of engenderment, the JPM also inherited and intentionally adopted traits of the counterculture into its forms of Pentecostalism. In this way the JPM demonstrates the qualities of elasticity and fluidity within Pentecostalism that enable it to engage with and to critically evaluate both new cultural ideologies

16. Ellwood, *Sixties,* 10.

17. Grenz, *Primer,* 10.

and conventional norms. It shows Pentecostalism's ability to adapt to and to adopt what its participants determine to be beneficial, and to discard what they determine to be either morally wrong or functionally valueless for their own self-actualizing and globalizing causes. Pentecostalism in the JPM succeeded at forming a contextualized sociological and theological hybridization; or more accurately a clustering of hybridizations and Pentecostalisms. It was a subculture with a contextual Pentecostal and Charismatic set of theologies engendered at the heart of the counterculture.

This perspective makes a break from the way many sociologists of the seventies normally imagined the JPM. For example, it is the opposite interpretation of Mauss and Peterson ("Les 'Jesus Freaks'") who saw the JPM as a "waystation." They presented the JP as passive, vulnerable, and "stigmatized," and as such in need of a phenomenon to lend them a hand at being "reabsorbed" back into American Christianity. There may have been some degree of stigmatization in the JPM. But seeing the JP's contribution as a newly created, subcultural form of Pentecostalism and as a bridge between conventional American Christianity and the countercultural values, presents them as intentionally engaging and responsible for shaping the ethos and outcome of the phenomenon. While Mauss and Peterson do acknowledge the migration into classical Pentecostal churches, their presentation of the JP as passive and vulnerable does not acknowledge the formidable controversy or the transformation initiated in classical Pentecostal churches as a consequence of this migration. Neither do they recognize the controversy surrounding the stream of the JPM birthed within the classical Pentecostal churches. The JP intentionally embattled their Pentecostal and counterculture values and as such offered much of American Christianity a helping hand at negotiating their way forward into post-sixties America. Without the JPM American Christianity and American Pentecostalism may have found itself rather marginalized and distant from the post-sixties changes in American culture.

The Jesus People Movement's Uniqueness within American Pentecostalism

Having considered some of the major contributions of the JP's Pentecostalism, attention will be turned to what makes the JPM different from classical Pentecostalism, the CR, and CCR movements in America. The uniqueness of the JPM is found in the context of engenderment; that is the combination of its historical, sociological, and theological qualities. So while other movements in American Pentecostalism may share one or two of these traits, it is the combination of these that make the movement unique. The first and perhaps most noted uniqueness of the JPM was the age of the participants; ranging from 13 to 30. The JPM and CCR were comparatively similar in the age of the participants, at least in the early years, as attested to by Kevin and Dorothy Ranaghan (*Catholic Pentecostals*), and M. Harrison ("Sources"). This was due to the CCR's origins which beginning "from university circles the movement spread from parishes to convents to monasteries."[18] The overlap in the CCR and JPM during these early years is more than likely reflected in the later statistics collected by Donald Miller that found 28 percent of "New Paradigm" churchgoers were from Catholic backgrounds.[19] The JPM offers a place for research into youth movements of Pentecostalism and in the origins of the CCR.

Another unique feature in the JPM was the high percentage of males and this meant that men were more prominent in leadership than was noted in the early days of classical Pentecostalism.[20] This also breaks from the general trend in Pentecostalism that indicates a majority female following.[21] While the large portion of men led Harder ("Sex Roles") to conclude that it reinforced the inferiority of women, others were convinced that it provided a new generation of male leadership into the end of the century. This high percentage of male participation and leaders in the JPM is most probably reflected in Stephen Hunt's later observation that "today's neo-Pentecostal new paradigm churches are nonetheless typically under the command of 'charismatic' male authority figures."[22]

The historical context of the sixties counterculture movement determined three particularities in the JPM: first, the communalism of the JPM has been unparalleled in any other Pentecostal and Charismatic movements in American history. Although the JP saw their communes as a restoration by the Spirit of Acts 2:42–47, it received its impetus from hippie communalism of the time and became part of the largest communal movement of American history. The second particularity were the streams of the JPM's located "outside" the established churches. The association of the JPM with the "cultic milieu" meant the JPM, its participants, its communes, music, and new ecclesiological bodies all faced a battle for legitimacy within Pentecostalism, something different than the Fundamentalist and modernist controversy of classical Pentecostalism's birth. The third uniqueness stemming

---

18. McDonnell, *Catholic Pentecostalism*, 23.

19. D. Miller, *Reinventing*, 198.

20. See Barfoot and Sheppard ("Prophetic vs. Priestly"), and A. Anderson, *Introduction*, 271–76.

21. Anderson et al., "Introduction," in *Studying Global Pentecostalism*, 3.

22. S. Hunt, *History of the Charismatic*, 328.

from the counterculture would be the movement's beginning and ending dates. While the CCR shared a similar start date in 1967, the ebb and flow of the JPM's heyday, unlike the CCR, was determined by its attachment to the counterculture. Another unique quality of the JP was their transience that resulted in a high level of mobility and in their willingness to move freely in and out of JP churches, CR, CCR, and Evangelical churches. Their transience also seemed to cultivate a greater interest in collective and unified celebrations, marches, outreaches, and outdoor festivals rather than in polemic and apologetic arguments over subsequence and consequence as in other movements.

The JPM's Historical Resemblance with American Pentecostalism

It is interesting to compare similarities between the JPM and other movements of American Pentecostalism in order to connect the JP's story with the larger narrative. Beginning first with history, it should be noted that the JPM, like the CM, ultimately traces its roots to the people, churches, and ministries that arose out of the revivals at the turn of the twentieth century. Killian McDonnell reportedly stated it this way, "Behind every neo-Pentecostal stood a classical Pentecostal."[23] Similarly, Stephen Hunt wrote, "Most obviously, neo-Pentecostalism is in many respects an extension of classical Pentecostalism, while the boundaries between the two are increasingly blurred. Thus the broader movement may be appraised as a single phenomenon that enthuses, no uncertain way, the Christian world across the continents."[24]

Some of the historical links from classical Pentecostalism to the CM were not shared by the JPM. For example, David du Plessis was dubbed "Mr Pentecost" due to his enormous role in the spread of Pentecostalism into Protestant Churches. For his work in spreading Pentecostalism in the Catholic Church, he was awarded the "Good Merit" medal by Pope John Paul II, and was, according to Vinson Synan, the first non-Catholic to be given this award.[25] Another classical Pentecostal mission popular in its day, Camps Farthest Out, was purportedly responsible for introducing the likes of Tommy Tyson, Harald Bredesen, and Don Basham to the BHS.[26] While, David du

23. Synan, *Century*, 361.

24. S. Hunt, *History of the Charismatic*, 3.

25. Synan, *Century*, 362.

26. D. Moore, *Shepherding Movement*, 34.

Plessis and Camps Farthest Out were critical links to Pentecostalism in the CR, CCR, and SM, they were completely unknown to most of the JP.[27]

While Sherrill's book *They Speak with Other Tongues* and Bennett's book *Nine O'clock in the Morning* were commonly read in the CR and the CCR, they were not as popular among the JP. However, David Wilkeson's *TCTS* and the FGBMFI were hugely responsible for infusing the JPM, the CR, and the CCR with Pentecostalism. The FGBMFI not only sponsored numerous JP outreaches, as early as 1962 they had begun holding meetings with Catholic priests, and had introduced healing revivalists such as Oral Roberts to Protestant church leaders. They also sponsored those associated with the Faith Movement such as Kenneth Hagin Sr. and Kenneth Copeland.[28] The timing of the FGBMFI's growth, from an attendance of 3,000 at the inaugural meeting in 1952 to a membership of 300,000 in 1972, gives some indication of their influence on the CM.

As for Wilkerson's *TCTS*, it is credited by Catholics as the main catalyst for launching the CCR in 1967, from Duquesne, where curious students discussed the book and then prayed for the BHS.[29] Frank Reynolds credited the beginnings of Pentecostalism in the United Methodist Church in Pennsylvania in 1969 to *TCTS*, saying it was "the key in creating a hunger for a personal encounter with the Holy Spirit."[30] Souring sales of *TCTS* not only made it a best seller of the 1960s, but also launched Wilkerson as a global, cross-denominational speaker.[31] The FGBMFI and *TCTS* stand apart as the two primary agencies responsible for spreading Pentecostalism through all the Charismatic Movements of the sixties and seventies.

The JPM's Sociological Resemblance with American Pentecostalism

Allan Anderson comments that "a broader definition should emphasize Pentecostalism's ability to 'incarnate' the gospel in different cultural forms."[32] Pentecostalism in the JPM shared a socio-cultural characteristic with other movements in of the sixties and seventies in that it demonstrated an ability to attach itself to a host, to animate the participants with Pentecostal spirituality, and to form unique Pentecostal identities within that host. While the

27. Michelmore, *Back to Jesus*, 113.

28. Hollenweger, *Pentecostalism*, 153; Zeigler, "Full Gospel Business," 653.

29. Laurentin, *Catholic Pentecostalism*, 11–13.

30. Reynolds, "David Ray Wilkerson," 1196.

31. Ibid.

32. A. Anderson, *Introduction*, 14.

hosts were different, the adaptation process and outcomes were the same. Pentecostalism in the CR interacted with established Protestant traditions, in the CCR with Catholicism, and in the JPM with a new religious phenomenon, hippiedom, in order to form variant forms of contextualized Pentecostal phenomena. In the same way, Pentecostalism in the early part of the century interacted with the hosts of the Holiness and Keswick movements, as well as Fundamentalism, to form a contextualized religious phenomenon known as classical Pentecostalism.

For some within classical Pentecostal churches the idea of mixing Pentecostalism with hippiedom or with Catholicism was regarded as syncretistic. This is evidenced in David Wilkerson's controversial "prophesy," given at the Second International Lutheran Conference on the Holy Spirit in 1973, in which he stated that CR and CCR participants would be forced to leave their churches.[33] It can also be seen in his campaign to warn the AG of the dangers of the JPM. This sort of tension is not new and it was the Theosophical societies that once led the way on discussions of syncretism or the "mixing" of religions (Kraft, "To Mix or Not to Mix"). More recently it is the globalization theorists that have led these sorts of discussions in the area of Pentecostalism, most often preferring the word hybridization to syncretism (Beyer and Beaman, *Religion and Globalization*). Although the socio-cultural contexts of the JPM, the CR, and CCR were different, there was a shared norm in Pentecostalism's ability to adapt itself to different contexts.

The JPM's Theological Resemblance
with American Pentecostalism

Using Donald Dayton's fourfold paradigm of Christ as Savior, as Baptizer with the Holy Spirit, as Healer, and as Coming King facilitates a brief comparative theological examination of the similarities and variations between the JP and the other movements of Pentecostalism.[34] Due to a the limitation of space most of this discussion is devoted to the BHS and tongues as these, along with healing, formed the most common trait of Pentecostal identity between the JPM and other movements in the century. However, before moving on to the BHS and tongues, it is necessary to very briefly touch on the similarities in the other areas of Dayton's paradigm.

33. Laurentin, *Catholic Pentecostalism*, 145.

34. Dayton, *Theological Roots*, 21–28. The intention here is not to argue for Dayton's fourfold paradigm, but simply to use it to help facilitate this discussion.

First, as for Christ as Savior, the normative christocentric pneumatology within American Pentecostalism was also common in the JPM; in fact it was engraved in their name "The Jesus People." Christocentric pneumatology gave a common theological theme that facilitated their cooperation with Evangelicalism, with classical Pentecostals, with the CR, and the CCR. Second, as for Christ as the coming King, it is possible to differentiate eschatological particularities, as in pre/post/amillennialism, or pre/post tribulational views, as Peter Alhouse wrote, "While Pentecostals and Charismatics both hope in the imminence of the end-time parousia, Pentecostals had an eschatology different from the Charismatics."[35] In this way, the Dispensational sensibilities of the JP establish a closer eschatological kinship with classical Pentecostals than with other concurrent movements. However, Peter Hocken correctly stated, "'While many charismatics think the end of the world will occur in the near future, the most widespread conviction is of the imminence of Christ's return."[36] Regardless of the eschatological particularities, the JP, classical Pentecostals, CR, and CCR participants, shared a strong and unifying belief that Jesus would return at any moment.

Third, Christ as healer was a unifying theme within all the movements of Pentecostalism in America up to the seventies, despite smaller debates on theological issues as in the healing in the atonement.[37] The JP's emphasis on healing from drug addiction was a unique variation on the healing theme, perhaps shared mostly with Wilkerson's TC. Because JP streams were birthed inside established churches and due to the JP's migrational transience the unique emphasis on healing was also embedded into the historical churches and classical Pentecostal churches. While testimonies of healing from drug addiction lessened over time, Vineyard has probably preserved the strongest emphasis on healing of all the JPM churches.

The BHS and speaking in tongues are the single most salient features of Pentecostalism, and yet they have also been some of the most hotly debated beliefs. The diversity in the BHS and tongues evident in the JPM, has also been present in other movements of American Pentecostalism. For this reason, it is not enough to see the BHS and tongues alone as what unifies these movements, but it is the diversity of belief on the BHS and tongues that it is a common theme throughout. First, written in Pentecostal and Charismatic literature is an amazing diversity of phrases that express the experience of the BHS and at times they are synonymously interchanged. These phrases

---

35. Alhouse, *Spirit of the Last Days*, 15–16.

36. Hocken, "Charismatic Movement," 519.

37. Arguments over healing in the atonement of Christ were not found in the JP testimonies.

include the Baptism "of," "in," and "with" the Holy Spirit, "the outpouring of the Holy Spirit," "the release of the Spirit," the Sprit "coming upon," the "anointing of the Spirit," the "filling of the Spirit," and "the empowerment of the Spirit," to mention but a few. For example, according to René Laurentin, "Come Holy Spirit" was a prominent Catholic Hymn sung to invoke the BHS during the early days of the CCR in 1967. As an interpretation of Acts 19:2, Larry Christenson and other leaders in Lutheran renewal mediated the invocation of the Holy Spirit through the prayer of "receive the Holy Spirit."[38] These varied expressions of BHS in other movements of American Pentecostalism were also evident in the JPM.

Second, the JP's variations in subsequence and consequence were not uncommon. Recent scholarship shows that classical Pentecostal beliefs were far more diverse than might be popularly assumed. For example, Gerald King shows that while most early Pentecostals agreed on subsequence, there were dissenters like Dougless Jacobsen, F. F. Bosworth, and Donald Dayton as well as debates between "three-stage" versus "two-stage" Pentecostals.[39] In his work on Joseph Smale and The First New Testament Church Los Angeles, Timothy Welch also wrote of a "plethora of Pentecostalisms" in existence in the early days of classical Pentecostalism.[40] He wrote, "There never was one exclusive 'Pentecostal' profile that emphasized *glossolalia* or other charisms."[41]

The diversity of Pentecostalism in the CR was meted out by an interaction between parishioners' claimed, individual experiences and the leaders' interpretation of established doctrines within their denomination. Consequently, between the 1940s and the 1970s Lutherans, Episcopalians, Baptists, Mennonites, Methodists, and Presbyterians all had their own denominational, renewal movements with particular beliefs on subsequence and consequence. Vinson Synan ("Role of Tongues," 75–82) gives evidence of the diversity of opinion between the CR leaders.[42] John Sherrill (*They Speak*) surveyed the experiences of many CR participants, from common people to leaders like Larry Christenson and E. Stanley Jones, from Lutherans to Baptists, and Mennonites. He recorded the claimed experiences of participants as including healings of the body and spirit, tongues, praise, prophecies, empowerment, and the call into missionary service. Then he

---

38. Laurentin, *Catholic Pentecostalism*, 12; Christenson, "Charismatic Movement," 7–8.

39. G. King, "Disfellowshiped," 8–12.

40. Welch, "God Found His Moses," 210–12, 232–34.

41. Ibid., 232.

42. Synan, "Role," 75–82.

wrote his conclusions of the diversity on the BHS and tongues, saying, "So here was the gamut of opinion on the importance of tongues in determining the Spirit's presence: from the 'essential' to 'helpful' to 'necessary.'"[43]

Some people in the CR were known to "tarry" in prayer and praise sometimes for days while others were baptized in the Holy Spirit the first time they requested in prayer.[44] Dennis Bennett was known for being a staunch supporter of subsequence and initial evidence, but Larry Christenson seemed more supportive of diversity when he wrote, "Sometimes the baptism with the Holy Spirit occurs spontaneously, sometimes through prayer and the laying on of hands. Sometimes it occurs after water baptism, sometimes before. Sometimes it occurs virtually simultaneously with conversion, sometimes after an interval of time. So there is considerable variety within the pattern."[45]

Within the CCR, tensions arose over reconciling the interpretation of parishioners' claimed experiences that were couched in a borrowed, Pentecostal rhetoric, with the Catholic Church's teachings and traditions on the sacraments of water baptism, spirit baptism, and the Church as the mediator of these experiences (Sullivan, "Ecclesiological Context"; *Charisms*).[46] According to Sullivan, Vatican II fostered the growth of the CCR stating, "the teaching on Vatican II on the charisms marks a break with a commonly held view."[47] To reconcile personal experience and church teaching, the Church interpreted parishioners' experiences as follow on "charisms" or as subsequent experiences stemming from the initial receiving of the Holy Spirit at salvation. They interpreted parishioners' experiences as a greater awareness of the Spirit's work or as "the 'coming into conscious experience' of the power of the Spirit," or as "a 'growth process.'"[48]

Killian McDonnell continued in the same vein as Sullivan using the words "release" or "actualization of the Spirit" to define the BHS.[49] Catholic Pentecostalism has, according to Synan, uniformly resisted subsequence and initial evidence in the classical Pentecostal way of speaking.[50] McDonnell stated, "The issue in Pentecostalism is not tongues, but fullness of life in

43. Sherrill, *They Speak*, 87. For his examples, see pages 85–97 and pages 124–31.

44. Ibid., 124.

45. Christenson, *Speaking in Tongues*, 38. For more on Christenson's position, see Hoekema, *Holy Spirit Baptism*, 11. For Bennett's position on subsequence and consequence, see Synan, *Spirit Said*, 60.

46. Sullivan, ""Ecclesiological Context," 123–35.

47. Ibid., 123.

48. Sullivan, *Charisms*, 68–69.

49. Synan, "Role," 77.

50. Ibid.

the Holy Spirit, openness to the power of the Spirit, and the exercise of all the gifts of the Spirit."[51] Simon Tugwell wrote, "[T]he New Testament does not put pressure on anyone to seek the gift of tongues, but it encourages those who use it to grow into a fuller and richer Christian life."[52] As for praxis, Sullivan and McDonnell summarized the normal manifestations of gifts of the Spirit at CCR meetings as including, unstructured joyful praise and prayer, prayers in tongues, consoling and exhorting prophecies, not usually predictive prophecies, healings, various kinds of miracles, a love for the Bible and for people, and the constant reference to the BHS.[53]

In summary, there has always been considerable variance among the movements of American Pentecostalism on the issue of the BHS and glossolalia. It is not enough to merely highlight the unifying theme of the BHS and tongues within these movements, attention must be drawn to the variations on the belief on the BHS and tongues. It is suggested that the JPM, because of its cross-pollination with classical Pentecostalism, the FGBMFI, *TCTS*, the CR, the CCR, Evangelicalism, and its own newly formed movements, represented elements of each of these individual movement's beliefs on the BHS, tongues, and other gifts of the Spirit. This may have resulted in the JPM being the most diverse movement in its beliefs and practices on gifts of the Holy Spirit in American Pentecostalism. Certainly the JPM significantly contributed to the trend in the 1970s, observed by David Barrett, for an exponential growth in hybrid Pentecostalisms within American Pentecostalism.[54]

Locating the JPM within American Pentecostalism

The JPM was not only a large phenomenon that overlapped with many other concurrent, religious movements, but it also demonstrated the hallmarks of Pentecostal spirituality and as such should be included in the story of American Pentecostalism. Yet, when searching for popular or scholarly assessments on the JPM in American Pentecostalism, it is rather surprising to find an utter paucity. The JPM is completely missing from the historiography. What miniscule mention could be found in books, articles, and encyclopedias during the 1980s has lessened over the years and in quite a few cases has now been omitted. For example, the very small entry on the

51. McDonnell, *Catholic Pentecostalism*, 9–10.

52. Hollenweger, *New Wine*, 45.

53. McDonnell, *Catholic Pentecostalism*, 17–35; Sullivan, *Charisms*, 9, 57.

54. Barrett, "Twentieth-Century," 119.

JPM in *The DPCM* (1988) has been omitted from *The NIDPCM* (2002).[55] At best, the comments on the JPM in the area of Pentecostal and Charismatic studies are limited to brief snippets, most often without citations, and at times with misinformation. While many scholars and popular writers in the 1970s interpreted the JPM to be a third, vibrant, charismatic movement that overlapped with the CR and the CCR, present day Pentecostal and Charismatic scholarship seems completely unaware of its existence and rather disinterested in acknowledging its significance.

There are two primary reasons why the JP is missing from twentieth-century American Pentecostal histories. First, the history of Pentecostalism is thoroughly underdeveloped and the fact that the JPM is missing from the American storyline is one more piece of evidence of "how young the field is; in fact is still coming of age."[56] Classical Pentecostals are investing more effort into their early histories, but the Pentecostal and Charismatic history of the 1960s and 1970s remains undisturbed by historical and theological scholars. The investment made in this research to understand the AG and ICFG's involvement in the JPM could be superseded by leaps and bounds with the focused attention of insiders who have far greater access to critical historical data. For there are many classical Pentecostal people, now aging ex-JP, affected by the JPM. Why more of them have not been interested in unearthing this period of their own history is puzzling. In addition, the JP in new churches and para-church organizations could contribute to a deeper historical understanding or an emic, self-understanding of their own community or movement. Also, the east coast JPM needs to be more thoroughly investigated and the JPM in the CG was not even touched by this research. With a very few exceptions in the CCR and one or two excellent works like David Moore's on the SM, the history of Pentecostalism in the 1960s and 1970s has for the most part been abandoned. What little is known rests primarily on a very few older works.[57]

There are a few exceptional individuals who include the JPM as part of their analysis of American Pentecostalism. Thirty years ago, Walter Hollenweger (*Pentecost*) made an appeal for the JPM to be considered as part of the story of American Pentecostalism. Although his views reflect the optimism towards ecumenicalism that was prevalent in Pentecostal and Charismatic studies in the 1970s, his hope for a long-term result from the JPM was fulfilled. Also, Allan Anderson has consistently included the JPM in his list

55. Bustraan, "Jesus People," 37.

56. Anderson et al., "Introduction," in *Studying Global Pentecostalism*, 6.

57. Bustraan, "Jesus People," 38.

of Charismatic movements in the sixties and seventies.[58] However, Stephen Hunt stands out as a near lone scholar who has of recent focused attention on the JPM and has included it in his analysis of American Pentecostalism.[59] As a sociologist, Hunt recognizes the cultural developments of the sixties and seventies and traces the JPM along the trajectory of the post-sixties changes in American culture and in American religion. He understands the JPM to be one of many "vibrant forms of neo-Pentecostalism outside the mainstream denominational Charismatic movement." He believes that the JP are among those who "proved to be culturally accommodating at the same time that they have proved to be world rejecting, using the media for their own purposes if the technology fitted the evangelization imperative."[60]

But there remains a pressing task for many new and thorough studies to be launched that deeply probe and examine the 1960s and 1970s. For example, at present, almost every "scholarly" work that mentions Dennis Bennett and St Mark's Episcopal Church cites exclusively from Bennett's own autobiography *Nine o'clock in the morning*. This clearly is an unacceptable level of source examination. A scholarly, biographical analysis on the life of Jean Stone would certainly be a good starting point for understanding more about the events at St Mark's Episcopal Church. She is the woman who helped coin the phrase "Charismatic" and for five years published *Trinity* magazine before moving to Hong Kong to minister to drug addicts. This is only one example of numerous other people and organizations that could be assessed and the results would most likely challenge many commonly held assumptions.

The second primary reason that the JPM is missing due to the terms and definitions used to describe American Pentecostalism. Pentecostal historiographical paradigms and taxonomies should be built upon thorough research, but in fact they opposite has occurred. While this era of Pentecostal history remains distressingly under researched, the paradigms and taxonomies have been firmly cemented into the jargon and narrative of historical literature. With the paradigms in place, critical historical thinking seems to have stopped and the paradigms now serve to foster the sense that there is nothing more to study.

---

58. See A. Anderson (*Introduction to Pentecostalism*; "Pentecostal and Charismatic Movements"; "Varieties").

59. See S. Hunt ("Deprivation"; "Were the Jesus People Pentecostals?"; *History of the Charismatic Movement*).

60. S. Hunt, *History of the Charismatic*, 344.

The Dominant Three-Wave Paradigm and Taxonomy

There is in Pentecostal and Charismatic literature a singular taken-for-granted paradigm that tells the story of American Pentecostalism as unfolding in three consecutive waves. This model is so well ingrained in literature on Pentecostalism that it seems unnecessarily redundant to repeat it. But for clarity, the First Wave is purportedly the classical Pentecostal era. The Second wave supposedly began with Dennis Bennett in 1960 and is "inside" the historical churches, and the Third Wave allegedly began around C. Peter Wagner in 1980. This Third Wave paradigm is called Wagner's Third Wave, named for C. Peter Wagner. There is also another Third Wave paradigm, David Barrett's Third Wave, that blends chronology —events unfolding sequentially— with spatial, locational context. Barrett's Third Wave uses the terms classical Pentecostal, Charismatic, and neo-Charismatic to dissect American Pentecostalism into three categories.

Three Problems with the Three Waves

There are three main problems with the Third Wave paradigms and taxonomies. First, authors frequently mingle the terminologies and paradigms and they do not clarify which Three Wave model they are writing about. Wagner coined the term "Third Wave" and, according to Vinson Synan, Barrett borrowed it. But both have different meanings. Wagner's term centers on himself and the Association of Vineyard Churches while Barrett's term describes those Pentecostalisms that emerged outside the classical and mainline Pentecostalisms. Wagner's third and final wave begins in 1980 with John Wimber's classes at Fuller Theological Seminary, and the foundation of Vineyard in 1982 as something partially attributable to himself. Barrett's third and final wave traces the collection of Pentecostalisms from the late 1960s into the 1970s that could not be classed within the classical Pentecostal or mainline CM.

Second, the paradigms unnecessarily magnify two individuals, C. Peter Wagner and Dennis Bennett, and draw hard and fast lines in history at the years 1960 and 1980 that never did exist. The firm delineations at 1960 and 1980 have caused Bennett's and Wagner's significance to be grossly overstated and a myriad of other people, churches, and movements to be completely ignored. Wagner can be found taking advantage of the confusion over the two paradigms to promote himself and his own Third Wave model. For example, writing in 1988, Wagner stated, "I see it [his Third Wave] as mainly a movement beginning in the 1980s and gathering momentum through the closing years of the twentieth century. Researcher David Barrett estimates 27 million third-wavers in 1988."[61] Wagner blends the two usages of third wave in a way "that leads the reader to believe that his Third Wave, which was in fact centered on a limited number of people and events in Southern California, had affected 27 million people worldwide."[62] Wagner's Third Wave never affected anywhere near this many people. He writes this same exaggerated way in his article on "The Third Wave" in the *DPCM*.[63] Wagner has continued inventing paradigms centered on himself, his newest being the "New Apostolic Churches." The *NIDPCM*, while omitting the JPM, has served Wagner's purposes well by continuing to include an entry on the "Third Wave" written by, C. Peter Wagner.

Wagner's Third Wave paradigm also over centralizes the Vineyard story in American Pentecostalism. As such it has created a magnetic effect in scholarly pursuits by dictating the loci of many theological and sociological discussions that have clustered around Vineyard and the Third Wave trajectory—the Toronto Blessing. John Wimber's willingness to attach himself to Wagner's Third Wave label may have also served to distract the scholarly eye even further from the JPM.[64] The problem in any case does not lie with Vineyard and Wimber, but with the lack of rigorous, critical reflexivity in historical scholarship that should interpret Vineyard as simply another new church movement rooted in the JPM and Wagner's Third Wave paradigm as opportunism.

The most ardent academic supporters of Wagner's Third Wave have been Margaret Poloma and Vinson Synan.[65] For example, Poloma's recent work mentions the JPM in a few cursory sentences reducing it to mere "seeds" of Wagner's Third Wave.[66] This further promotes the false notion that the JPM was an incidental precursor of something far larger, the Wagner's Third Wave. With attention diverted, the JPM, incomparably larger and far more influential than events unfolding around Wagner, has almost vanished from the historical narrative of American Pentecostalism. Consequently, JPM church movements as large as PHCF with 1,400 affiliate churches have emerged undetected and unexamined. And ministers as prominent as Larry

---

61. P. Wagner, *Third Wave*, 18.

62. Bustraan, "Jesus People," 41.

63. P. Wagner, "Third Wave," 844.

64. S. Hunt, "Anglican Wimberites," 105.

65. See Poloma (*Charismatic Movement*, "Spirit Movement," *Main Street Mystics*), Poloma and Green (*Assemblies of God*), and Synan (*Spirit Said "Grow,"* "Role of Tongues," *Holiness Pentecostal Tradition*).

66. Poloma, *Assemblies of God: Godly Love*, 3.

Lea and The Church on the Rock, when briefly referenced, are done so without their proper historical connection to the JPM.

Problems with Barrett's Third Wave

In 1997 Walter Hollenweger wrote his book *Pentecostalism* in which he not only proposed a new paradigm for understanding Pentecostalism based on five roots, but he argued the need for a reclassification of taxonomies and definitions. According to Stanley Burgess, Barrett and Johnson responded in the year 2000 with the term "neo-Charismatic."[67] However, far from the serious reconsideration Hollenweger had envisioned, this was little more than a tautological exercise that exchanged the word "Third Wave" for "neo-Charismatic."[68] Thus the term "neo-Charismatic" was introduced as a replacement for term Barrett's "Third Wave," a "catchall" for 18,810 independent churches that did not qualify to fit into the other two categories.[69] Barrett's neo-Charismatic taxonomy has added to the confusion rather than resolve it, since at times authors interchange the terms Third Wavers, neo-Charismatics, neo-Pentecostals more for stylistic variance than for definitional clarity.

The JPM, however, breaks down the assumption undergirding Barrett's "neo-Charismatic" paradigm; that strong dividing lines existed between the three waves to form a definitive, triadic taxonomy. For there were significant JPM streams that not only crossed over into the Protestant, Catholic, and classical Pentecostal churches, but that were, in part, responsible for their growth and transformation. Or for example, Hope Chapel is a new church movement that has arisen within a previously existing classical Pentecostal denomination, the ICFG, and it cannot be located "outside" the first two waves.

The implications provoke numerous research questions. For example, what is the correlation between the ebb and flow in the CR and the JPM? The assumption guiding Pentecostal and Charismatic scholarship is that the CR was initiating a phenomenon and the unidirectional flow spilled over and resulted in new church movements and defectors migrating into classical Pentecostal churches. But the flow was, in fact, two directional, a reciprocal interchange through which the CR and CCR also received a portion of their revitalization and numerical growth from the JPM. Was the decline in the CR in the mid to late seventies caused by the demise of the JPM and the migration of young JP away from historical churches and into new JPM

67. Burgess, "Neocharismatics," 329.

68. Burgess, "Neo-Charismatics," 928.

69. Burgess, "Neocharismatics," 329.

churches, classical Pentecostal churches, and Evangelical churches? The inflexibility in Barrett's delineations between neo-Charismatic, Charismatic, and classical Pentecostal taxonomies does not recognize any reciprocal interchange. Thus it precludes any considering of the mutual qualitative and quantitative benefit between the First, Second, and Third Waves that occurred in the JPM.

Including the JPM into the present paradigms and taxonomies also challenges many of the statements made about American Pentecostalism in this era. For example, Peter Hocken wrote, "Since the 1970s, CM-CR has had two major contrasting expressions: on the one hand, the new charismatic churches and networks, and on the other hand renewal within the historic churches. The 1990s have seen the new churches and networks expand on a massive scale, not widely paralleled by CR within the historic churches."[70] His conclusions exclude the JPM from the 1970s Pentecostalism and his inflexibility of "two major contrasting expressions" unnecessarily dichotomizes between "inside" and "outside" the historical churches. It does not recognize the reciprocal interchange between the JPM and the CM in the 1970s. And his conclusion regarding the 1990s new church movements outside the historical churches needs to recognize the JPM's contribution to this phenomenon.

Hocken also wrote, "Holy Spirit renewal regularly brings a heightened urgency for evangelism. This was more evident in the 1990s than in the 1970s."[71] This simply is not true. If the JPM were included in the history of Pentecostalism it would demonstrate a heightened urgency for evangelism in the 1970s. These are only two examples, but they demonstrate that the implications for including the JPM into the story of American Pentecostalism are devastating to many assumptions and conclusions that have been formulated on the present paradigms and taxonomies. Locating the JPM simply as a neo-Charismatic movement, and thus "outside" the historical churches, is not being true to the historical evidence and it robs the rich nature of the reciprocal interchange that was occurring between the JPM and the various movements of Pentecostalism in the 1960s and 1970s. Barrett's Third Wave falls apart when locating the JPM into it.

The Problems with the "Second Wave" and "Neo-Charismatic"

The notion that the CM began in 1960 from Dennis Bennett ignores the evolutionary process within Pentecostalism that was taking place long before

70. Hocken, "Charismatic Movement," 515.

71. Ibid.

Bennett's BHS. For example, if there is a need to choose such a "founder" why does the CM begin with Bennett's BHS in 1959, instead of with Harald Bredesen's in 1946?[72] After all, being a reformed minister qualified him to be "within the mainline churches." In addition, he was purportedly responsible for influencing the likes of Pat Robertson, Pat Boone, John Sherrill and apparently Benny Hinn and Don Moen.[73] That Bennett influenced the spread of Pentecostalism in the American Episcopal and other Protestant churches is not doubted, but there were numerous other individuals in Protestant churches before, during, and after Bennett's own spiritual experiences that also were affecting the lives of those in mainline Protestant churches.

Another serious problem with the Second Wave paradigm is that it forces historical classifications to work with a system that reflects where Pentecostalism was in the 1960s. Time has moved on and the sense of new in "neo" Charismatic sounds rather "old" and dated fifty years after the alleged second wave began. This seems to suggest that every subsequent movement to arise after the 1960s historical churches' renewal, whether it be for the next two hundred years, should be called "neo."

But there is a more substantial problem with the taxonomies. The label "Charismatic" and the notion of a "Second Wave" emerged from Pentecostalism's legitimacy and credibility battle in the historical churches. That is to say, the CR and the CCR leaders wanted to legitimize the Pentecostalism in their churches and their association with classical Pentecostals threatened their credibility. Classical Pentecostals were seen as people of lower echelons in society who practiced an inferior, unthinking, and experience-driven form of religion. Any association with classical Pentecostals threatened to delegitimize the CM. To help legitimize their own movements CR and CCR leaders downplayed or concealed their associations with classical Pentecostals and even invented another term to describe their form of Pentecostalism, the Charismatic Movement.

Catholics have been the most forthcoming on this issue and have published materials that discuss this legitimacy battle.[74] The CR leaders have been less forthcoming on this issue and this holds true even to the present day. For example, Dennis Bennett wrote *Nine o'clock in the morning* using people's first names only. And he limited his links to Pentecostalism to a fellow Episcopalian priest named Frank (Frank Maguire) and a couple from Maguire's church known only as John and Joan. The closest Bennett comes

72. Hocken, "Harald Bredesen," 441–42.

73. Ibid.

74. See Fitcher ("Liberal and Conservative"), C. Harper ("Spirit-Filled Catholics"), M. Harrison ("Sources of Recruitment"), McDonnell (*Catholic Pentecostalism*; *Holy Spirit*), and Laurentin (*Catholic Pentecostalism*).

to admitting his links to classical Pentecostalism is one brief sentence in which John and Joan announce that they were introduced to the BHS at "a neighborhood prayer meeting."[75] Consequentially, Bennett succeeded at concealing his links to classical Pentecostalism and at presenting himself as the founder of a new "Charismatic" movement that emerged ex-nihilo from St. Mark's Church in Van Nuys, California. Peter Hocken's PhD thesis reveals communications between Frank Maguire and other Episcopalian clergy in which they talked about their public disassociation with classical Pentecostals. Maguire said, "They [classical Pentecostals] mean well, and we can learn a great deal from them in private discussions, but *NEVER, NEVER, NEVER,* have them at prayer meetings where there are sensitive people present."[76]

These previous comments are not intended to fault the CR and CCR leaders for their concerns or methods of legitimization. In fact, classical Pentecostals and the JP all faced the same struggle and used means to gain credibility. However, as with Wagner's Third Wave, the fault lies in the lack of rigorous and critical, historical scholarship that has demonstrated very little critical reflexivity in its acceptance of the Second Wave and neo-Charismatic paradigms.

In the 1960s context of legitimacy, there was nothing "new" in the "neo-Charismatic" movements that occurred outside the historical churches. Instead, there was something "other," something "deviant." In other words, "neo-Charismatic" has become the default dumping ground for any Pentecostalism since the 1970s that has not fit neatly into the first two categories. This unfairly elevates classical Pentecostals and Charismatics—first and second wavers—to the position of primary definers of American Pentecostalism. And as such all "others" or "neos" are inferior offspring whose taxonomical legitimacy is gained solely on the grounds of their ability to prove their comparative historical, theological, and sociological merits. Under Barrett's Three Wave paradigm, the location of any movement is determined by understanding if it is not classical Pentecostal and second if it is not renewal within the mainline churches. If the answer to both of these questions is no, then it is an "other" or "deviant" Pentecostalism.

Not only does the JPM struggle to find a place under this schema, but it also raises questions about many "other" people and movements that have emerged in American Pentecostalism. For example, where do Oral Roberts, Demos Shakarian, David du Plessis, Kathryn Kuhlman, Tommy

---

75. Bennett, *Nine O'clock*, 19.

76. Letter from Frank Maguire to Michael Harper, September 10, 1963, in Hocken, "Baptised in the Spirit," 166–68.

Tyson, Harald Bredesen, Derick Prince, and Don Basham belong? Where does the Latter Rain Movement, the FGBMFI, the SM, Orthodox Renewal, AfricanAmerican and Latin American Charismatics, the Faith Movement, the Messianic Movement, the Metropolitan Community Church, and the National Gay Pentecostal Alliance locate? The JPM shares a common dilemma with these "other" movements, in that they are rather thoughtlessly dropped into the leftover category of deviants. Ironically, this "other," default category has had so many Pentecostalisms loaded into it that according to Stanley Burgess, its adherents are now more numerous than the first two categories combined; 60 percent being neo-Charismatics as of 2005.[77] Or as it has also been stated, "The rapid expansion of Pentecostalism has pushed so-called mainstream Protestantism into a minority position."[78]

Conclusions

If the present paradigms and taxonomies must be used they are rather problematic, but a few suggestions are forwarded. First, Wagner's Third Wave paradigm should be jettisoned as being completely incompatible with the historical, theological, and sociological research presented here on the JPM. Second, although Barrett's Third Wave or neo-Charismatic taxonomy seriously depreciates the JPM by its relegation to "otherness," it is a little more workable. Using Barrett's paradigm the JPM would be best located as a classical Pentecostal (or First Wave), as a Charismatic (or Second Wave), and as a neo-Charismatic movement with its majority portion in the neo-Charismatic camp. While recognizing the overlap with the classical Pentecostalism, the CM, and Evangelicalism, it must be acknowledged that the JPM's Pentecostalism was unique and that there were large new ministries and new churches initiated. It bears resemblance to other concurrent movements in Pentecostalism, but especially with the healing revivals of the late 1800s, the 1940s and 1950s.

It is suggested that the JPM was far more transformational of all of American Pentecostalism than is acknowledged in the footnote mentions it receives in Pentecostal scholarly assessments. And it has been far more enduring and revitalizing of American Christianity into the present day than is given credit. Not only is it impossible to locate the JPM in a single "wave" category, but it also impossible to understand the latter half of twentieth-century American Pentecostalism without the story of the JP. Donald Miller's bold assessment deserves attention. He envisions the JPM and its

---

77. Burgess, "Neocharismatics," 329.

78. Anderson et al., "Introduction," in *Studying Global Pentecostalism*, 2.

"new paradigm churches" as a "revolution" comparable to the Protestant Reformation and he believes that is only in its initial stages.[79]

The JPM and its aftermath is a microcosm of a global trend of hybridizations in Pentecostalisms since the 1970s which, according to Allan Anderson, is so vast that even the global statistical experts of Johnstone and Mandryk, and Barrett and Johnson differ over who to include in which circles.[80] This trend highlights the problem with assigning labels in an increasingly pluralistic and rapidly changing labyrinth of Pentecostalisms. The heart of the challenge in taxonomies and paradigms lies in the necessity to find something more equitable and unifying while not overriding diversity. There is also a need to recognize the overlap, the reciprocal interchange, the porous borders, and the evolutionary process within American Pentecostalism, while at the same time recognizing the unique contribution made by individuals and movements. The present conversation of Pentecostalism in the 1960s and 1970s is too insular and it needs to be more connected with the massive shifts in the social, political, and religious trends within America during this same era.

There was a Jesus Revolution and it took place at a time when America shifted from a pre-sixties to a post-sixties culture. The JPM and the other movements of the counterculture revolution transformed the American landscape, leaving the 1980s and the 1990s and up to the present day in its aftermath. There is an ongoing transformation of a post-1960s Christianity that is attributable to this thirteen year, religious movement known as the Jesus People Movement. It is hoped that this work becomes a spark of inspiration for many others to research its history, sociology, and theology and to understand its contribution to American Pentecostalism.

79. D. Miller, *Reinventing*, 2, 11–18.
80. A. Anderson, *An Introduction*, 11.

Bibliography

All articles in the *PE* were accessed online from the Flower Pentecostal Heritage Center "2nd Chapter of Acts." Online: http://www.2ndchapterofacts.com/History.html.

The 5th Dimension. "Aquarius/Let the Sunshine In." Liberty Records, 1969.

"Abbott Loop Community Church, History." Online: http://www.abbottloop. org/?q=node/10.

Adams, David. "Jesus People." Pyramid Films, 1972. Online: http://www. hollywoodfreepaper.org.

Adams, Robert Lynn, and Robert Jon Fox. "Mainlining Jesus: The New Trip." *Society* 9/4 (1972) 50–56.

Addington, Larry H. *America's War in Vietnam: A Short Narrative History*. Indianapolis: Indiana University Press, 2000.

Aiken (SC) Standard and Review. "Coffee House for Teens Draws Capacity Crowd." November 24, 1969. Online: NewspaperArchive.com.

Albright, Thomas. "Visuals: How the Beats Begat the Freaks." In *The Rolling Stone Book of the Beats, the Beat Generation and the Counterculture*, edited by Holly George-Warren, 353–56. London: Bloomsbury, 1999.

Allitt, Patrick. *Religion in America since 1945: A History*. New York: Columbia University Press, 2003.

Alpert, Richard, and Timothy Leary. "The Politics of Consciousness Expansion." *Harvard Review* 1/4 (1963) 33–37. Online: http://www.lysergia.com/FeedYourHead/FYH_LearyAlpert1963.htm.

Althouse, Peter. *Spirit of the Last Days: Pentecostal Eschatology in Conversation with Jürgen Moltmann*. London: T. & T. Clark, 2003.

Anderson, Allan. *An Introduction to Pentecostalism*. Cambridge: Cambridge University Press, 2004.

———. "The Pentecostal and Charismatic Movements." In *The Cambridge History of Christianity*, edited by Hugh McLeod, 89–106. Cambridge: Cambridge University Press, 2006.

———. *Spreading Fires: The Missionary Nature of Early Pentecostalism*. London: SCM, 2007.

———. "Varieties, Taxonomies, and Definitions." In *Studying Global Pentecostalism: Theories and Methods*, edited by Allan Anderson et al., 13–29. Berkeley, CA: University of California Press, 2010.

Anderson, Allan, et al., editors. *Studying Global Pentecostalism: Theories and Methods*, Berkeley: University of California Press, 2010.

Anderson, Mapes Robert. *Vision of the Disinherited: The Making of American Pentecostalism.* Oxford: Oxford University Press, 1979.

Aquirre, Adalberto. *Racial and Ethnic Diversity in America: A Reference Book.* Santa Barbara: ABC CLIO, 2003.

Archer, Kenneth J. *A Pentecostal Hermeneutic for the Twenty-First Century: Spirit, Scripture, Community.* New York: T. & T. Clark, 2004.

Assemblies of God. "Core Doctrines: The Second Coming." Online: http://agchurches. org/Sitefiles/Default/RSS/IValue/Resources/Teaching%20Outline/Second%20 Coming%20Outline.pdf.

Assemblies of God. "Statement of Faith." Online: http://ministers.ag.org/ pdf/16Fundamentals.pdf.

Associated Press. "Army Wants No Hippie Chaplain." *Free Lance Star*, December 2, 1967. Online: http://news.google.com/newspapers.

———. "Compound Leader Tony Alamo Arrested in Child Porn Probe." September 25, 2008. Online: http://www.foxnews.com/story/0,2933,428241,00.html.

———. "Hip Heckling Hits Sermon In Bay Area." *Modesto Bee,* January 29, 1968. Online: http://news.google.com/newspapers.

———. "Jesus People Leave City for Good." *Indiana (PA) Evening Gazette,* June 26, 1972. Online: NewspaperArchive.com.

———. "'Jesus People' Winning over Street Youth in Southland." *Press Telegram (CA),* February 04, 1971. Online: NewspaperArchive.com.

———. "Junkies Get Help From Rustic Home." *Lawrence Journal-World (KS),* August 06, 1966. Online: http://news.google.com/newspapers.

———. "Lifelight Festival Draws Huge Crowd." September 03, 2008, Online: http:// www.keloland.com/NewsDetail6162.cfm?Id=73475.

———. "Pat Boone Baptizes in His Swimming Pool." *Hutchinson (KS) News,* December 4, 1971. Online: NewspaperArchive.com.

———. "Rev. Howard Conatser." *Toledo Blade*, June 21, 1978, 8. Online: http://news. google.com/newspapers.

———. "Salvation Army is 'Groovy.'" *Evening Independent (FL)*, August 24, 1967. Online: http://news.google.com/newspapers.

———. "'Underground Church' Spreads in U.S." *The Sarasota Herald-Tribune*, February 17, 1967, 25. Online: http://newsgoogle.com/newspapers.

———. "Village Priest Offers to Be Teenager-Parent Go-Between." *Daytona Beach Morning Journal,* March 27, 1968. Online: http://news.google.com/newspapers.

Aune, Kristin. "Between Subordination and Sympathy: Evangelical Christians, Masculinity and Gay Sexuality." In *Contemporary Christianity and LGBT Sexualities,* edited by Stephen Hunt, 39–49. Surrey, UK: Ashgate, 2009.

Baker, Paul. *Why Should the Devil Have All the Good Music.* Waco, TX: Word, 1979.

Balmer, Randall Herbert. "Linda Meissner." In *Encyclopedia of Evangelicalism.* Louisville: Westminster John Knox, 2002.

———. *Mine Eyes Have Seen the Glory: A Journey into the Evangelical Subculture in America.* Oxford: Oxford University Press, 1993.

Balmer, Randall Herbert, and Todd, Jesse T., Jr. "Calvary Chapel Costa Mesa California." In *American Congrgations Volume 1: Portraits of 12 Religious Communities*, edited by James P. Wind et al., 663–98. London: University of Chicago Press, 1994.

Balswick, Jack. "The Jesus People Movement: A Generational Interpretation." *Journal of Social Issues* 30/3 (1974) 23–42.

Baptist Press. "1181 Decisions Reported In Dayton Encounter Crusade." July 27, 1967. Online: http://media.sbhla.org.s3.amazonaws.com/2436,27-Jul-1967.pdf.

Baptist Press Release. "Golden Gate Seminary Report to the SBC." May 31, 1967. Online: http://media.sbhla.org.s3.amazonaws.com/2400,31-May-1967.pdf.

————. "Ron Willis Named Street Minister in San Antonio," July 6, 1972. Online: http://media.sbhla.org.s3.amazonaws.com/3406,06-Jul-1972.pdf.

Barfoot, Charles H., and Gerald T. Sheppard. "Prophetic Vs. Priestly Religion: The Changing Role of Women Clergy in Classical Pentecostal Churches." *Review of Religious Research* 22/1 (1980) 2–17. Online: http://www.jstor.org/pss/3510481.

Barnes, Hazel. "Teen-Agers Aided." *Spokane Daily Chronicle*, September 24, 1965. Online: http://www.facebook.com/photo.php?fbid=412827131814&set=t.1457623490&type=3&theater.

Barrett, David B. "The Twentieth-Century Pentecostal/Charismatic Renewal in the Holy Spirit with Its Goal of World Evangelization." *International Bulletin of Missionary Research* 12/3 (1988) 119. Online: http://www.internationalbulletin.org/archive/all/1988/7.

Barrett, David B., et al., editors. "The Catholic Charismatic Renewal 1959–2025." In *World Christian Trends, AD 30–AD 2200: Interpreting the Annual Christian Megacensus*, 1:278. Pasadena, CA: William Carey Library, 2001.

Bastien, Brian. "Hollywood Boulevard: One Way." *CT*, January 2, 1970.

Beaty, Kim. "The Jesus People: Where Are They Now? How Have They Changed?" *Virtue*, January–February 1992.

Bebbington, David W. *The Dominance of Evangelicalism: The Age of Spurgeon and Moody*. Downers Grove, IL: InterVarsity, 2005.

"Belmont Church." Online: http://www.belmont.org/assem/history.asp.

Bennett, Dennis J. *Nine O'clock in the Morning*. New ed. London: Coverdale House, 1974.

Berg, Robert A. "Relationship to Neo-Pentecostal Christians." In *Encyclopedia of Pentecostal and Charismatic Christianity*, edited by Stanley M. Burgess. London: Routledge, 2006.

Berger, Peter L. *The Sacred Canopy: Elements of a Sociological Theory of Religion*. Garden City, NY: Doubleday, 1967.

Berman, Paul. *A Tale of Two Utopias: The Political Journey of the Generation of 1968*. London: Norton, 1996.

Beyer, Peter, and Lori G. Beaman. *Religion and Globalization, Theory, Culture & Society*. London: Sage, 1994.

Bindas, Kenneth J., and Kenneth J. Heinman. "Image Is Everything? Television and the Counter-Cultural Message During the 1960s." *Journal of Popular Film and Television* 22/1 (1994) 22–37. Online: http://members.tripod.com/anthony_giacalone/tv_counterculture.html.

Bisceglia, Bronya. "'Jesus Movement' Attracts Following across Country, on Campuses." *New Castle (IN) News*, January 13, 1972. Online: NewspaperArchive.com.

Black Demographics. "Middle Class." Online: http://blackdemographics.com/middle_class.html.

Blessitt, Arthur. *Turned on to Jesus*. London: Word, 1971.

Bloch-Hoell, Nils. *The Pentecostal Movement: Its Origin, Development, and Distinctive Character*. London: Allen & Unwin, 1964.

Blumhofer, Edith W. *The Assemblies of God: A Chapter in the Story of American Pentecostalism.* Vol. 1, *To 1941.* Springfield, MO: Gospel, 1989.

———. *Restoring the Faith: The Assemblies of God, Pentecostalism, and American Culture.* Champaign: University of Illinois Press, 1993.

"Bob Jones University Residence Hall Life." Bob Jones University. Online: http://www.bju.edu/become-a-student/accepted-students/expectations/residence.php.

Bodroghkozy, Aniko. *Groove Tube: Sixties and the Youth Rebellion.* Durham, NC: Duke University Press, 2001.

Bookchin, Murray. *Post-Scarcity Anarchism.* 3rd ed. Oakland: AK, 2004.

Boyce, Wayne. "Father Bennett's Mission." *Brandon (Manitoba) Sun,* April 21, 1973. Online: NewspaperArchive.com.

Bozeman, John. "Jesus People USA." In *The Encyclopedia of Cults, Sects, and New Religions,* edited by James R. Lewis. New York: Prometheus, 1998.

Braunstein, Peter. "Forever Young: Insurgent Youth and the Sixties Culture of Rejuvenation." In *Imagine Nation: The American Counterculture of the 1960s and '70s,* edited by Peter Braunstein and Michael William Doyle, 243–74. New York: Routledge, 2002.

Braunstein, Peter, and Michael William Doyle. "Historicizing the American Counterculture of the 1960s and '70s." In *Imagine Nation: The American Counterculture of the 1960s and '70s,* edited by Peter Braunstein and Michael William Doyle, 5–15. London: Routledge, 2002.

Braunstein, Peter, and Michael William Doyle, editors. *Imagine Nation: The American Counterculture of the 1960s and '70s.* New York: Routledge, 2002.

Brotzman, Harry, Jr. "A Deaf Hippie Finds Christ." *PE,* September 29, 1968.

Burgess, Stanley M. "Neo-Charismatics." In *NIDPCM,* 928.

———. "Neocharismatics." In *Encyclopedia of Pentecostal and Charismatic Christianity,* edited by Stanley M. Burgess. London: Rutledge, 2006.

Burns, Gary. "Trends in Lyrics in the Annual Top Twenty Songs in the United States, 1963–1972." In *American Popular Music Volume 2: The Age of Rock,* edited by Timothy E. Scheurer, 129–41. Bowling Green: Bowling Green State University Popular Press, 1989.

Bush, Brentice. "Christian Witness at Hippie Festival." *PE,* September 27, 1970.

Bustraan, Richard. "The Jesus People Movement and the Charismatic Movement: A Case for Inclusion." *Pentecostudies* 10/1 (2011) 29–49.

"Calvary Chapel." Online: http://www.calvarychapel.com/.

Calvary Chapel. "Calvary Chapel Association." Online: http://calvarychapelassociation.com.

Calvary Chapel. "Statement of Faith." Online: http://calvarychapelassociation.com/general-information/statement-of-faith/

"Calvary Chapel Tri-City." Online: http://www.calvarytricity.com/about.php.

Campbell, Colin. "Clarifying the Cult." *The British Journal of Sociology* 28/3 (1977) 375–88.

———. "The Cult, the Cultic Milieu and Secularization." In *The Cultic Milieu: Oppositional Subcultures in an Age of Globalization,* edited by Jeffrey Kaplan and Heléne Lööw, 12–25. Walnut Creek, CA: AltaMira, 2002.

———. "The Secret Religion of the Educated Classes." *Sociological Analysis* 39/2 (1978) 146–56. Online: http://www.jstor.org/stable/3710214.

"Campus Crusade for Christ International: US Staff Personnel Handbook." November 1981.

Canadian Press. "Church Hall Raid Nets Drug Users." *Windsor Star (Ontario)*, January 09, 1968. Online: http://news.google.com/newspapers.

———."Jesus People's Army Meets for Vancouver Rock Revival." *Sarasota (FL) Herald Tribune*, August 29, 1970. Online: NewspaperArchive.com.

Cartledge, Mark. "Interpreting Charismatic Experience: Hypnosis, Altered States of Consciousness and the Holy Spirit?" *The Journal of Pentecostal Theology* 6/13 (1998) 117–32.

———. *Testimony in the Spirit*. Bodmin, UK: Ashgate, 2010.

Cassels, Louis (AP). "Young Life Group Reaches Turned-Off Young People." *Playground Daily News (FL)*, November 23, 1973. Online: NewspaperArchive.com.

Castaneda, Carlos. *The Teaching of Don Juan: A Yaqui Way of Knowledge*. Berkeley: University of California Press, 1968.

CBN. "Interview." Online: http://www.cbn.com/media/player/index.aspx?s=/vod/ScottRoss_Interview1.

———. "John Gimenez: The Legacy of a Powerhouse Preacher." Online: https://www.cbn.org/media/player/index.aspx?s=/vod/AR49V1.

Chandler, Russell. "Melodyland School: The Spirit's Tune." *CT*, July 20, 1973.

Channels.com. "Maharishi Mahesh Yogi." Online: http://www.channels.com/episodes/show/10225573/Maharishi-on-History-Channel.

Chauncey, George. "Long-Haired Men and Short-Haired Women—Building a Gay World in the Heart of Bohemia." In *Greenwich Village: Culture and Counterculture*, edited by Rick Beard and Leslie Cohen Berlowitz, 151–63. New Brunswick: Rutgers University Press, 1993.

Chippindale, Peter. "Jesus People 'Reformation.'" *Guardian (UK)*, April 10, 1973. Online: ProQuest Historical Newspapers (0307795715).

Chrasta, Michael James. "Jesus People to Promise Keepers: A Revival Sequence and Its Effect on Late Twentieth-Century Evangelical Ideas of Masculinity." PhD diss., The University of Texas at Dallas, 1998. Online Preview: http://proquest.umi.com. ATT 9910768.

"Christ Is the Answer." Online: http://www.citatoday.com/christ_is_the_answer/missions/missions_index.asp.

Christenson, Larry. "The Charismatic Movement: An Historical and Theological Perspective." *Lutheran Forum* 43/3 (2009) 1–27. Online: http://www.lutheranrenewal.org/The_Charismatic_Movement.pdf.

———. *Speaking in Tongues and Its Significance for the Church*. London: Coverdale, 1968.

Claussen, Dane S., editor. *The Promise Keepers: Essays on Masculinity and Christianity*. Jefferson, NC: McFarland, 2000.

Coleman, Margo. "Religious Movement Is Misunderstood." *Derrick (PA)*, July 19, 1971. Online: NewspaperArchive.com.

Coleman, Simon. "The Faith Movement: A Global Religious Culture?" *Culture and Religion* 3/1 (2002) 3–19.

Connor, Steve. *Postmodernist Culture: An Introduction to Theories of the Contemporary*. Cambridge: Blackwell, 1997.

Conover, Patrick W. "Communes and Intentional Communities." *Nonprofit and Voluntary Sector Quarterly* 7/5 (1978) 5–17. Online: http://nvs.sagepub.com/cgi/reprint/7/3/5.

Copley News Service. "'Jesus People' Are out to Convert the World." *Naples (FL) Daily News,* August 03, 1973. Online NewspaperArchive.com.

Cording, Bob, and Hardenbrook, Weldon. "The Son Worshippers." Gospel Media, Los Angeles, CA, 1972. Online: http://www.youtube.com/watch?v=CvHSP3kT16A.

Cornell, George. "Church Leaders Note Dangers in Youthful Jesus Movement." *Newport (RI) Daily News,* February 08, 1973. Online: NewspaperArchive.com.

——— (AP). "Jesus People' Call Nation Back to God." *Press Courier (CA),* July 11, 1971. Online: NewspaperArchive.com.

——— (AP). "N.Y. Youths Embrace Jesus Movement." *Albuquerque (NM) Journal,* May 12, 1972. Online: NewspaperArchive.com.

Corry, Geoffrey. *Jesus Bubble or Jesus Revolution: The Growth of Jesus Communes in Britain and Ireland.* London: British Council of Churches Youth Department, 1973.

Cox, Claire (CNS). "Jesus Movement Continues Strong." *Odessa American (TX),* July 28, 1973. Online: NewspaperArchive.com.

Cox, Harvey. *Fire from Heaven: The Rise of Pentecostal Spirituality and the Reshaping of Religion in the Twenty-First Century.* London: Cassell, 1996.

———. *The Secular City: Secularization and Urbanization in Theological Perspective.* London: SCM, 1968.

"Creation Northeast." Online: http://www.creationfest.com/ne.

Creech, Joe. "Visions of Glory: The Place of the Azusa Street Revival in Pentecostal History." *American Society Church History* 65/3 (1996) 405–24. Online: http://www.jstor.org/stable/pdfplus/3169938.pdf.

Cronn, Jason "Jason Questions a Jesus Freak." Peninsula Bible Church. Online: http://www.pbc.org/messages/17925.

Cunningham, George. "Theater-in-the-Round: Center Stage for the Gospel Melodyland Christian Center Anaheim, California Ralph Wilkerson, Pastor." In *The Complete Book of Church Growth,* by Elmer L. Towns, John N. Vaughan, David J. Seifert, 22–26. Wheaton, IL: Tyndale, 1978.

CT. "The Great Camp Meeting in 1973." July 6, 1973.

———. "Jesus Newspapers." May 10, 1974.

———. "The Man with the Plan." October 27, 1972.

———. "Skinner Gets Them Together." June 9, 1972.

Cutten, George. *Speaking with Tongues: Historically and Psychologically Considered.* New Haven: Yale University Press, 1927.

Daily Chronicle (WA). "Christian Couples Club Will Hear Mrs. Neal," February 22, 1973. Online: NewspaperArchive.com.

Daily Courier (AZ). "Mario Murillo Featured Speaker at Living Faith," April 25, 2003. Online: news.google.com/newspapers.

Daily News (PA). "Only Another 'Trip,'" August 02, 1971. Online: NewspaperArchive.com.

Daily News of Port Angeles (WA). "Jesus People Leave Streets of Spokane," June 25, 1972. Online: NewspaperArchive.com.

Dalton, Dudley (NYT). "Charismatics to Begin 'Great Revival.'" *Hutchinson News (KS),* December 27, 1975. Online: NewspaperArchive.com.

"Dave Anderson." Online: http://daveanderson.name/?page=bio.

"David Hoyt." Online: http://www.davehoytgallery.com/index.php?p=1_4_About-Us.

Davidsson, Tommy Henrik. "Lewi Pethrus' Ecclesiological Thought 1911–1974: A Transdenominational Pentecostal Ecclesiology." PhD diss., University of Birmingham, 2012.

Davis, Rex. *Locusts and Wild Honey: The Charismatic Renewal and the Ecumenical Movement. Geneva*: World Council of Churches, 1978.

Dayton, Donald W. *Theological Roots of Pentecostalism*. Peabody, MA: Hendrickson, 1987.

Deloria, Philip. "Counterculture Indians and the New Age." In *Imagine Nation: The American Counterculture of the 1960s and '70s*, edited by Peter Braunstein and Michael William Doyle, 159–88. New York: Routledge, 2002.

Denscomb, Martyn. *The Good Research Guide: For Small-Scale Research Projects.* Maidenhead, NY: Open University Press, 2007.

Der Speigel. "Gott Sein Ist Ein Harter Job." February 14, 1972. Online: http://www. spiegel.de/spiegel/print/d-43019123.html.

———. "Jesus-Revolution Im Nächsten Jahr?" August 30, 1971. Online: http://www. spiegel.de/spiegel/print/d-43175388.html.

"Diggers." Online: http://www.diggers.org/history.htm.

Di Sabatino, David. "Frisbee: The Life and Death of a Hippie Preacher." USA: Jester Media, 2005.

———. *The Jesus People Movement: An Annotated Bibliography and General Resource.* Lake Forest: Jester Media, 2004.

———. "The Jesus People Movement: Counterculture Revival and Evangelical Renewal." Master's thesis, McMaster Divinity College, 1994.

———. "Lonnie Frisbee: A Modern Day Sampson." In *The Jesus People Movement: An Annotated Bibliography and General Resource*, by David Di Sabatino, 205–12. Lake Forest: Jester Media, 2004.

Doty, Mark. "From the Poem That Changed America: 'Howl' Fifty Years Later." *The American Poetry Review* 35/2 (2006) 3, 8. Online: http://gateway.proquest.com/ openurl?ctx_ver=Z39.88-2003&xri:pqil:res_ver=0.2&res_id=xr.

Droogers, André. "Essentialist and Normative Approaches." In *Studying Global Pentecostalism: Theories and Methods*, edited by Allan Anderson et al., 30–50. London: University of California Press, 2010.

———. "The Normalization of Religious Experience: Healing, Prophecy, Dreams, and Visions." In *Charismatic Christianity as a Global Culture*, edited by Karla Poewe, 33–49. Columbia: University of South Carolina Press, 1994.

Duffield, Guy P., and Nathaniel M. Van Cleave. *Foundations of Pentecostal Theology*. Los Angeles: Life Bible College, 1983.

Durkin, Jim. "The Bold Confession." In *Practice the Word*. Radiance Media Ministry, 1973. Online: http://goalumni.homestead.com/Bold_Confession.html.

———. *Living the Word: How to Apply the Scripture to Your Life*. Ann Arbor: Servant, 1979.

Durkin, Jim, et al. *The Coming World Crisis*. Plainfield: Haven, 1980.

"Eagles Communications." Online: http://www.eagles.com.sg/aboutUs.html.

Eastman, Dick. "Prayer Power and the Jesus Movement." *PE*, August 22, 1971.

———. *Up with Jesus*. Grand Rapids: Baker, 1971.

Echols, Alice. *Shaky Ground: The Sixties and Its Aftershocks*. New York: Columbia University Press, 2002.

Eggebroten, Anne. "Rally Round the Cross." *The Christian Century*, August 21, 1970.

Ellensburg Daily Record (WA), "Evangelist to Speak Sunday," August 28, 1969. Online: http://news.google.com/newspapers.

Ellwood, Robert, Jr. *One Way: The Jesus Movement and Its Meaning*. Englewood Cliffs, NJ: Prentice-Hall, 1973.

————. *The Sixties Spiritual Awakening: American Religion Moving from Modern to Postmodern*. New Brunswick, NJ: Rutgers University Press, 1994.

Enroth, Ronald M. *Churches That Abuse*. Grand Rapids: Zonvdervan, 1992.

————. *A Guide to Cults and New Religions*. Downers Grove, IL: InterVarsity, 1983.

————. *Recovering from Churches That Abuse*. Grand Rapids: Zondervan, 1994.

————. "Where Have All the Jesus People Gone?" *Eternity*, October 1973.

————. *Youth, Brainwashing, and the Extremist Cults*. Exeter, UK: Paternoster, 1977.

Enroth, Ronald M., et al. *The Story of the Jesus People: A Factual Survey*. Exeter, UK: Paternoster, 1972.

Eshelman, Paul. *The Explo Story: A Plan to Change the World*. Glendale, CA: Regal, 1972.

Eskridge, Larry. "God's Forever Family: The Jesus People Movement in America, 1966–1977." PhD diss., Sterling University, 2005. Online: uk.bl.ethos.427916.

————. "Jesus People." In *The Encyclopedia of Christianity*, edited by Erwin Fahlbusch et al. Grand Rapids: Eerdmans, 1999.

————. "'One Way': Billy Graham, the Jesus Generation, and the Idea of an Evangelical Youth Culture." *The American Society of Church History* 67/1 (1998) 83–106. Online: http://www.jstor.org/stable/3170772.

————. "The 'Praise and Worship' Revolution." *CT*, October 29, 2008. Online: Http://www.christianitytoday.com/ch/thepastinthepresent/storybehind/praiseworshiprevolution.html?start=2.

Eskridge, Larry, and David Di Sabatino. "Remembering the Jesus Movement." *One-Way.org*. Online: one-way.org, 2004. http://www.one-way.org/jesusmovement/index.html: one-way.org, 2004.

"Every Home for Christ." Online: http:// http://www.ehc.org/about-us-dick-eastman.

"Ex-family." Online: http://www.exfamily.org/index.htm.

Farber, David. "The Intoxicated State/Illegal Nation: Drugs in the Sixties Counterculture." In *Imagine Nation: The American Counterculture of the 1960s and '70s*, edited by Peter Braunstein and Michael Doyle, 17–40. New York: Rutledge, 2002.

"The Farm Website." Online: http://thefarmcommunity.com/about_the_farm/brief_history.asp.

"Fisherman's Net Revival Center." Online: http://fishermansnetchurch.org/fishermansnetchurch/about_the_Pastor.html.

"Fishnet Ministries." Online: http://www.fishnetministries.org/general-info/about/from-the-president.html.

Fiske, Edward B. (NYT). "Religious Authority Reasserted." *European Stars and Stripes*, July 22, 1973. Online: NewspaperArchive.com.

Fitcher, Joseph H. "Liberal and Conservative Catholic Pentecostals." *SC* 21/3 (1974) 303–10. Online: http://scp.sagepub.com/cgi/reprint/21/3/303.

Fitzgerald, Francis. *Cities on a Hill*. New York: Simon & Schuster, 1987.

Flowers, James. "So I'm a Square." *News Courier (NY)*, May 17, 1968. Online: http://news.google.com/newspapers.

Foursquare Church. "Beliefs: Spirit Filled Life." Online: http://www.foursquare.org/about/what_we_believe/spirit_filled_life.

———. "Declaration of Faith." Online: http://www.foursquare.org/images/assets/Declaration_of_Faith.pdf.

Fromm, Charles. "Textual Communities and New Song in the Multimedia Age: The Routinization of Charisma in the Jesus Movement." PhD diss., Fuller Theological Seminary, 2006.

Funnell, David. "Some Memories of Jim Durkin." Verbo Christian Ministries. Online: http://www.verbo.org/site/memoirs.htm.

Gerlach, Luther P., and Virginia H. Hine. "Five Factors Crucial to the Growth and Spread of a Modern Religious Movement." *JSSR* 7/1 (1968) 23–40. Online: http://www.jstor.org/stable/1385108.

Gessell, Paul. "Bible-Carrying 'Freaks' Out to Conquer the World." *Leader-Post (Saskatchewan)*, December 17, 1970. Online: NewspaperArchive.com.

Gilbreath, Edward. "Why Pat Boone Went 'Bad': His Controversial Mission to Interpret Pop Culture for Cranky Christians." *CT*, October 4, 1999. Online: http://www.christianitytoday.com/ct/1999/october4/9tb056.html?start=5.

Gillian, Frank. "Discophobia: Antigay Prejudice and the 1979 Backlash against Disco." *Journal of the History of Sexuality* 16/2 (2007) 276–306. Online: http://muse.jhu.edu/journals/journal_of_the_history_of_sexuality/vo16/16.2frank.pdf.

Gillon, Steve. *Boomer Nation: The Largest and Richest Generation Ever, and How It Changed America*. New York: Free, 2004.

———. "Hippies: Why Were College Campuses Such Seedbeds of Unrest?" Online: http://link.history.com/services/link/bcpid1329229825/bctid1329241557.

"GO Alumni." Online: http://goalumni.homestead.com/.

Godec, Frank. "They're High on Jesus: This Coffee House Alters Lives." *European Stars and Stripes*, December 9, 1971. Online: NewspaperArchive.com.

Goffard, Christofer. "God's Word, Plus Static, on Calvary Satellite Network." *Los Angeles Times*, February 27, 2007. Online: http://www.religionnewsblog.com/17612/calvary-chapel.

Goldman, Marion S. "Continuity in Collapse: Departures from Shiloh." *JSSR* 34/3 (1995) 342–54. Online: http://ww.jstor.org/stable/1386883.

Goldman, Marion S., and Lynne Isaacson. "Enduring Affiliation and Gender Doctrine for Shiloh Sisters and Rajneesh Sannyasins." *JSSR* 38/3 (1999) 411–22. Online: http://www.jstor.org/stable/1387761.

Goldstein, Richard. "Love a Groovy Thing While He Lasted." In *Imagine Nation: The American Counterculture of the 1960s and '70s*, edited by Peter Braunstein and Michael William Doyle, 14. New York: Routledge, 2002.

Goodall, Wayde I. "Ask the Superintendent—Ministering to Today's Youth." *Enrichment Journal*, Winter, 2001. Online: http://enrichmentjournal.ag.org/200101/index.cfm.

Gordon, David F. "The Jesus People: 'An Identity Synthesis.'" *Urban Life and Culture* 3/2 (1974) 159–78. Online: http://jce.sagepub.com./cgi/reprint/3/2/159.

Graham, Billy. *The Jesus Generation*. London: Hodder & Stoughton, 1971.

Green, Melody, and David Hazard. *No Compromise: The Life Story of Keith Green*. Naskville: Nelson, 2008.

Grenz, Stanley J. *A Primer on Postmodernism*. Grand Rapids: Eerdmans, 1996.

———. *Welcoming but Not Affirming: An Evangelical Response to Homosexuality*. Louisville: Westminster John Knox, 1998.

Griffith, Jack Garrison, Jr. "Press Coverage of Four Twentieth-Century Evangelical Religious Movements, 1967–1997." PhD diss., University of Southern Mississippi, 2004. Online preview: http://proquest.umi.com. ATT 3149887.

Guffin, Scott Lee. "An Examination of Key Foundational Influences on the Megachurch Movement in America, 1960–1978." PhD diss., Southern Baptist Theological Seminary, 1999. Online Preview: http://proquest.umi.com. ATT 9929995.

Halcli, Abigail. "Social Movements." In *Understanding Contemporary Society*, edited by Abigail Halcli, Gary Browning, and Frank Webster, 463–75. London: Sage, 2000.

Halliday, Jerry. *Spaced out and Gathered In*. Old Tappan, NJ: Revell, 1972.

Harder, Mary W. "Sex Roles in the Jesus Movement." *SC* 21/3 (1974) 345–53. Online: http://scp.sagepub.com/cgi/reprint/21/3/345.

Harper, Charles L. "Spirit-Filled Catholics Some Biographical Comparisons." *SC* 21/3 (1974) 311–24. Online: http://scp.sagepub.com/cgi/reprint/21/3/311.

Harper, Michael. *A New Way of Living: How the Church of the Redeemer, Houston Found a New Life-Style*. London: Hodder & Stoughton, 1973.

Harrel, Mel. "Awakening in Reedley." *PE*, November 11, 1971.

Harris, Harriet A. *Fundamentalism and Evangelicals*. Oxford: Clarendon, 1998.

Harrison, Michael I. "Sources of Recruitment to Catholic Pentecostalism." *JSSR* 13/1 (1974) 49–64. Online: http://www.jstor.org/stable/pdfplus/1384800.pdf.

Harrison, William C. (AP). "Hippies Find Golden Gate Damp and Cold." *Pittsburgh Post-Gazette*, September 16, 1967. Online: NewspaperArchive.com.

Hart, John. "Top Army Chaplain: Jesus Movement Praised." *European Stars and Stripes*, October 7, 1972. Online: NewspaperArchive.com.

"Harvest Crusade." Online: http://www.harvest.org/crusades/events/archives.html.

Harvey, Paul. "Jesus Freaks—a Fad or a Trend?" *News Tribune (FL)*, April 29, 1971. Online: NewspaperArchive.com.

Hayford, Jack W., and David S. Moore. *The Charismatic Century: The Enduring Impact of the Azusa Street Revival*. New York: Warner Faith, 2006.

Heinz, Donald. "The Christian World Liberation Front." In *The New Religious Consciousness*, edited by Charles Y. Glock and Robert N. Bellah, 143–61. Berkeley: University of California Press, 1976.

Hendershot, Heather. *Shaking the World for Jesus: Media and Conservative Evangelical Culture*. Chicago: University of Chicago Press, 2004.

Heritage. "The Men Who Have Led the A/G." Spring 1982. Online: http://ifphc.org/pdf//Heritage/1982_01.pdf.

Hess, Catherine M.D. "National Institute on Drug Abuse Report on Teen Challenge— Summary Page: U.S. Department of Health, Education, and Welfare, 1975." *TeenChallange*. Online: http://www.teenchallengeonline.com/about/nida-report.shtml.

Hills, James W.L. "The New Charismatics 1973." *Eternity*, March 1973.

Hine, Virginia H. "Pentecostal Glossolalia toward a Functional Interpretation." *JSSR* 8/2 (1969) 211–26. Online: http://www.jstor.org/stable/1384335.

"History of Hope Chapel." Online: http://www.hopechapel.org/HChistory.htm.

Hocken, Peter Dudley. "Baptised in the Spirit: The Origins and Early Development of the Charismatic Movement in Great Britain." PhD diss., University of Birmingham, 1984.

———. *The Challenges of the Pentecostal, Charismatic and Messianic Jewish Movements: The Tensions of the Spirit*. Burlington, UK: Ashgate, 2009.

———. "Charismatic Movement." In *NIDPCM*, 417–519.

———. "Harald Bredesen." In *NIDPCM*, 441–42.

Hoekema, Anthony. *Holy Spirit Baptism*. Exeter, UK: Paternoster, 1972.

Hollenweger, Walter J. *New Wine in Old Wineskins: Protestant and Catholic Neo-Pentecostalism*. Gloucester: Fellowship, 1973.

———. *Pentecost Between Black and White: Five Case Studies on Pentecost and Politics*. Belfast: Christian Journals, 1974.

———. *Pentecostalism: Origins and Developments Worldwide*. Peabody, MA: Hendrickson, 1997.

Hollingshead, Michael. "The Man Who Turned on the World." London: Blond & Briggs, 1973. Online: http://www.psychedelic-library.org/hollings.htm.

Hollywood Free Paper. "A Brief History of the Jesus Movement." Online: http://www.hollywoodfreepaper.org/portal.php?id=2.

———. "Duane's Interview with Josh Tinley, 13 December 2007." Online: http://www.hollywoodfreepaper.org/interview.php?id=3.

———. "Victory for Jesus in Scandinavia," Winter 1972. Online: http://www.hollywoodfreepaper.org/archive.php?id=66.

———. "World Revival," Vol. 1 No. 2, Spring 1972. Online: http://www.hollywoodfreepaper.org/archive.php?id=67.

Hope Chapel. "Statement of Faith." Online: http://www.hopechapel.org/hcmi/index.php?option=com_content&view=article&id=64&Itemid=71.

Horsley, Richard A., and John S. Hanson, *Bandits, Prophets and Messiahs: Popular Movement in the Time of Jesus*. Minneapolis: Winston, 1985.

Howard, John Robert. "The Flowering of the Hippie Movement." *The Annals of the American Academy of Political and Social Science* 382 (1969) 43–55.Online: http://ann.sagepub.com/cgi/reprint/382/1/43.

"The Human Be-In poster." for January 14, 1967.

Hummel, Charles. *Fire in the Fireplace*. London: Mowbrays, 1979.

Hunt, James D. "'Jesus People' Are Locating in County." *Daily News (PA)*, March 30, 1976. Online: NewspaperArchive.com.

Hunt, Stephen. "The Alpha Course and Its Critics: An Overview of the Debates." *PentecoStudies* 4 (2005) 1–22.

———. "Anglican Wimberites." *PNEUMA* 17/1 (1995) 105–18.

———. "Deprivation and Western Pentecostalism Revisited: The Case of 'Classical' Pentecostalism." *PentecoStudies* 1/1 (2002a) 1–32.

———. "Deprivation and Western Pentecostalism Revisited: Neo-Pentecostalism." *PentecoStudies* 1/2 (2002b) Online: http://www.glopent.net/pentecostudies/2008-vol-7/no-1-spring/hunt-08.

———. *A History of the Charismatic Movement in Britain and the United States of America: The Pentecostal Transformation of Christianity Book 1*. Lampeter, UK: Mellen, 2009a.

————. *A History of the Charismatic Movement in Britain and the United States of America: The Pentecostal Transformation of Christianity Book 2.* Lampeter, UK: Mellen, 2009b.

————. "The Radical Kingdom of the Jesus Fellowship." *PNEUMA* 20/1 (1998) 21–41.

————. "Saints and Sinners: Contemporary Chrisianity and LGBT Sexualities." In *Contemporary Christianity and Lgbt Sexualities,* edited by Stephen Hunt, 1–22. Surrey, UK: Ashgate, 2009c.

————. "Were the Jesus People Pentecostals?" *PentecoStudies* 7/1 (2008) 1–33.

Hunter, Andrea. "Kenn Gulliksen: Surprised by Grace and Rescued by Love." *ASSIST News Service* (ANS), January 26, 2007. Online: http://www.assistnews.net/ Stories/2007/s07010146.htm

Hunter, James Davison. *American Evangelicalism: Conservative Religion and the Quandary of Modernity.* New Brunswick, NJ: Rutgers University Press, 1984.

————. *Culture Wars: The Struggle to Define America.* New York: Basic, 1990.

Iannaccone, Laurence R. "A Formal Model of Church and Sect." *American Journal of Sociology* 94/s (1988) s241–s68. Online: http://www.jstor.org/stable/2780248.

"ICFG History 1944—Present." Camp McPherson. Online: http://www. campmcpherson.org/content.cfm?id=292.

Imperi, Lillian L., et al., "Use of Hallucinogenic Drugs on Campus." *Journal of the American Medical Association* 12/204 (1968) 1021–24.

Independent Press Telegram (CA), "Advertisement for Runaway Generation," March 23, 1968. Online: NewspaperArchive.com.

———— *(CA),* "Advertisement for Runaway Generation," April 04, 1970. Online: NewspaperArchive.com.

Intervarsity. "Core Values." Online: http://www.Intervarsity.Org/About/Our/Our-Core-Values.

————. "Our Doctrinal Basis." Online: http://www.Intervarsity.Org/About/Our/Our-Doctrinal-Basis.

Isaacson, Lynne Marie. "Delicate Balances: Rearticulating Gender Ideology and Rules for Sexuality in a Jesus People Communal Movement." PhD diss., University of Oregon, 1996. Online Preview: http://proquest.umi.com. ATT 9706741.

Jackson, Dave. *Coming Together: All Those Communities and What They're up To.* Minneapolis: Bethany, 1978.

Jackson, Dave, and Neta Jackson. *Living Together in a World Falling Apart.* 4th ed. Carol Stream, IL: Creation House, 1976.

Jacob, Michael. *Pop Goes Jesus: An Investigation of Pop Religion in Britain and America.* London: Alden, 1972.

Jacobson, Cardell K., and Thomas J. Pilarzyk. "Croissance, Développement Et Fin D'une Secte Conversioniste: Les Jesus People De Milwaukee." *SC* 21/3 (1974) 255–68. Online: http://scp.sagepub.com/cgi/reprint/21/3/255.

Jenkins, Philip. *Mystics and Messiahs: Cults and New Religions in American History.* Oxford: Oxford University Press, 2000.

Jennings, George J. "An Ethnological Study of Glossalalia." *Journal of the American Scientific Affiliation* 20/1 (1968) 5–16. Online: http://www.asa3.org/ASA/ PSCF/1968/JASA3–68Jennings.html.

Jensen, Lori Jolene. "(Re)Discovering Fundamentalism in the Cultural Margins: Calvary Chapel Congregations as Sites of Cultural Resistance and Religious

Transformation." PhD diss., University of Southern California, 2000. Online Preview: http://proquest.umi.com. ATT 3018093.

"Jesus People." Online: http://www.jesuspeople.nl/.

John, Elton, and Taupin, Bernie. "Tiny Dancer." DJM Records, recorded 9 August 1971.

Johns, Jackie D. "Pentecostalism and the Postmodern Worldview." *The Journal of Pentecostal Theology* 3/7 (1995) 73–96.

Johnston, Hank. "The Marketed Social Movement: A Case Study of the Rapid Growth of TM." *The Pacific Sociological Review* 23/3 (1980) 333–54. Online: http://www.jstor.org/stable/1388826.

Jones, Bob. *Is Jesus a Revolutionary?* Greenville, SC: Bob Jones University Press, 1970.

Jones, Bob, III. *Look Again at the Jesus People*. Greenville, SC: Bob Jones University Press, 1972.

Jorstad, Erling. *That New Time Religion: The Jesus Revival in America*. Minneapolis: Augsburg, 1972a.

"JPUSA." Online: http://www.jpusa.org/meet.html.

Juster, Daniel, and Peter Hocken. "The Messianic Jewish Movement." *Toward Jerusalem Council II, 2004*. Online: http://www.tjcii.org/userfiles/Image/messianic-jewish-movement-an-inttroduction-Eng.pdf.

Kaiser, Kurt. "Pass It On." Bud John Songs, 1969.

Kalapathy, Ernest. "Chicago Hebrew Mission Dedicated." *PE*, June 28, 1970.

Kane, Tim. "Global U.S. Troop Deployment, 1950–2003." The Heritage Foundation, 2004. Online: http://www.heritage.org/Research/NationalSecurity/cda04-11.cfm?renderforprint=1.

Kanter, Rosabeth Moss. "Commitment and the Internal Organization of Millennial Movements." *American Behavioral Scientist* 16 (1972) 219–43. Online: http://abs.sagepub.com/cgi/reprint/16/2/219.

Kaplan, Jeffrey, and Heléne Lööw, eds. *The Cultic Milieu: Oppositional Subcultures in an Age of Globalization*. Walnut Creek, CA: AltaMira, 2002.

Kärkkäinen, Veli-Matti. *An Introduction to Ecclesiology*. Downers Grove, IL: InterVarsity, 2002.

———. "Pneumatologies in Systematic Theology." In *Studying Global Pentecostalism: Theories and Methods*, edited by Allan Anderson et al., 223–44. Berkeley: University of California Press, 2010.

———. *Toward a Pneumatological Theology: Pentecostal and Ecumenical Perspectives on Ecclesiology, Soteriology, and Theology of Mission*. Edited by Amos Yong. Lanham, MD: University Press of America, 2002.

Kay, William. *Pentecostalism*. London: SCM, 2009.

Kelley, Barry. "Christ: Revolutionary or Rebel?" *CT*, May 22, 1970.

Kelley, Dean M. *Why Conservative Churches Are Growing: A Study in Sociology of Religion*. New York: Harper & Row, 1972.

———. "Why Conservative Churches Are Still Growing." *JSSR* 17/2 (1978) 165–72. Online: http://www.jstor.org/stable/1386160.

King, Gerald. "Disfellowshiped: Pentecostal Responses to Fundamentalism in the United States, 1906–1943." PhD diss., University of Birmingham, 2009.

King, Pat. *The Jesus People Are Coming*. Plainfield, NJ: Logos, 1971.

———. "What Ever Happened to the Jesus People?" *Christian Life*, June 1974.

Kinsolving, Lester. "A Rector, a Church and the Hippies." *The Christian Century*, May 17, 1967.

Knight, Walker L. *Jesus People Come Alive*. London: Coverdale, 1971.

Koch, J.R., et al., "Body Art, Deviance, and American College Students." *Western Social Science Association* 47/1 (2010) 151–61.

Kraft, Siv Ellen. "'To Mix or Not to Mix': Syncretism/Anti-Syncretism in the History of Theosophy." *Numen* 49/2 (2002) 142–77. Online: http://www.jstor.org/stable/3270480.

Lammers, Matthew, and Todd E. Lewis. "Tony Alamo Materials (MC 1673)." In *University of Arkansas Libraries Special Collections*, 2008. Online: http://libinfo.uark.edu/SpecialCollections/findingaids/mc1673.asp.

"Last Days Ministries." Online: http://www.lastdaysministries.org/Groups/1000008637/Last_Days_Ministries/LDM/Our_Story/Our_Story.aspx.

Lattin, Don. *Jesus Freaks: A True Story of Murder and Madness on the Evangelical Edge*. New York: HarperOne, 2007.

Laurentin, René. *Catholic Pentecostalism*. Translated by Mathew O'Connell. London: Darton, Longman & Todd, 1977.

Leary, Timothy. *Flashbacks, an Autobiography: A Personal and Cultural History of an Era*. New York: Putnam, 1990.

Lee, Dallas. "'Gut-Level Witnessing' Urged among the Hippies." *Baptist Press Release*. October 14, 1968. Online: http://media.sbhla.org.s3.amazonaws.com/2671,14-Oct-1968.PDF.

Leen, Jeff. "The Vietnam Protests: When Worlds Collided." *Washington Post*, September 27, 1999. Online: http://washingtonpost.com/wp-srv/local/vietnam092799.htm.

Lindberg, Carter. *The Third Reformation: Charismatic Movements and the Lutheran Tradition*. Macon, GA: Mercer University Press, 1983.

Lindsey, Hal. *The Late Great Planet Earth*. Grand Rapids: Zondervan, 1970.

Little, Marti. "Jesus People Find 'Sign' in New Movement." *El Paso Herald-Post*, February 4, 1972. Online: NewspaperArchive.com.

"The Lord's Land—a Brief History." Online: http://www.lordsland.org/History.html.

Lovelace, Richard F. *Dynamics of Spiritual Life: An Evangelical Theology of Renewal*. Exeter, UK: Paternoster, 1979.

"LSD." Online: http://www.lysergia.com/FeedYourHead/FYH_LearyAlpert1963.htm.

Lynch, Dudley Morton. "Pat Boone and the Charismatics." *The Christian Century*, October 6, 1971.

Lynch, Lydia. "The Originator: Herbert Huncke." In *The Rolling Stone Book of the Beats, the Beat Generation and the Counterculture*, edited by Holly George-Warren, 287–89. London: Bloomsbury, 1999.

Lyra, Synesio, Jr. "The Rise and Development of the Jesus Movement." *Calvin Theological Journal* 8 (1973) 40–61.

MacDonald, John A. *House of Acts*. Carol Stream, IL: Creation House, 1970.

MacIntosh, Michael K. and Raul A. Ries. "A Venture of Faith: The History and Philosophy of the Calvary Chapel Movement." Film, Logos Media Group, 1992.

MacRobert, Iain. *The Black Roots and White Racism of Early Pentecostalism in the USA*. London: Macmillan, 1988.

"Mario Murillo." Online: www.mariomurillo.com/.

Martin, David. *Pentecostalism: The World Their Perish*. Oxford: Oxford University Press, 2002.

———. "Undermining the Old Paradigms: Rescripting Pentecostal Accounts." *PentecoStudies* 5/1 (2006) 18–38.

Martin, Sandra Pratt. *Bite Your Tongues.* Fort Worth: McElhaney, 1976.

Maseko, Achim N. "Potter's House Christian Fellowship, Neo-Charismatic Churches Part 4." In *Church Schism & Corruption.* Durban: Lulu.com, 2008. Online: http://www.lulu.com/items/volume_65/7248000/7248562/1/print/book_4.pdf.

Mauss, Armand L., and Donald W. Peterson. "Les 'Jesus Freaks' Et Le Retour À La Respectabilité" *SC* 21/3 (1974) 283–301. Online: http://scp.sagepub.com/cgi/reprint/21/3/283.

May Fourth Task Force. "President's Commission on Campus Unrest." Washington DC: Government Printing Office, 13 June 1970. *Kent State University.* Online: http://www.library.kent.edu/page/14424#P.

Mayers, Marvin H. "The Behavior of Tongues." *Journal of the American Scientific Affiliation* 23/3 (1971) 89–95. Online: http://www.asa3.org/ASA/PSCF/1971/JASA9-71Mayers.html.

McCartney, Paul, and John Lennon. "All You Need Is Love." EMI/Olympic Studios, recorded 14 and 19–26 August 1967.

McCleary, John, and Joan Jeffers. *The Hippie Dictionary: A Cultural Encyclopedia of the 1960s and 1970s.* Berkeley, CA: Ten Speed, 2004.

McClung, Floyd. "I Visited a Jesus Movement Church." *Evangel,* May 10, 1971.

McDonnell, Killian. *Catholic Pentecostalism: Problems in Evaluation.* Pecos, NM: Dove, 1970.

———. *The Holy Spirit and Christian Initiation.* The Holy Spirit and Power: The Catholic Charismatic Renewal. Garden City, NY: Doubleday, 1975.

McGee, Gary B. *Miracles, Missions, & American Pentecostalism.* American Society of Missiology Series 45. Maryknoll, NY: Orbis, 2010.

McKenzie, Scott. "San Francisco: Be Sure to Wear Flowers in Your Hair." Ode Records, United States, 1967.

McLeod, Hugh. *The Religious Crisis of the 1960s.* Oxford: Oxford University Press, 2007.

McLeod, Hugh, and Werner Ustorf, editors. *The Decline of Christendom in Western Europe, 1750–2000.* Cambridge: Cambridge University Press, 2003.

McLoughlin, William. *Revivals, Awakenings, and Reforms: An Essay on Religion and Social Change in America, 1607–1977.* London: University of Chicago Press, 1978.

McPherson, William. *Ideology & Change: Radicalism and Fundamentalism in America.* Palo Alto: National Press, 1973.

Mellis, Charles J. *Committed Communities: Fresh Streams for World Missions.* South Pasadena: William Carey Library, 1976.

Melton, Gordon. "The Modern Anti-Cult Movement in Historical Perspective." In *The Cultic Milieu: Oppositional Subcultures in an Age of Globalisation*, edited by Jeffrey Kaplan and Heléne Lööw, 265–89. Walnut Creek, CA: AltaMira, 2002.

———. "Metropolitan Community Churches, Universal Fellowship Of." In *The Encyclopedia of American Religions*, edited by Gordon Melton. Detroit: Gale, 1989.

———. "Salem Acres." In *The Encyclopedia of American Religions*, edited by Gordon Melton. Detroit: Gale, 1989.

Menzies, William W. "The Reformed Roots of Pentecostalism." *PentecoStudies* 6/2 (2007) 78–99. Online: http://www.glopent.net/pentecostudies/2007/fall-2/menzies-2007a.

"Merry Berg." Online: http://www.xfamily.org/index.php/Merry_Berg.

"Metropolitan Community Church." Online: http://mccchurch.org/overview/our-purpose/.

Meyer, Ilan H. "Prejudice, Social Stress, and Mental Health in Lesbian, Gay, and Bisexual Populations: Conceptual Issues and Research Evidence." *Psychological Bulletin* 129/5 (2003) 674–97.

Michelmore, Peter. *Back to Jesus*. Greenwich: Fawcett, 1973.

Miller, Donald E. *Reinventing American Protestantism: Christianity in a New Millennium*. Berkley: University of California Press, 1997.

———. *Global Pentecostalism: The New Face of Christian Social Engagement*. Berkeley: University of California Press, 2007.

Miller, Timothy. *The 60s Communes: Hippies and Beyond*. Syracuse: Syracuse University Press, 1999.

———. *The Hippies and American Values*. Knoxville: University of Tennessee Press, 1991.

———. "The Sixties-Era Communes." In *Imagine Nation: The American Counterculture of the 1960s and '70s*, edited by Michael William and Doyle Peter Braunstein, 327–52. New York: Routledge, 2002.

Mills, Carol. "Jesus People Rapping with God." *Daily Review (CA)*, February 21, 1971. Online: NewspaperArchive.com.

Modesto Bee, "Church Delegate from the Haight-Ashbury Arouses Smiles," October 22, 1967. Online: http://news.google.com/newspapers.

———. "Parley Faces Major Issues In One Session," October 22, 1967. Online: http://news.google.com/newspapers.

Mohler, Albert R., Jr. "Faithfully Proclaim the Truth — an Interview with John F. Macarthur." *Preaching*. Online: http://www.preaching.com/resources/features/11563456/page1/archive1/.

Moody, Jess. *The Jesus Freaks*. Waco: Word, 1971.

Moore, David S. *The Shepherding Movement: Controversy in Charismatic Ecclesiology*. London: T. & T. Clark, 2003.

Moore, Paul, and Joe Musser. *The Shepherd of Times Square*. Nashville: Nelson, 1979.

Moore, Ralph. *Let Go of the Ring: The Story of Hope Chapel*. 3rd ed. Kaneohe, HI: Straight Street, 1993.

"Moriel Ministries." Online: http://www.moriel.org/About_Moriel/About_Moriel-Jacob.html.

Morris, Michael W., et al., "Views from inside and Outside: Integrating Emic and Etic Insights About Culture and Justice Judgment." *Academy of Management* Review 24/4 (1999) 781–96. Online: http://www.columbia.edu/~da358/publications/etic_emic.pdf.

Mortenson, Eric. "Thousands Bid Pastor Farewell." *Eugene Register Guard*, February 16, 1994. Online: http://news.google.com/newspapers.

Moses, Anne B. "The Runaway Youth Act: Paradoxes of Reform." *Social Service Review* 52/2 (1978) 227–43. Online: http://pao.chadwyck.co.uk/PDF/1295956138784.pdf.

Mullen, Peter. "The Curse of the Hallelujah Chorus." *Guardian (UK)*, July 28, 1984. Online: ProQuest Historical Newspapers (05577311232).

Munstra, Ron. "Evangelism among Hippies and Other Sub-Culture Groups." In *Let the Earth Hear His Voice: International Congress on World Evangelization, Lausanne, Switzerland, 16–25 July 1974*, edited by J. D. Douglas, 800–805. Minneapolis: World Wide, 1975.

Nathan, Rich, and Ken Wilson. *Empowered Evangelicals: Bringing Together the Best of the Evangelical and Charismatic Worlds.* Rev. ed. Boise: Ampelon, 2009.

National Association of Evangelicals. "Statement of Faith." Online: http://www.nae.net/about-us/statement-of-faith.

New York Times. "'Jesus People' Puzzle the Pope." *Salina (KS) Journal,* December 16, 1971. Online: NewspaperArchive.com.

New Zealand Herald. "10,000 March for Jesus," May 06, 1972.

Nicholson, William F. (AP). "Jesus People Move to Latin America." *Nashua (NH) Telegraph,* June 11, 1973. Online: NewspaperArchive.com.

Niebuhr, Richard H. *The Social Sources of Denominationalism.* New York: Holt, 1929. Reprint, New York: Meridian, 1957.

Noll, Mark A. "Where We Are and How We Got Here." *CT,* October 2006. Online: http://www.christianitytoday.com/ct/2006/october/16.42.html?start=5.

Norman, Larry. *Upon This Rock.* Capital, 1969.

Northup, Paul. "Turning Thirty." London: Greenbelt Festivals, 2004.

Oakland (CA) Tribune, "Trips Festival," January 23, 1966. Online: NewspaperArchive.com.

Old, Hughes Oliphant. *The Reading and Preaching of the Scriptures in the Worship of the Christian Church.* Grand Rapids: Eerdmans, 2010.

One-Way.org. "Oden Fong interview." http://www.one-way.org/jesusmusic/.

"Operation Mobilisation International Policy Manual 2004." Operation Mobilization. Online: www.omusa.org/resources/ . . . care/ . . . policy-manuals/ . . . policy-manual/download.

Ortega, Ruben. *The Jesus People Speak Out.* London: Hodder & Stoughton, 1972.

Owen, Bob. *Jesus Is Alive and Well: The Truth Behind the Stickers and Slogans.* Aylesbury: Hunt Barnard, 1972.

Palms, Roger C. *The Jesus Kids.* London: SCM, 1972.

Pattison, Mansell E. M.D. "Behavioral Science Research on the Nature of Glossolalia." *Journal of the American Scientific Affiliation* 20/3 (1968) 73–86. Online: http://www.asa3.org/ASA/PSCF/1968/JASA9-68Pattison.html.

Patton, Michael Quinn. *Qualitative Research and Evaluation Methods.* London: Sage, 2002.

PBS. "The American Experience, Summer of Love." Online: http://www.pbs.org/wgbh/amex/love/sfeature/timeline.html.

PE. "1,000 'Jesus People' Baptized in Ocean Off California." June 13, 1971.

———. "Assemblies of God Jewish Evangelism at a Glance." May 18, 1969.

———. "Baptist Ask Charismatics to 'Desist or Withdraw.'" December 8, 1974.

———. "Baptists Moving to Detente with Glossolalia Groups?" June 23, 1974.

———. "Chapel of Jesus Christ Ministers to Berkeley Students." August 20, 1972.

———. "Church Sponsors Outreach Ministry to Youth through Coffeehouse." March 10, 1974.

———. "Coffeehouse Ministers to College Students." August 20, 1972.

———. "Executive Reviews Success of Teen Challenge Work." June 28, 1970.

———. "Few Blacks Seen in Jesus Movement." August 15, 1971.

———. "'Jesus People' Seminar Draws Crowds to Protestant and Catholic Churches." January 23, 1972.

———. "Jewish Ministry Flourishes in Florida." March 26, 1978.

———. "Mennonites Hold First Charismatic Conference." November 10, 1974.

———. "Mountain Spa Is Opened by 'Jesus Freaks.'" August 23, 1970.

———. "New Michigan Teen Challenge Expands Outreach." February 27, 1972.

———. "Rock and the Church." October 24, 1971.

———. "Teen Challenge." January 24, 1971.

———. "Teen Challenge Centers Merge." February 22, 1970.

Perrin, Robin D., and Armand L. Mauss. "Strictly Speaking . . . : Kelley's Quandary and the Vineyard Christian Fellowship." *JSSR* 32/2 (1993) 125–35. Online: http://www.jstor.org/stable/1386792.

Perry, Charles. *The Haight-Ashbury: A History.* New York: Random House, 1984.

Perry, Helen. *The Human Be-In.* London: Lane, 1970. Online: http://www.erowid.org/library/books_online/human_be_in.pdf.

Peterson, Donald W., and Armand L. Mauss. *The Cross and the Commune.* Religion in Sociological Perspective. Belmont, CA: Wadsworth, 1973.

Peterson, Richard G. "Electric Sister." In *The God Pumpers: Religion in the Electronic Age,* edited by Marshall William Fishwick and Ray Broadus Browne, 116–40. Bowling Green: Bolwing Green State University Popular Press, 1987.

Philpott, Kent. *Awakenings in America and the Jesus People Movement.* San Rafael, CA: Earthen Vessel, 2011.

———. "The Jesus People Movement: A Fourth Great Awakening?" Mill Valley, 2002.

———. *The Third Sex?: Six Homosexuals Tell Their Stories.* Plainfield, NJ: Logos, 1975.

Pin, Emile Jean. "En Guise D'introduction, Ou Comment Se Sauver De L'anomie Et De L'aliénation: Jesus People Et Catholiques Pentecostaux" *SC* 21/3 (1974) 227–39. Online: http://scp.sagepub.com/cgi/reprint/21/3/227.

Plowman, Edward E. "2,000 Christian Youth Reach out at Olympics." *CT,* September 29, 1972.

———. "Explo '72 'Godstock' in Big D." *CT,* July 7, 1972.

———. *The Jesus Movement: Accounts of Christian Revolutionaries in Action.* London: Hodder & Stoughton, 1972.

———. "Report from Europe — 'a Rustling in the Leaves.'" *CT,* October 13, 1972.

———. "Turning on to Jeshua." *CT,* December 17, 1971.

———. "Urbana '73: 'a Way I Can Help.'" *CT,* January 18, 1974.

———. "Where Are All the Children Now?" *CT,* April 27, 1973.

Poloma, Margaret. *The Assemblies of God at the Crossroads: Charisma and Institutional Dilemmas.* Knoxville: University of Tennessee Press, 1989.

———. "Charisma and Structure in the Assemblies of God: Revisiting O'Dea's Five Dilemmas." Manuscript prepared as the Assemblies of God "Case Study" for the Organizing Religious Work Project. University of Akron, Akron, OH, February 6, 2002. Online: http://www3.uakron.edu/sociology/AoGPastors02.pdf.

———. *The Charismatic Movement: Is There a New Pentecost?* Boston: Twayne, 1982.

———. *Main Street Mystics: Toronto Blessing & Reviving Pentecostalism.* Lanham, MD: AltaMira, 2003.

———. "The Spirit Movement in North America at the Millennium: From Azusa Street to Toronto, Pensacola and Beyond." *The Journal of Pentecostal Theology* 6/12 (1998) 83–107.

Poloma, Margaret, and John Green. *The Assemblies of God: Godly Love and the Revitalization of American Pentecostalism.* New York: New York University Press, 2010.

Port Angeles (WA) Evening News, "Children of God Seen Two Ways," November 28, 1971. Online: NewspaperArchive.com.

"The Potter's House." The Christian Research Institute. Online: http://www.caic.org.au/biblebase/potters/potter1.htm.

"Praise Chapel International." Online: http://www.praisechapel.com/PCI/?page_id=21.

Rainey, Dennis. "Campus Ministry Recruiting Task Force Proposal." Campus Crusade for Christ, 25 June 1987.

Ranaghan, Kevin, and Dorothy Ranaghan. *Catholic Pentecostals.* New York: Paulist, 1969.

Redlands (CA) Daily Facts. "Jesus People Festival set next week at Bowl," August 21, 1971. Online: NewspaperArchive.com.

Reich, Charles. *The Greening of America.* New York: Random House, 1970.

Reid, Alvin Lee. "The Impact of the Jesus Movement on Evangelism among Southern Baptists." PhD diss., Southwestern Baptist Theological Seminary, 1991.

Religious News Service. "'Jesus People' Settle in U.K." *Winnipeg (Manitoba) Free Press,* January 27, 1973. Online: NewspaperArchive.com.

———. "'Jesus People' Worry Rabbi, Meeting Told." *Winnipeg (Manitoba) Free Press* July 10, 1971. Online: NewspaperArchive.com.

Reyonlds, F. M. "David Ray Wilkerson." In *NIDPCM*, 1195–96.

Richardson, James T. "Definitions of Cult: From Sociological-Technical to Popular-Negative." *Review of Religious Research* 34/4 (1993b) 348–56.

———. "Financing New Religions: Comparative and Theoretical Considerations. *JSSR* 21/3 (1982) 255–68. Online: http://www.jstor.org/stable/1385890.

———. "From Cult to Sect: Creative Eclecticism in New Religious Movements." *The Pacific Sociological Review* 22/2 (1979) 139–66. Online: http://www.jstor.org/stable/1388875.

———. "The Jesus Movement." In *Encyclopedia of Religion* Number 7, edited by Lindsey Jones. London: Gale, 2005.

———. "Mergers, 'Marriages,' Coalitions, and Denominationalization: The Growth of Calvary Chapel." *SYZYGY: Journal of Alternative Religion and Culture* 2/3–4 (1993) 205–23.

———. "New Religious Movements in the United States: A Review." *SC* 30/1 (1983) 85–110. Online: http://scp.sagepub.com/cgi/reprint/30/1/85.

———. "Regulating Religion: A Sociological and Historical Introduction." In *Regulating Religion: Case Studies from Around the Globe,* edited by James T. Richardson, 1–21. New York: Kluwer Academic, 2004.

Richardson, James T., and Rex Davis. "Experiential Fundamentalism: Revisions of Orthodoxy in the Jesus Movement." *Journal of the American Academy of Religion* 51/3 (1983) 397–425. Online: http://www.jstor.org/stable/1463099.

Richardson, James T., and M. T. V. Reidy. "Form and Fluidity in Two Contemporary Glossolalic Movements." *The Annual Review of the Social Sciences of Religion* 4 (1980) 183–220.

Richardson, James T., and Mary Stewart. "Conversion Process Models and the Jesus Movement." *American Behavioural Scientist* 20/6 (1977) 819–38. Online: http://abs.sagepub.com/cgi/content/abstract/20/6/819.

Richardson, James T., et al. "Thought Reform and the Jesus Movement." *Youth Society* 4/2 (1972) 185–202. Online: http://yas.sagepub.com/cgi/reprint/4/2/185.

Richardson, James T., et al. *Organized Miracles: A Study of a Contemporary, Youth, Communal, Fundamentalist Organization.* New Brunswick: Transaction Books, 1979.

Riss, Richard M. *A Survey of 20th century Revival Movements in North America.* Peabody, MA: Hendrickson, 1988.

Robbins, Thomas, et al., "Theory and Research on Today's 'New Religions.'" *Sociological Analysis* 39/2 (1978) 95–122. Online: http://www.jstor.org/stable/3710211.

Robertson, Roland. "Global Millennialism: A Postmortem on Secularization." In *Religion, Globalization, and Culture,* edited by Peter Beyer and Lori Beaman, 9–34. Leiden: Brill, 2007.

———. "Glocalization: Time-Space and Homogeneity-Heterogeneity." In *Global Modernities,* edited by Mike Featherstone et al., 25–44. London: Sage, 1995.

"The Rock Church." Online: http://www.rockchurchinternational.com/.

Rockument.com. "Allen Cohen on the San Francisco Oracle." Online: http://www.rockument.com/WEBORA.html.

Rodney, Les. "Calls Jesus People 'Faddists, Not 1st Century Christians.'" *Independent Press Telegram (CA),* September 4, 1971. Online: NewspaperArchive.com.

Romanowski, William D. "Rock'n'religion: A Sociocultural Analysis of the Contemporary Christian Music Industry." PhD diss., Bowling Green State University, 1990. Online Preview: http://proquest.umi.com. ATT 9122799.

Rome, Adam. "Give Earth a Chance: The Environmental Movement and Sixties." *The Journal of American History* 90/2 (2003) 525–54. Online: www.historycopperative.org.

Rossinow, Doug. "The Revolution Is About Our Lives: The New Left's Counterculture." In *Imagine Nation: The American Counterculture of the 1960s and '70s,* edited by Peter Braunstein and Michael William Doyle, 99–124. London: Routledge, 2002.

Roszak, Theodore. *The Making of a Counter Culture: Reflections on the Technocratic Society & Its Youthful Opposition.* London: Latimer Trend, 1970.

———. *Unfinished Animal: The Aquarian Frontier and the Evolution of Consciousness.* London: Faber, 1976.

Runge, David A. "Jesus People Rally Here." *Milwaukee Journal,* March 20, 1971. Online: http://news.google.com/newspapers.

San Mateo (CA) Times. "Kesey Klan in South." February 05, 1966. Online: NewspaperArchive.com.

Saskatoon Star-Phoenix, "Leighton Ford speaks out on love, hippies, humanists," October 13, 1967. Online: http://news.google.com/newspapers.

Scalf, Daniel. "Early Days." Jesus People USA. Online: http://www.facebook.com/jesuspeople?v=app_2373072738#!/topic.php?uid=117320356814&topic=13134.

Schenkel, Albert Frederick. "New Wine and Baptist Wineskins: American and Southern Baptist Denominational Responses to the Charismatic Renewal, 1960–80." In *Pentecostal Currents in American Protestantism,* edited by Edith Blumhofer et al., 152–67. Urbana: University of Illinois Press, 1999.

Scholtes, Peter. "They'll Know We Are Christians by Our Love." N.p.: F. E. L., 1966.

Schwein, Margaret. "'Jesus People' Here Eager to Serve." *Atchison (KS) Daily Globe,* February 20, 1972. Online: NewspaperArchive.com.

Scott, Steve. "'Jesus People' Really Doing Good Job." *Nashua (NH) Telegraph,* August 14, 1971. Online: NewspaperArchive.com.

Seesholtz, Mel. "Remembering Dr. Timothy Leary." *Journal of Popular Culture* 38/1 (2004) 106–23. Online: http://web.ebscohost.com/ehost/detail?vid=1&hid=6&sid=f01b0567–394a-42cf-b599-d6a389f7efe4%40sessionmgr2.

"Shepherds Inn Canton Ohio Jesus People." Online: http://www.shepherdsinncanton.com/CantonJP.htm.

Sherrill, John L. *They Speak with Other Tongues.* London: Hodder & Stoughton, 1965.

Sherrill, John L., and Elizabeth Sherrill. *Scott Free.* Old Tappan, NJ: Chosen, 1976.

Shires, Preston. *Hippies of the Religious Right.* Waco: Baylor University Press, 2007.

Simmonds, Robert B. "Conversion or Addiction: Consequences of Joining a Jesus Group Movement." *American Behavioral Scientist* 20/6 (1977a) 909–24. Online: http://abs.sagepub.com/cgi/reprint/20/6/909.

———. "Organizational Aspects of a Jesus Movement Community." *SC* 21 (1974) 269–81. Online: http://scp.sagepub.com/cgi/content/abstract/21/3/269.

———. "The People of the Jesus Movement: A Personality Assessment of Members of a Fundamentalist Religious Community." PhD diss., University of Nevada, 1977b. Online Preview: http://proquest.umi.com. ATT 7716668.

Simmonds, Robert B., et al. "A Jesus Movement Group: An Adjective Check List Assessment." *JSSR* 15/4 (1976) 323–37. Online: http://www.jstor.org/stable/1385635.

Simpkins, Ron. *An Open Door.* Prescott, AZ: Potters, 1985.

Smith, Christian. *Moral, Believing Animals: Human Personhood and Culture.* Oxford: Oxford University Press, 2003.

Smith, Christian, et al. *American Evangelicalism: Embattled and Thriving.* Chicago: University of Chicago Press, 1998.

Smith, Chuck. *Calvary Chapel Distinctives: Foundational Principles of the Calvary Chapel Movement.* Costa Mesa, CA: Word for Today, 2000.

———. *Charisma vs. Charismania.* Eugene, OR: Harvest House, 1983.

———. *End Times Report: Future Survivors.* Costa Mesa, CA: Word for Today, 1978.

———. "The History of Calvary Chapel." *Last Times* 1981.

———. "Revelation 2, 3." *TWFT.* Online: http://www.twft.com/?page=C2000.

Smith, Chuck, and Tal Brooke. "Harvest." Costa Mesa, CA: Word for Today, 1987. Online: http://www3.calvarychapel.com/library/smith-chuck/books/harvest.htm.

Smith, Chuck, and Hugh Steven. *The Reproducers: New Life for Thousands.* Glendale, CA: Regal, 1972.

Smith, Kevin John. "The Origins, Nature, and Significance of the Jesus Movement as a Revitalization Movement." DMiss thesis, Asbury Theological Seminary, 2003. Online: http://proquest.umi.com. ATT 3085530.

———. *The Origins, Nature, and Significance of the Jesus Movement as a Revitalization Movement.* Lexington, KY: Emeth, 2011.

Sofranko, Steven Jude. "Where the Jesus People Went: A Survey of Santa Rosa Christian Church and an Intersection of Religious Movements." MA thesis, Graduate Theological Union, 2000. Online: http://www.archive.org/details/wherejesuspeopleoosofrrich.

"The Sojourner's." Online: http://http://sojo.net/about-us/history.

Sparks, Jack. *God's Forever Family.* Grand Rapids: Zondervan, 1974.

Spittler, Russell P. "Are Pentecostals and Charismatics Fundamentalists?" In *Charismatic Christianity as a Global Culture,* edited by Karla Poewe, 103–16. Columbia: University of South Carolina Press, 1994.

Spokane Daily Chronicle, "1000 Attracted to Gospel Meets," May 28, 1965. *Online:* http://news.google.com/newspapers.

———. "Coffee House Operator to Make Seminar Plans," January 10, 1969. Online: http://www.facebook.com/photo.php?fbid=412827116814&set=t.1457623490&type=3&theater.

———. "Jesus People Plan to Take Word Abroad," February 02, 1972. Online: http://news.google.co.uk/newspapers.

Spokesman Review (WA), "Central Lutheran Concert," January 11, 1975. Online: http"//news.google.com/newspapers.

Stafford, Tim, and James Beverley. "Conversations: God's Wonder Worker." *CT*, July 14, 1997. Online: http://www.christianitytoday.com/ct/1997/july14/7t8046.html?start=3.

Stark, Rodney. "Psychopathology and Religious Commitment." *Review of Religious Research* 12/3 (1971) 165–76. Online: http://www.jstor.org/stable/3510420.

———. "Secularization R.I.P." *Sociology of Religion* 60/3 (1999) 249–73.

Stark, Rodney, and William Sims Bainbridge. "Of Churches, Sects, and Cults: Preliminary Concepts for Theory of Religious Movements." *JSSR* 18/2 (1979) 117–31. Online: http://www.jstor.org/stable/1385935.

———. *The Future of Religion: Secularization, Revival, and Cult Formation*. Berkeley: University of California Press, 1985.

Stegemann, Ekkehard W., and Wolfgang Stegemann. *The Jesus Movement: A Social History of Its First Century*. Edinburgh: Fortress, 1999.

Stertzer, Carol Chapman. "A Journey toward Healing." *Charisma*, January 12, 2002. Online: http://www.charismamag.com/index.php/features2/346-special-interview/5257-a-journey-toward-healing?format=pdf.

Stevens, Marsha. "For Those Tears I Died." Bud John Songs, 1969.

Stewart, David Tabb, and James T. Richardson. "Mundane Materialism: How Tax Policies and Other Governmental Regulation Affected Beliefs and Practices of Jesus Movement Organizations." *Journal of the American Academy of Religion* 67/4 (1999) 825–47. Online: http://www.jstor.org/stable/1466272.

Stibal, Mary E. "Disco. Birth of a New Market System." *Journal of Marketing* 41/4 (1977) 82–88. Online: http://www.jstor.org/stable/pdfplus/1250240.pdf.

Stones, Christopher R. "The Jesus People: Fundamentalism and Changes in Factors Associated with Conservatism." *JSSR* 17/2 (1978) 155–58.

Strang, S. "Weiner, Robert Thomas." In *NIDPCM*, 1186–87.

Streiker, Lowell D. *The Jesus Trip: The Advent of the Jesus Freaks*. Nashville: Abingdon, 1971.

Sullivan, Francis, A. *Charisms and Charismatic Renewal*. Dublin: Gill & Macmillan, 1982.

———. "The Ecclesiological Context of the Charismatic Renewal." In *The Holy Spirit and Power: The Catholic Charismatic Renewal*. Garden City, NY: Doubleday, 1975.

Summer of Love. "Frequently Asked Questions." Online: http://www.summeroflove.org/faq.html.

Sumner, Colin. *The Sociology of Deviance: An Obituary*. Buckingham: Open University Press, 1994.

Swaim, Lawrence. "Hippies: The Love Thing." *North American Review* 252/5 (1967) 16–18.

Synan, Vinson. *The Century of the Holy Spirit: 100 Years of Pentecostal and Charismatic Renewal, 1901–2001*. Nashville: Nelson, 2001.

———. *The Holiness Pentecostal Tradition: Charismatic Movements in the Twentieth Century*. 2nd ed. Grand Rapids: Eerdmans, 1997.

———. "The Role of Tongues as Initial Evidence." In *Spirit and Renewal: Essays in Honor of J. Rodman Williams*, edited by Mark W. Wilson, 67–82. Sheffield: Sheffield Academic, 1994.

———. *The Spirit Said "Grow."* Monrovia: Marc, 1992.

"The Tab World." Online: http://www.thetabworld.com/Johnny_Cash_biography.html.

"Tanignak Productions." Online: http://www.tanignak.com/WilsonMcKinleyInfoPage.htm.

Taslimi, Cheryl Rowe, et al. "Assessment of Former Members of Shiloh: The Adjective Check List 17 Years Later." *JSSR* 30/3 (1991) 306–11. Online: http://www.jstor.org/stable/1386975.

Taylor, Charles. *A Secular Age*. London: Belknap, 2007.

"Ted Patrick." Online: http://www.xfamily.org/index.php/Ted_Patrick.

Thomas, Daren. "The Keith Green Story." Sparrow Records, 2002. Online: http://www.youtube.com/watch?v=G6hOyx8LF4I.

Thompson, Donald W. "A Thief in the Night." Mark IV Pictures Incorporated, 1972. Online: http://www.youtube.com/watch?v=Ly4CPRE_Keo.

Thompson, Lewis. "'FAD' in 2000th Year." *Daily Chronicle (WA)*, July 19, 1971. Online: NewspaperArchive.com.

Thomson, Noah. "Children of God: Lost and Found (a First-Person Account of Growing up in an Evangelical Christian Cult)." Home Box Office, 2007. Online: http://www.youtube.com/watch?v=Ud4Z9xkre6g.

Tiegel, Elliot. "Pat Boone Opens Centre to Aid Jesus Music." *Billboard*, June 3, 1972.

Time. "The Alternative Jesus: Psychedelic Christ." June 21, 1971. Online: http://www.time.com/time/magazine/article/0,9171,905202,00.html.

———. "The Hippies: The Philosophy of a Subculture." July 7, 1967. Online: http://www.time.com/time/magazine/article/0,9171,899555–51,00.html.

———. "Is God Coming Back to Life." December 26, 1969. Online: http://www.time.com/time/covers/0,16641,19691226,00.html.

———. "Is God Dead?" April 8, 1966. Online: http://www.time.com/time/covers/0,16641,19660408,00.html.

———. "The Jesus Evolution." September 24, 1973. Online: http://www.time.com/time/magazine/article/0,9171,1122006,00.html?iid=sphere-inline-sidebar.

———. "Street Christians: Jesus as the Ultimate Trip." August 3, 1970. Online: http://www.time.com/time/magazine/article/0,9171,876689–81,00.html.

Tipton, Steven M. *Getting Saved from the Sixties: Moral Meaning in Conversion and Cultural Change*. London: University of California Press, 1982.

"Trinity Gospel Temple." Online: http://www.trinitybrotherdave.org/html/broadcast.html.

"The Trips Festival Movie Introduction Audio Mp3." The Trips Festival. Online: http://www.thetripsfestival.com/audio.html.

Trott, Jon, and Mike Hertenstein. "The Selling of Satan: The Tragic History of Mike Warnke." *Cornerstone* 21/98 (1992). Online: http://www.cornerstonemag.com/features/iss098/sellingsatan.htm.

Trott, Walt. "Hanau Gl Freaks out' with Jesus as Member of New Religious Cult." *European Stars and Stripes*, August 3, 1971. Online: NewspaperArchive.com.

———. "Johnny Cash . . . Modern-Day Folk Hero." *European Stars and Stripes*, March 3, 1972. Online: NewspaperAchive.com.

"Uncle Tim'$ Children." *Digger Archives*. Online: http://www.diggers.org/bibscans/cc030a_m.gif.

United Press International, "Flower-Pelting Hippies Trip Anti-Hippie Melee." *Sarasota Journal,* June 2, 1967. Online: http://news.google.com/newspapers.

The United States Census Bureau. "Statistical Abstracts 1951–1994." *U.S. Department of Commerce.* Online: http://www.census.gov/prod/www/abs/statab1951–1994.htm.

The University of Missouri-Kansas City School of Law. "Chicago 7 Trial: Transcript of Allan Ginsberg's Testimony." Online: http://www.law.umkc.edu/faculty/projects/ftrials/Chicago7/Ginsberg.html.

Vachon, Brian. "The Jesus Movement Is Upon Us." *Look,* February 9, 1971.

———. *A Time to Be Born.* New Jersey: Prentice-Hall, 1972.

Vahanian, Gabriel. *The Death of God: The Culture of Our Post-Christian Era.* New York: Braziller, 1961.

Vanguard. "Building Kid's Character." Winter 2008. Online: http://www.vanguard.edu/about/wp-content/uploads/2011/02/VUmag_Winter2008_BuildingKidsCharacter.pdf.

"Verbo Christian Ministries." Online: http://www.verbo.org/cms/.

Victoria (TX) Advocate, "Rallies Planned for Youths Here," January 11, 1973. Online: http://www.pipelinechurch.com/staff.html.

Vines, Jerry. *Spirit Works: Charismatic Practices and the Bible.* Nashville: Broadman & Holdman, 1999.

"Vineyard History." Online: http://www.vineyardusa.org/site/about/vineyard-history.

Vineyard USA. "Statement of Faith." Online: http://www.vineyardusa.org/site/files/about/statement-of-faith.pdf.

Wacker, Grant. "Are the Golden Oldies Still Worth Playing? Reflections on History Writing among Early Pentecostals." *PNEUMA* 8/2 (1986) 81–100.

———. *Heaven Below.* London: Harvard University Press, 2001.

Wadleigh, Michael. "Woodstock." Wadleigh-Maurice, 1970. Online: http://www.youtube.com/watch?v=IQpaN66GRic.

Wagner, C. Peter. *On the Crest of the Wave: Becoming a World Christian.* Ventura, CA: Gospel Light, 1983.

———. "The Third Wave." In *NIDPCM,* 1141.

———. *The Third Wave of The Holy Spirit.* Ann Arbor: Vine, 1988.

———. "Wimber, John." In *NIDPCM,* 1199–1200.

Wagner, Frederick Norman. "A Theological and Historical Assessment of the Jesus People Phenomenon." DMin thesis, Fuller Theological Seminary, 1971.

Wallace, Anthony F.C. "Revitalization Movements." *American Anthropologist* 58/2 (1956) 264–81. Online: http://www.jstor.org/stable/pdfplus/665488.pdf.

Walter, Robert G. *The "Jesus Movement" under the Searchlight of Scripture.* Collingswood, NJ: Bible for Today, 1973.

Ward, Hiley H. (AP). "Are Jesus People Fundamentalists? Fundamentalists Don't Think So." *Chronicle Telegram,* May 6, 1972. Online: NewspaperArchive.com.

———. *The Far-Out Saints of the Jesus Communes: A Firsthand Report and Interpretation of the Jesus People Movement.* New York: Association, 1972a.

Warner, Stephen R. *New Wine in Old Wineskins: Evangelicals and Liberals in a Small-Town Church.* Berkeley: University of California Press, 1988.

Warner, Stephen R., and Judith G. Wittner. *Gatherings in Diaspora: Religious Communities and the New Immigration.* Philadelphia: Temple University Press, 1998.

Warner, W. E. "Hicks, Roy, W." In *NIDPCM*, 712.

"Watch Unto Prayer." Online: http://watch.pair.com/cult-scp1.html.

"Wayman Mitchell." Online: http://www.waymanmitchell.com/.

"Weiner Ministries." Online: http://www.youthnow.org/

Weiner, Bob. *Take Dominion: Display the Works of God in Your Life.* Old Tappan, NJ: Chosen, 1988.

Welch, Timothy Bernard. "God Found His Moses: A Biographical and Theological Analysis of the Life of Joseph Smale (1867–1926)." PhD diss., University of Birmingham, 2009.

Westhues, Kenneth. "Hippiedom 1970: Some Tentative Hypothesis." *Sociological Quarterly* 13/1 (1972) 81–89. Online: http://pao.chadwyck.co.uk//PDF/1220277192337.pdf.

Whelan, Brent. "'Further': Reflections on Counter-Culture and the Postmodern." *Cultural Critique* 11 (1988–1989): 63–86. Online: http://www.jstor.org/stable/1354244.

Wilkerson, Austin W. "The Jesus Movement—God's Answer to Our Church's Prayer." *PE*, September 16, 1973.

Wilkerson, David. *The Cross and the Switchblade.* Old Tappan, NJ: Revell, 1964.

———. "Dave Wilkerson's Open Letter to Campus Rebels." *PE*, August 17, 1969.

———. "A Desperate Effort to Lose Identity and Become Detached." *PE*, May 3, 1970.

———. "God Is for Squares." *PE*, April 28, 1968.

———. *Purple-Violet-Squish.* London: Zondervan, 1969.

Williams, Don. *Call to the Streets.* Minneapolis: Augsburg, 1972.

Williams, John Rodman. "Preface—A Theological Pilgrimage." *Renewal Theology: Featuring the Works of Theologian J. Rodman Williams.* Online: http://www.renewaltheology.net/A_Theological_Pilgrimmage/TP_Preface.html.

———. *Renewal Theology: God, the World, and Redemption.* Vol. 1. Grand Rapids: Zondervan, 1996.

———. *Renewal Theology: Systematic Theology from a Charismatic Perspective.* Vol. 2. Grand Rapids: Zondervan, 1996.

Wilson, Doneva. "Earp Has Three-Pronged Ministry: Work at Agape Inn Takes Much Time." *Abilene Reporter-News,* July 21, 1972. Online: NewspaperArchive.com.

Wilson, Ian. *In Pursuit of Destiny: Biography of Wayman Mitchell.* Barrie, ON: Northstar, 1996.

Wimber, Carol. *John Wimber: The Way It Was.* London: Hodder & Stoughton, 1999.

Wimber, John. *Power Evangelism.* London: Hodder & Stoughton, 1985.

Winter, Ralph D. "Is a Big New Student Mission Movement in the Offing?" *CT*, May 10, 1974.

Wolfe, Tom. *The Electric Kool-Aid Acid Test.* 13th ed. New York: Bantam, 1972.

"World Challenge." Online: http://www.worldchallenge.org/about_david_wilkerson/dw_fullbio.

Yablonski, Lewis. *The Hippie Trip.* New York: Pegasus, 1968.

Yong, Amos. *Spirit-Word-Community: Theological Hermeneutics in Trinitarian Perspective*. Hants, UK: Ashgate, 2002.

Young, James Lee. "Writer-Photographer Meets 'Jesus People,' Joins Them." *Baptist Press*, February 9, 1971. Online: http://media.sbhla.org.s3.amazonaws.com/3134,09-Feb-1971.pdf.

"Youth Encounter." Online: http://old.youthencounter.rg/about_ye/history.asp.

"YWAM Denmark." Online: http://ywam.dk/content/view/22/56/lang,en-GB/.

"YWAM History." Online: http://www.ywam.org/About-YWAM/Who-we-are/The-History-of-YWAM.

"YWAM Netherlands." Online: http://www.ywam.eu/regions/countries/netherlands.php.

Zeigler, J. R. "Full Gospel Business Men's Fellowship International." In *NIDPCM*, 653–54.

———. "Shakarian, Demos." In *NIDPCM*, 1058.

Zellner, William W., and Marc Petrowsky. "Sects, Cults, and Spiritual Communities: A Sociological Analysis." *In Religion in the Age of Transformation*, edited by William W. Zellner and Marc Petrowsky, 27–40. Westport, Conn: Praeger, 1998.

Zidock, Alex, Jr. "Jesus People Gather in Paradise to Praise Him." *Bucks County (PA) Courier*, August 19, 1973. Online: NewspaperArchive.com.

Index

Made in the USA
Middletown, DE
06 September 2023

38126559R00146